Assessing
Individuals
With Disabilities

Assessing
Individuals
With Disabilities

in Educational, Employment,
and Counseling Settings

Edited by
Ruth B. Ekstrom and
Douglas K. Smith

American Psychological Association
Washington, DC

Published by
American Psychological Association
750 First Street, NE
Washington, DC 20002
www.apa.org

To order
APA Order Department
P.O. Box 92984
Washington, DC 20090-2984
Tel: (800) 374-2721, Direct: (202) 336-5510
Fax: (202) 336-5502, TDD/TTY: (202) 336-6123
Online: www.apa.org/books/
Email: order@apa.org

In the U.K., Europe, Africa, and the Middle East, copies may be ordered from
American Psychological Association
3 Henrietta Street
Covent Garden, London
WC2E 8LU England

Typeset in Goudy by EPS Group Inc., Easton, MD

Printer: Data Reproductions, Auburn Hills, MI
Cover designer: Naylor Design, Washington, DC
Production Editor: Catherine Hudson
Project Manager: Debbie Hardin, Carlsbad, CA

The opinions and statements published are the responsibility of the authors, and such opinions and statements do not necessarily represent the policies of the American Psychological Association.

Library of Congress Cataloging-in-Publication Data
Assessing individuals with disabilities in educational, employment, and counseling settings / edited by Ruth B. Ekstrom and Douglas K. Smith.—1st ed.
    p. cm.
   Includes bibliographical references and index.
   ISBN 1-55798-874-9 (alk. paper)
    1. Handicapped—Functional assessment. 2. People with disabilities—Employment. 3. People with disabilities—Education. 4. Developmentally disabled—Employment. I. Ekstrom, Ruth B. II. Smith, Douglas K.
RM930.8 .A85 2002
362.4—dc21

2002018249

British Library Cataloguing-in-Publication Data
A CIP record is available from the British Library.

Printed in the United States of America
First Edition

IN MEMORIAM

Douglas K. Smith died suddenly in April 2001, just as we were putting the final touches on this book. All of those who worked with him, especially the members of the Joint Committee on Testing Practices, had the highest regard for his expertise in disability issues. We will miss him.

—Ruth B. Ekstrom

CONTENTS

CONTRIBUTORS

Peter Behuniak, Connecticut State Department of Education, Hartford
Gwyneth Boodoo, Educational Testing Service, Princeton, NJ
Susanne M. Bruyère, Cornell University, Ithaca, NY
Wayne Camara, The College Board, New York
Wanda J. Campbell, Edison Electric Institute, Washington, DC
Ruth B. Ekstrom, Educational Testing Service, Princeton, NJ
William E. Foote, Albuquerque, NM
Heather Roberts Fox, Towson University, Towson, MD
John Fremer, Educational Testing Service, Princeton, NJ
Kurt F. Geisinger, University of St. Thomas, Houston, TX
Sharon Goldsmith, Washington, DC
Janet E. Helms, Boston College
Shelby Keiser, National Board of Medical Examiners, Philadelphia
William A. Mehrens, Michigan State University, East Lansing
Julie P. Noble, ACT, Inc., Iowa City, IA
Carole Perlman, Chicago Public Schools
Diana Pullin, Boston College
Audrey Qualls, University of Iowa, Iowa City
Michael Rosenfeld, Educational Testing Service, Princeton, NJ
Douglas K. Smith, University of Wisconsin—River Falls (deceased)
Donald L. Stovall, University of Wisonsin—River Falls
Nancy Tippins, Personnel Research Associates, Dallas
Nicholas A. Vacc, University of North Carolina at Greensboro
Janet E. Wall, Sage Solutions, Rockville, MD, and Pebble Beach, CA

Assessing
Individuals
With Disabilities

INTRODUCTION

RUTH B. EKSTROM AND DOUGLAS K. SMITH

About 20% of the U.S. population has a disability according to estimates by the Census Bureau (McNeil, 1997, 2001). Nearly 10% are estimated to have a severe disability.

Under the Americans With Disabilities Act (ADA), individuals with disabilities:

- Have a physical or mental impairment that substantially limits a major life activity;
- Have a record of such an impairment; or
- Are regarded as having such an impairment.

In the Census Bureau report, an individual with a disability was someone age 15 or older who met one or more of the following criteria: (a) used a wheelchair or was a long-term user of a cane, crutches, or walker; (b) had difficulty with one or more functional activities, such as seeing, hearing, speaking, walking, lifting/carrying, or using stairs; (c) had difficulty with one or more activities of daily living, such as bathing, dressing, eating, or toileting; (d) had difficulty with an instrumental activity of daily living, such as keeping track of money and bills, preparing meals, doing light housework, or using a telephone; (e) had a learning disability, mental retardation, or other developmental disability, Alzheimer's disease, or some other type of mental or emotional disability; (f) were between the ages of 16 and 67 and limited in their ability to work at a job or business; or (g) were receiving federal benefits based on an inability to work. Children aged

3

6 to 14 were defined as having a disability if they (a) were unable to perform the functional activities of seeing, hearing, walking, running, and using stairs; (b) were unable to perform activities of daily living; (c) used a wheelchair, cane, or crutches; (d) were unable to do regular schoolwork; or (e) had a learning disability, mental retardation, or some other developmental disability, or any other developmental condition for which they received therapy or diagnostic services.

Disability increases with age, affecting about 9% of individuals age 14 or younger, 19% between the ages of 15 and 64, and 52.5% of individuals age 65 and older. Males under the age of 16 are more likely to have a disability than females. At the older ages, females are more likely to have a disability than males. There are also differences in the proportion of individuals with disabilities in different racial and ethnic groups.

For children under the age of 18, the most common disabilities are learning disability, speech problem, mental retardation, asthma, mental or emotional problem, blindness or vision problem, deafness or hearing problem, cerebral palsy, and epilepsy or seizure disorder (McNeil, 1997). The U.S. Department of Education reported that more than 5.5 million children with disabilities were served in 1997 to 1998 under Chapter 1 and the Individuals With Disabilities Education Act (U.S. Department of Education, 2000). About half of these were children with specific learning disabilities. The number of students with disabilities in federal programs was approximately 12% of the school population in 1995 to 1996, according to the U.S. Department of Education (1997). About 1 in 11 first-time, full-time college freshmen in 1998 reported having a disability (Henderson, 1999).

The 1994 to 1995 Census Report indicated that 77% of individuals between the ages of 21 and 64 with a nonsevere disability and 26% of individuals with a severe disability had a job or business (as compared to 82% of individuals in this age group without a disability). However, the presence of a disability appeared to be associated with lower earnings.

EQUITY ISSUES

Equity is the most important factor in the assessment of individuals with disabilities. Equity requires that appropriate assessments be available to all individuals with disabilities. This means providing assessments in a place and manner that is accessible. Equity also requires that an assessment reflect the abilities of the individual, not the disability. This may mean providing tests specifically designed for individuals with disabilities or providing testing accommodations or modifications on standardized tests. *Equitable* does not mean *identical*. Therefore, testing accommodations must be individualized, because no single type of accommodation can be adequate or appropriate for all of the individuals with a given type of impairment or disability. Finally, it is essential that testing professionals do not hold biased or stereotyped views about individuals with disabilities. Testing professionals have the responsibility to become informed about disabilities and appropriate assessment procedures for individuals with disabilities. They should seek the advice of experts when they are uncertain about how to proceed.

Given the prevalence of disabilities, it is likely that anyone involved in assessment will at some time face the challenge of how best to test an individual with a disability. This book is intended to provide assistance in meeting this challenge. Readers should note that the material in this volume is the authors' interpretation of current laws, policies, and recommendations for best practice. Because these are interpretations and because the laws and regulations may change over time, this material does not have the force of law. Readers should consult with appropriate experts when questions arise.

OVERVIEW

The book is divided into six parts. Part I covers legal, policy, and psychometric issues affecting all types of assessment. Part II covers testing accommodations, documentation, and score reporting. These two sections, as well as Part VI on additional sources of information, should be of interest to all assessment professionals. The remaining three parts focus on specific types of assessment, covering the assessment of people with disabilities in clinical and counseling settings (Part III), educational settings (Part IV), and assessment for employment, certification, and licensing (Part V).

Part I

The individual carrying out assessments of people with disabilities must first of all be aware of the legal requirements that exist. These include Section 504 of the Rehabilitation Act of 1974, the Individuals With Disabilities Education Act, and the Americans With Disabilities Act. In chapter 1 Diana Pullin discusses these laws and the challenge of reconciling social science and social policy when testing individuals with disabilities. The effect of test accommodations on test validity is a major concern when assessing individuals with disabilities. Kurt Geisinger, Julie Noble, and Gwyneth Boodoo discuss this and related psychometric issues in chapter 2.

Part II

The process of assessing an individual with a disability must begin with determining if the individual will require some modification of the test or assessment and, if so, developing a rationale for the selection of a modification. Examples of testing accommodations are provided by Peter Behuniak in chapter 3. Testing professionals may be asked to provide documentation of a disability to support the need for testing accommodations or to help plan for services and educational programs for individuals with disabilities. In chapter 4 Nicholas Vacc and Nancy Tippins discuss documentation both from the perspective of the testing professional preparing such material and from the perspective of the testing professional who must use documentation information to make decisions about test accommodations. In chapter 5 Douglas Smith tells how to develop a rationale for the selection of a testing accommodation. Reporting scores when test accommodations have been made raises a number of problems related to test validity and the rights of individuals with disabilities; William Mehrens and Ruth Ekstrom explore some of these issues in chapter 6.

Part III

One of the first and most important steps in assessing individuals with disabilities occurs as part of testing for rehabilitation. Another important step is testing to determine if the person qualifies as disabled under various pieces of legislation. Both of these are most likely to occur in clinical and health care settings and are discussed by William Foote in chapter 7. Counseling also plays an important part in the rehabilitation and education of people with disabilities. In chapter 8, Janet Helms and Ruth Ekstrom discuss special concerns when testing individuals with disabilities in various types of counseling settings.

Part IV

Within the area of educational testing the laws and procedures for assessing individuals with disabilities vary considerably. Testing that centers on the individual (such as developing an individual educational plan) is covered by different requirements than testing in which the individual with a disability is being compared with a larger group of people (such as testing to make decisions about college admissions or in a state or district testing program). It is important for school administrators and policy makers to know how students with disabilities are faring in the educational system and to be able to compare their progress with that of other students. In chapter 9 Peter Behuniak, Audrey Qualls, and Carole Pearlman cover the issues that arise when individuals with disabilities are included in large-scale state and local assessments. School psychologists carry out much of the individual testing required under the IDEA. In chapter 10 Douglas Smith and Don Stoval discuss some of the common types of individual ability and achievement tests used in school settings. Still other issues arise when students with disabilities are tested for college admission, as discussed by Julie Noble, Wayne Camara, and John Fremer in chapter 11.

Part V

An overview of issues related to the employment testing of individual with disabilities is discussed by Wanda Campbell and Heather Roberts-Fox in chapter 12. In chapter 13, Susanne Bruyère describes how to attain disability nondiscrimination in the employment process. The implications of the ADA for employment testing are discussed by Nancy Tippins in chapter 14. The section concludes with chapter 15 by Michael Rosenfeld, Shelby Keiser, and Sharon Goldsmith on the use of certification and licensing examinations with individuals who have a disability.

Part VI

The book ends with a chapter by Janet Wall that includes a list of sources for further information about disabilities and about the assessment of people with disabilities. This section also includes the list of references.

CONCLUSION

We discussed, and decided not to include in this book, a section dealing with the assessment of individuals with specific types of disabilities. In 1998 APA Books published *Test Interpretation and Diversity*. This book includes chapters on the assessment of deaf and hearing-impaired people, people with visual impairments, people with learning disabilities, and a chapter covering conditions such as intellectual disabilities, emotional disturbances, autism, brain injury, metabolic disorders, endocrine disorders, and motor handicaps. We felt that it would be redundant to add similar material to this volume.

This book is designed to serve as a reference for the testing professional. The material in Parts I and II is applicable to most, if not all, testing professionals, and Parts III through V focus on specific settings. Whenever possible, chapter authors have cross-referenced material in their chapters with similar material that may be covered in more depth elsewhere in this book. These references as well as the resource material in chapter 16 are valuable sources of more detailed and, in the case of Internet sources, updated information on the assessment of individuals with disabilities.

The assessment of individuals with disabilities is a dynamic field. Definitions of what constitutes a disability continually change as a result of court rulings and subsequent legislation. Testing procedures continually improve with the introduction of new instruments and techniques, especially those involving new technology.

Our goals in developing this book have been to provide the testing professional with current and useful information about assessing individuals with disabilities; to provide sources of detailed information on specific topics; and to acquaint the testing professional with important issues affecting practice in this challenging field.

REFERENCES

Henderson, C. (1999). *College freshmen with disabilities.* Washington, DC: HEATH Resource Center, American Council on Education.

McNeil, J. M. (1997, Aug.). *Americans with disabilities: 1994–95* (Publication No. 70-61). Washington, DC: U.S. Census Bureau.

McNeil, J. M. (2001, Feb.). *Americans with disabilities: 1997* (Publication No. 70-73). Washington, DC: U.S. Department of Education.

U.S. Department of Education. (1997). *Mini Digest of Education Statistics.* Washington, DC: U.S. Department of Education.

U.S. Department of Education. (2000). *Twenty-second annual report to Congress on the implementation of the Individuals with Disabilities Education Act.* Washington, DC: U.S. Department of Education.

I

LEGAL, POLICY, AND PSYCHOMETRIC ISSUES

1

TESTING INDIVIDUALS WITH DISABILITIES: RECONCILING SOCIAL SCIENCE AND SOCIAL POLICY

DIANA PULLIN

The participation of individuals with disabilities in our society has grown enormously in the past two decades, and this trend will continue. As a result of dramatic advances in the medical sciences, there are more individuals with disabilities, living longer lives, than ever before. An aggressive social and political movement on behalf of this population, arising out of the race- and gender-based civil rights movement of the middle of the twentieth century, resulted in a national commitment to the policy goal of full inclusion of individuals with disabilities in all aspects of our economic, social, and political life. These social policy goals were written into strong new federal laws to protect this population.

Psychologists, educators, employers, test developers, and test users face significant challenges in attempting to make lawful, efficient, valid, and reliable decisions concerning the assessment and testing of individuals who have been diagnosed with disabilities. Identifying those individuals with disabilities who should receive accommodations or modifications can be challenging. Once this has been accomplished, determining the appropriateness of an accommodation can also be challenging. Sometimes necessary accommodations or modifications are not available. At other times, accommodations or modifications may be made available, but little evidence is provided concerning comparability of scores from administrations with accommodations compared with those from typical administrations. Standardized testing programs have often been unable to provide modified tests that are demonstrated to be technically comparable to unmodified tests. Yet the legal provisions designed to eliminate discrimination on the basis of disabilities and professional standards of practice for testing require that tests used to inform important educational or employment decisions must be both valid and reliable and offered with reasonable accommodations.

The challenges resulting from the social policy goals and legal issues confronting test developers, test administrators, and test users in the testing and assessment of individuals with disabilities are substantial. This chapter summarizes these social policy and legal issues, focusing on three examples of these problems: those arising in selection testing in higher education, in employment testing, and in accountability testing in elementary and secondary education. The chapter also compares professional standards with legal requirements. Finally, the chapter issues a call for widespread new research and implementation of appropriate practices for testing individuals with disabilities.

FEDERAL DISABILITY RIGHTS STATUTES

The intent of laws governing the testing of individuals with disabilities is to promote fair treatment and access. For example, the statutory and regulatory provisions designed to protect individuals with disabilities from discrimination would bar the use of information about the nature or existence of a disability in preemployment inquiries before an individual is hired. Similarly, inquiries into the existence of a disability are barred in educational admissions decisions unless the use of the information was narrowly limited to a determination of whether an individual was "otherwise qualified" to participate in a particular educational program. The same legal provisions require the use of properly validated tests in selections for employment or admissions decisions or in education, yet there is often insufficient evidence of that validity.

Recently, at the same time that the new civil rights of individuals with disabilities were being implemented, Congress addressed the social policy goals associated with full inclusion as part of its initiatives to promote reform of public elementary and secondary education nationwide. Instead of simply barring discrimination against individuals with disabilities, legislation was enacted to ensure that this population was both fully included in reform initiatives and fully counted in accountability reports on whether and how education reform was working (Heubert & Hauser, 1999).

There are two broad federal civil rights statutes that bar discrimination against persons with disabilities: Section 504 of the Rehabilitation Act and the Americans With Disabilities Act.

Section 504 of the Rehabilitation Act

Section 504 of the Rehabilitation Act of 1973 provides the following protection:

> No otherwise qualified individual with a disability . . . shall, solely by reason of his or her disability, be excluded from the participation in, be denied the benefits of, or be subjected to discrimination under any program or activity receiving Federal financial assistance. . . . (29 U.S.C. § 794(a))

By its terms, this law applies only to activities that occur in institutions with federally funded activities. This covers all public elementary and secondary education programs and the educational and employment activities in the vast majority of public and private institutions of higher education.

A private testing/assessment organization or practitioner also needs to take into account the legal requirements imposed on those engaged in activities involving individuals with disabilities. The provisions of Section 504 can apply to a private organization that receives federal financial assistance or to the use of a private contractor's test or test results by a federally funded program or agency.

The provisions of Section 504 and its implementing regulations are designed to ensure equal opportunities for persons with disabilities to "benefit" from educational programs and activities and to participate in employment and other life activities without discrimination. Under Section 504, it is, for example, a prohibited discriminatory practice for public school systems, on the basis of disability, to

> (i) [d]eny a qualified handicapped person the opportunity to participate in or benefit from . . . [an] aid, benefit or service; (ii) [a]fford a qualified handicapped person an opportunity to participate in or benefit from . . . [an] aid, benefit, or service that is not equal to that afforded others; (iii) [p]rovide a qualified handicapped person with an aid, benefit or service that is not as effective as that provided to others; [or] (iv) [p]rovide different or separate aid, benefits or services to any handicapped person or to any class of handicapped person unless such action is necessary to provide qualified handicapped persons with aid, benefits, or services that are as effective as those provided to others. (34 C.F.R. § 104.4(b)(1))

The Section 504 regulations require that programs and services for persons with disabilities be equally effective compared to those received by others and that an aid, benefit, or service "must . . . afford [disabled] persons equal opportunity to obtain the same result, to gain the same benefit, or to reach the same level of achievement. . . ." (34 C.F.R. § 104.4(b)(2)). Routinely excluding students with disabilities from testing or assessment programs would violate their rights under Section 504 to receive the same benefits and services provided to nondisabled students. On the other hand, simply allowing all individuals with disabilities to participate in testing or assessment in the same way as persons without disabilities presents opportunities for other forms of discrimination (McDonnell, McLaughlin, & Morison, 1997; Pullin & Heaney, 1997; Pullin & Zirkel, 1988).

Section 504 clearly requires individualized determinations on the need for accommodation and the nature of a reasonable accommodation. This presents challenges both in determining the nature and impact of a disability and in assessing the consequences of making an accommodation on the technical qualities of a test. Section 504 requires reasonable accommodations in programs for persons with disabilities to ensure that any qualified individual with a disability will not, solely on the basis of disability, be denied participation in or the benefits of a program or activity receiving federal financial assistance (29 U.S.C. § 794(a)). As the U.S. Supreme Court has stated,

> An otherwise qualified handicapped individual must be provided with meaningful access to the benefit that the grantee offers. The benefit itself, or course, cannot be defined in a way that effectively denies otherwise qualified handicapped individuals the meaningful access to which they are entitled; to assure meaningful access, reasonable accommodations in the grantee's program or benefit may have to be made. (*Alexander v. Choate*, 1985, p. 301)

Consideration of the "reasonableness" of a particular accommodation can be difficult. Courts addressing these types of disputes have tended to give great deference to the judgment of professionals and have recognized that accommodations that alter the essential nature of a program are not "reasonable."

Although there have been only a limited number of cases involving issues of alleged violations of Section 504 in testing or assessment programs, those cases have demonstrated the willingness of courts to impose statutory and regulatory constraints on some practices. The courts have made clear that they will not require test users to change their standards for either admission or successful program participation in a way that would substantially alter any core component or requirement of a program (Pullin & Heaney, 1997). Those administering a test or assessment have the responsibility for determining whether a requested accommodation is reasonable, but if they do not have sufficient evidence to support their decision making about accommodations, then courts may defer to the service providers or care givers of the individual with the disability (*D'Amico v. New York State Board of Bar Examiners*, 1993). The "reasonableness" of a requested accommodation can be taken into account by those administering a test or assessment. Reasonable accommodations are only required in response to "known physical or mental limitations" that are either on record, known about, or disclosed by the individual with a disability. Both the ADA and Section 504 allow refusal to provide an accommodation that would cause "undue hardship." "Undue hardship" has been defined as an action requiring significant difficulty or expense considered in light of the nature and cost of the accommodation; the overall size, nature, and financial resources of the entity being asked for an accommodation; and the type of program involved.

In one case involving the use of multiple-choice exams in a medical school course and a request from a student with dyslexia for another type of testing format, a federal appellate court formulated the following test to determine whether an educational institution has met its obligation of providing reasonable testing accommodations under Section 504:

> If the institution submits undisputed facts demonstrating that the relevant officials within the institution considered alternative means, their feasibility, cost and effect on the academic program, and came to a rationally justifiable conclusion that the available alternatives would result either in lowering academic standards or require substantial program alteration, the court could rule as a matter of law that the institution had met its duty of seeking reasonable accommodation. (*Wynne v. Tufts University School of Medicine*, 1991, p. 26)

This court also stated that accommodations that alter the essential nature of a program are not "reasonable" (*Wynne v. Tufts University*, 1991).

There have also been several decisions by federal administrative hearing officers concerning assessment or testing programs. Administrative hearing officers of the Office for Civil Rights (OCR) of the U.S. Department of Education (1990, 1996, 1997, 1998) have made a distinction between providing accommodations to individuals capable of mastering the skills/subject being tested but who have disability-based difficulty in demonstrating their knowledge/mastery, and making modifications in requirements for individuals who, because of a disability, cannot master the subject matter and skills being tested Where a test or assessment would not be valid if an accommodation is made, then the accommodation has not been required.

Accommodation decisions need to be individualized, taking into account the specific nature of an examinee's capabilities. The past history of accommodations provided in educational or employment settings may be relevant in making a decision about the appropriate accommodations for a test or assessment. The OCR (U.S. Department of Education, 1987a, 1987b) has also found that a state education agency violated Section 504 when, as a result of a blanket policy allowing only blind students to have readers, it refused to provide a reader for a student with a learning disability during a high school graduation examination even though the student had received that accommodation during his high school studies.

Americans With Disabilities Act

The second disability-related federal civil rights law is an even broader nondiscrimination law than Section 504, applying to almost all educational testing or assessment programs. The Americans With Disabilities Act (ADA) expressly prohibits public entities and public and private employers from discrimination on the basis of disability, from "[p]rovid[ing] different or separate aids, benefits or services [to persons with disabilities] that are not as effective as those provided to others" (42 U.S.C. § 12101 et seq.). Title II of the ADA prohibits any state, school district, or school from excluding from participation, denying benefits, aids, or services, or otherwise discriminating against a qualified individual with a disability, on the basis of his or her disability (42 U.S.C. § 12131 et seq.). Title III of the law bars disability-based discrimination in "public accommodations and services operated by private entities" (42 U.S.C. § 12181–12189).

The ADA includes a specific provision governing examinations:

> Any person that offers examinations or courses related to applications, licensing, certification, or credentialing for secondary or post-secondary education, professional, or trade purposes shall offer such examinations or courses in a place and manner accessible to persons with disabilities or offer alternative accessible arrangements for such individuals. (42 U.S.C. § 12189)

The regulations under the ADA include a specific provision requiring nondiscrimination in the administration of examinations (42 U.S.C. § 12189). These provisions include ADA regulations requiring that testing sites be physically accessible (29 C.F.R. § 418 (appendix; 1993)) and that test formats be "the most effective manner" for persons to demonstrate that they can perform necessary job-related skills and knowledge (42 U.S.C. § 12112(b)(7); 29 C.F.R. § 418 (appendix; 1993); 45 C.F.R. § 84.12(b)(2) (1993)). When an individual with a disability notifies a test administrator that he or she would like an alternative format for a test, or a portion of the test, this accommodation must ordinarily be made available unless the individual is not covered by the protections of the disability law or the requested accommodation or modification would mean that the new form of the test no longer measured the job-related skills the test was designed to measure.

Those giving tests are allowed to inquire before the test whether an individual needs an accommodation and, if so, what the requested accommodation would be (29 C.F.R. § 1630.14(a) app.). There is also an obligation, once an educator, employer, or test administrator becomes aware of the possible existence of a disability, to initiate discussion and consideration of a possible reasonable accommodation (29 C.F.R. § 1630.14(a)).

Although the statute is so new there is as yet little case law interpreting these provisions, the U.S. Supreme Court has recently issued several decisions significantly reducing the scope of the law. First, the Supreme Court, emphasizing that determinations under the Act must be made on an individualized basis, determined that the disabilities covered under the law must be substantial and do not include those such as the need to wear eyeglasses or contact lenses or to take medication that mitigate the disability (*Albertsons, Inc. v. Kirkingburg*, 1999; *Murphy v. United Parcel Service*, 1999; *Sutton v. United Air Lines*, 1999). Second, the Supreme Court decided that Congress had no authority to allow state employees to use the Americans With Disabilities Act to file discrimination lawsuits against the state agencies or institutions that employ them (*Board of Trustees of the University of Alabama v. Garrett*, 2001). There are several cases pending or recently settled out of court involving examination contexts, such as professional school admissions or licensure testing (Slobodzian, 1997a, 1997b). One of the issues yet to be resolved is whether the provisions of part III apply only to physical accessibility or should be regarded as broader nondiscrimination provisions. The matter is perhaps somewhat moot for testing and assessment programs where it may not be possible to draw a bright line around what is and is not a "physical" accommodation. The statute specifically requires the removal of many architectural barriers as a form of physical accommodation. Although a large print version of a test is probably a "physical accommodation," is extended time, for example, a "physical" accommodation? These "accessibility" requirements will require considerable attention on the part of testing/assessment companies and practitioners.

EMPLOYMENT TESTING

Both Section 504 and the ADA bar discrimination on the basis of disability when private or local government employers use job criteria that intentionally or unintentionally screen out individuals with disabilities who are capable of performing the job in question (Bergdorf, 1995). Preemployment inquiries on the existence or nature of a disability are barred. However, once an applicant discloses a disability, the employer is required to make reasonable accommodations for that disability. A test or assessment should not be used as a job requirement if it bars individuals with disabilities from employment unless the test can be shown to be job-related and necessary to meet legitimate business needs for a particular position (42 U.S.C. § 12112(b)(6)). Therefore, if a test is to be used as a requirement for qualifying for a job, then there must be evidence that the test measures an essential function of the job, that it is "job related" (42 U.S.C. § 12112(b)(7); 29 C.F.R. Pt. 1630, app. (1993)).

To establish that a program is fair or nondiscriminatory, it is ordinarily required that an employer, if challenged, is able to prove the necessity of the program. The ADA includes a "job-relatedness" requirement if a test "screen[s] out or tends to screen out . . . individuals with disabilities unless the . . . test . . . is shown to be job-related for the position in question and is consistent with business necessity" (42 U.S.C. § 12112(a)). Even if there is a sufficient business justification for a test or assessment, use of the test may still be unlawful under the civil rights laws if there is a reasonable alternative that would have a lesser adverse impact. The justification for the use of a particular test or assessment will therefore require both evidence that the skills and knowledge being measured are appropriate for the training program, certification, or licensure for which the test is being used as well as evidence that the test is a valid measure of those skills and knowledge.

Both the ADA and Section 504 provisions require that test scores give an accurate reflection of what an individual can do, rather than merely reflecting a disability. Ordinarily, employers must select and administer tests concerning employment to ensure that test results accurately reflect the applicant's or employee's job skills, aptitude, or whatever other factor the test purports to measure rather than reflecting the applicant's or employee's impaired sensory, manual, or speaking skills. The only exceptions would be when those skills are the factors that the test purports to measure for some business-related reason (29 C.F.R. § 1614.203).

One federal appeals court has determined that the ADA requires accommodations or modifications that would afford a person with a disability a chance to take an exam "on a level playing field with other applicants," including such accommodations as a reader and extended time (*Bartlett v. New York State Board of Law Examiners*, 1998). A requested accommodation or modification is not required under the law if it would impair the accurate assessment of a person's actual ability to perform the essential functions of a job (29 C.F.R. § 1630.10 app.), including the possibility of performing the job with reasonable accommodation (29 C.F.R. § 1630.15(b)(1), (c), & app.). Therefore, each time a need to accommodate on a test is considered, it is important to know clearly both the essential requirements of the job and the impact of a particular test accommodation on the assessment of the abilities to perform essential job tasks.

MAKING ACCOMMODATIONS DETERMINATIONS

The first consideration in making accommodations for persons with disabilities is determining the existence of a disability and the extent to which the disability could affect test performance. Once the need for accommodations is ascertained, there are generally four broad types of accommodations: changes in presentation of the test (such as a Braille or large-print form); changes in response mode (such as the use of a scribe); changes in timing for timed tests; and changes in the setting in which the test is given (such as a special desk). Sometimes, combinations of these approaches are used (McDonnell, McLaughlin, & Morison, 1997). The most typical types of reasonable accommodations or modifications are alterations in the format of a test (such as the provision of large-print, audiotape, reader, or braille formats) or extended time to take a test (Thurlow, Ysseldyke, & Silverstein, 1995). In educational testing, most alternative formats require extended time for test administration (see chapters 7 and 13, this volume). For some examinees, extended time alone is sufficient and reasonable accommodation (Wightman, 1993; Willingham, Ragosta, Bennett, Braun, Rock, & Powers, 1988). Care should be taken to ensure, however, that extended time and format changes do not allow an opportunity for a test-taker with a disability to be either advantaged or disadvantaged by the accommodation and to ensure that the score on a modified version of a test is as much as possible comparable to a score on an unmodified version. Two types of steps can be taken to achieve these goals.

First, tests should be reviewed to determine the extent to which timed administrations are essential for measuring the underlying construct being assessed. For assembly line workers, speed in performing tasks involving manual dexterity may be an appropriate factor to assess. In jobs in which speed is not as critical an issue, such as insurance brokers, speed is probably not relevant and examinations could appropriately be untimed. Avoiding timed tests will eliminate the need for the most requested form of accommodation, extended test administration time (Nestor, 1985). Sometimes the speed with which a person can perform particular tasks is essential to determine whether or not a person can perform a particular job; many times speed should not be a factor in successful test performance because it is not required for successful job performance.

Second, test items or tasks should all be reviewed to ensure that the most straightforward means for assessing a skill or knowledge is being used for all test takers. For example, on a test of basic communications competency and the ability to spell and use appropriate grammar, it does not make sense to measure those skills using a dictation exercise in which examinees listen to an audiotape and then are asked to transcribe the taped passage, with proper spelling and usage. The task may not be content-valid as a measure of the skills of spelling and usage and may be more a test of an individual's ability to take dictation, a skill that may not even be required in the job at issue. If the test is being used to assess applicants for secretarial positions in which dictation or transcription is required, then the dictation test might be job-related. If, however, the only real job-related skills that need to be assessed are spelling and usage, then a more direct measure of those skills would be more legally defensible. In addition, the selection of the dictation exercise presents an obvious, and unnecessary, burden on many individuals with disabilities, such as hearing-impaired persons who cannot hear the tape. In addition, the use of a likely accommodation for the dictation exercise, a sign language interpretation, would result in an entirely different test because sign language is not the same language as English.

A small percentage of individuals with disabilities may be entitled to alternative or different assessments. It may be possible to substitute items on a test or to assess some alternate content and still be measuring the same skills and knowledge that the unmodified version of a test measures. If so, the alternative approach would be legally preferable.

SELECTION TESTING FOR HIGHER EDUCATION ADMISSIONS

A growing proportion of the individuals taking large-scale admissions examinations, such as the SAT (Scholastic Assessment Test) or the LSAT (Law School Admissions Test) request special accommodations in testing to address needs associated with their disabilities (American Council on Education, 1992). Nondiscrimination laws require that steps are taken to ensure that qualified students with disabilities are not being denied appropriate modifications in testing or being discriminated against on the basis of their disabilities (U.S. Department of Education, 1996). Thus, test administrators face the dilemmas of how to determine and make reasonable accommodations on admissions tests. At the same time, attention must be paid to the validity and reliability of the inferences made from scores on modified tests.

Once a determination has been made to allow an accommodation in the administration of a test, significant questions still remain about how to report the score on the accommodated administration (Heaney & Pullin, 1998; Pullin & Heaney, 1997). After any significant modification in the standardized administration of a test or assessment has been made, a determination has to be made whether to include in the score reporting a designation or explanation of the deviation from the standardized administration. This presents a second dilemma for test administrators because involuntary preadmissions disclosures of the existence of a disability are to be avoided, according to the nondiscrimination requirements in the federal laws.

The 1999 *Test Standards* state, "when there is credible evidence of score comparability across regular and modified administrations, no flag should be attached to a score" (Standard 10.11, AERA/APA/NCME, 1999). The same standard goes on to indicate that where score comparability is not evident, specific information on the type of modification provided should be given with the score report "if permitted by law." This last phrase appears to recognize the possibility that legal standards could potentially overrule the professional standard of practice.

A technical guidance manual for Section 504 was produced in 1978 under a contract from the U.S. Department of Education Office of Civil Rights (OCR) to address the question of notifying institutions of nonstandard administrations of admissions tests for students with disabilities (Silverstein, Kamil, Delaney, & Cassidy, 1979). This manual set out an interim OCR policy that the testing services will be allowed to continue to notify their users that tests were taken under nonstandard conditions.

This so-called interim policy has been in place for more than 18 years. However, OCR has begun a new effort to formally review this matter to consider revision, or final adoption, of its interim policy, although no new policy has yet been announced (Board on Testing and Assessment, National Research Council/National Academy of Sciences, 1997; personal communication with Eileen Hanrahan, U.S. Office for Civil Rights, September 20, 1996).

OCR, in its administrative determinations on complaints of discrimination in testing individuals with disabilities, has consistently upheld the use of test scores in admissions decisions where there exists substantial other evidence of an applicant's overall inability to meet program requirements, based on criteria other than test scores and in comparison to admitted applicants with stronger records (Milani, 1996). It has issued several decision letters in which it has stated that it is not, in and of itself, unlawful for universities to receive flagged test scores (*University of Michigan*, 1991; see also Milani, 1996). However, OCR later stated that universities may not treat flagged scores from the nonstandardized administration of tests differently from the way other scores on the same test are treated (*SUNY Health Science Ctr. at Brooklyn-College of Medicine*, 1993; see also Milani, 1996; Tucker, 1996).

In a significant development concerning the use of test-score flagging, Educational Testing Service recently reached a partial settlement of a court case challenging flagging of its graduate admissions tests. Under the agreement, ETS agreed to stop score flagging for the accommodation of extended time on its Graduate Record Examinations, the Graduate Admission Test, the Test of English as a Foreign Language, Praxis, and many other of its tests. The flagging agreement does not, as of this time, include the College Board exams that ETS administers. A panel of experts will be asked to evaluate aspects of the flagging practice and to make recommendations (Disability Rights Advocates, 2001; ETS, 2001).

FEDERAL LAWS ON ACCOUNTABILITY TESTING IN ELEMENTARY AND SECONDARY SCHOOLS

As a part of the recent trend in education reform and increased public accountability for the nation's public elementary and secondary schools, a large wave of state and federal legislation has resulted in significant increases in the use of standardized tests of students. The federal government has created incentives and encouragement for states and local districts to use standards-based, test-driven education reforms, and all fifty states have followed suit.

The Goals 2000 Educate America Act and the Improving America's Schools Act

The Goals 2000 Educate America Act (20 U.S.C. § 5801 et seq.) and the Improving America's Schools Act (20 U.S.C. § 6301 et seq.) embody the principles that all children can learn and achieve to high standards and that *all* students are entitled to participate in a broad and challenging curriculum. These principles of high standards and achievement for all have clear implications for the education of students with disabilities, who have often not been well-served by the nation's schools. Goals 2000 and the Improving America's Schools Act of 1994 evince an intent that a single, unified set of content and performance standards will be developed for, and applied to, students with and without disabilities.

To ensure that students are attaining the performance standards, Goals 2000 requires that state improvement plans must include a process for developing and implementing nondiscriminatory and reliable state assessments, which are aligned with state content standards, involve multiple measures of student performance, and provide for participation of students with diverse learning needs including students with disabilities (20 U.S.C. § 5886(c)(1)(B)). Title I of the Elementary and Secondary Education Act of 1965, reauthorized by the Improving America's Schools Act of 1994 (IASA), is the source of significant federal funding to aid low-income, low-achieving students throughout the nation. Under Title I, a school must provide opportunities for "all" children, including those with disabilities, to meet the state's student performance standards. Yearly assessments must provide for participation of "all" students, with "the reasonable adaptations and accommodations for students with diverse learning needs, necessary to measure the achievement of such students relative to State content standards" (20 U.S.C. § 6311(b)(3)(F)(i), (ii)).

Each state Title I plan must demonstrate that state has adopted a set of high-quality, yearly student assessments in at least reading and math that will be the primary means of determining yearly performance of the school district and school in enabling all children to meet state's performance standards. Such assessments shall "be the same assessments used to measure the performance of all children and be used so as to be "valid and reliable, and . . . consistent with relevant, nationally recognized professional and technical standards. . . ." (20 U.S.C. § 6311(b)(3)).

State assessments must "provide individual student interpretive and descriptive reports," including scores, or other information on attainment of performance standards, and such results must be disaggregated within each state, local educational agency, and school, including disaggregation of scores for students with disabilities as compared to nondisabled students (20 U.S.C. § 6311(b)(3)(H), (I)).

The detailed provisions in IASA regarding including students with disabilities in education reform initiatives clearly indicate the intent of Congress to ensure that all students, including all students with disabilities, should be fully included in the accountability initiatives.

The Individuals With Disabilities Education Act (IDEA) and Section 504

In the United States for the past 25 years, federal and state statutes and regulations have played a dominant role in the education of students with disabilities. In 1975, the U.S. Congress passed a law designed to require that states and local school districts provide all children with disabilities in need of special education an appropriate education at public expense that was designed on an individual basis to meet the unique needs of the child and be provided in the least restrictive environment. The law, now amended several times by the Congress and known as the Individuals With Disabilities Education Act (IDEA; 20 U.S.C. § 1400 et seq.) and its implementing regulations (34 C.F.R. § 300 and 303), also set forth detailed procedural protections for children and their families to ensure compliance with the law, including the right to use the federal court system to obtain enforcement of these legal rights, if necessary. All of the states have analogous, or sometimes more extensive (such as in Massachusetts) state statutes governing special education.

Congress has maintained a strong commitment to the goal of full inclusion of students with disabilities in education, and this social policy goal resulted, in the 1997 reauthorization of the law, in a clear and strong affirmation that state education reform initiatives must fully include students with disabilities (Pub. L. No. 105-17). This means that in a system of standards-based reform, special education and related services for students with disabilities must meet the IDEA requirement for providing an appropriate education. The new provisions of the IDEA require states to include specialized instruction and support services aligned with the state's general curriculum content and performance standards for students with disabilities.

Under the 1997 amendments to the IDEA, the federal law explicitly requires that students with disabilities participate in state and local school reform efforts. Students with disabilities must be included in state and local assessment and accountability or alternative assessments must be developed for students with disabilities who are legitimately exempted from assessments. The nature and extent of each student's participation in these initiatives must be determined on an individual basis by the team of educators and parents formulating a student's individualized educational program (IEP). The IEP must specify the nature of the student's participation and must state the appropriate modifications/accommodations that should be made for the student to participate in state or district-wide assessment programs (20 U.S.C. § 1414(d) (1997), Pub. L. No. 105-17 § 101).

In many respects, in most public schools, the provisions of Section 504 are identical to the provisions of the IDEA. However, there are different groups of persons covered under the IDEA and Section 504. There are some students with disabilities who are not covered under the IDEA but are covered by Section 504. Students with disabilities who do not need special education are not covered by the IDEA and most analogous state laws but are covered by Section 504. For example, a student with a mild learning disability might only need extended time for testing or in-class assignments and has no need for special education, but is entitled to receive accommodations or related services under Section 504.

Before the passage of the most recent revisions of the federal laws, there were few court decisions regarding the applicability of the federal special education laws to standards-based education reform. However, there were determinations that the denial of diplomas to students with disabilities who have been receiving the special education and related services required by the IDEA but are unable to pass a state competency test does not constitute a denial of free appropriate education required under the Act. However, under the IDEA, students with disabilities are entitled to the provision of IEPs designed to address their participation in the program (*Brookhart v. Illinois State Board of Education*, 1983). One state court has held that denial of high school diplomas where students completed IEPs but did not pass a state competency test does not violate federal special education statutes (*Board of Educ. of Northport-East Northport Union Free School Dist. v. Ambach*, 1983).

The issue of accommodations in diagnostic or evaluative testing and assessment and the use of nonstandardized administrations for individuals with disabilities have been addressed in the latest regulations under the

IDEA. The regulations give the student's IEP team of educators and the family the responsibility for determining how the child will participate in the state accountability system. The regulations also require that if an assessment is conducted under nonstandard conditions, information about the nature of the variations from standard conditions, including the qualifications of the person administering the assessment, must be included in the evaluation report (34 C.F.R. § 300.532(c)(2)).

There have also been state administrative hearings decisions addressing the nature of accommodations that should be provided to students with disabilities. For example, one state hearing officer determined that when an accommodation in the form of reading aloud portions of the math and language assessments was requested by an IEP team for a student with a learning disability, refusal to provide the accommodations did not constitute the denial of a free appropriate education when there was evidence that the student had previously been receiving an appropriate education, as evidenced by passing grades in his classes and where the accommodation requested for the assessment was not one that the student had been given previously in his academic career (*Mobile County Bd. of Educ.*, 1997).

A small percentage of disabled students require alternative or different assessment because their curriculum does not completely match the content and performance standards being assessed by the state or district-wide test. One state estimated that less than 2% of the total school population would fall in to this group, and this proportion has been widely adopted in discussions elsewhere (McDonnell et al., 1997, p. 175). Within this subset, however, are at least two groups of students: Students who are expected to master a state's content standards but because of their particular disability, need an alternative method for assessing a particular competency; and those students with disabilities so severe that alternative content and performance standards are more appropriate than standards generally applied to all students. The presumption recognized by the federal laws is that both types of students are entitled to a program of high standards and appropriate accountability (Heubert & Hauser, 1999).

VALIDITY ISSUES IN TESTING INDIVIDUALS WITH DISABILITIES

Careful attention to issues of including individuals with disabilities in testing programs and reporting their scores is of paramount importance in ensuring not only the fairness of the test for these individuals but also the validity of the inferences made as the result of a test score (Mehrens, 1997; Messick, 1993; Nestor, 1985; Phillips, 1994). Validation of a test requires the collection of sufficient empirical evidence to allow a judgment that the existing evidence supports the intended use of the test (Messick,

1993). In admissions and employment testing, validity evidence necessarily focuses on the predictive capabilities of test scores. Some accommodations may be unreasonably extensive and result in an overprediction of an applicant's potential for success in a job or an educational program. A flagged score from a modified administration of an admissions or accountability test may also encourage the test score recipient to discount the evidence about a candidate, thereby compromising the validity of inferences based on the score.

Test administrators must determine whether a particular individual has the claimed disability, what accommodations are required for that disability, and whether those accommodations are appropriate (Ragosta & Wendler, 1992). A low population size in many groups of test takers with disabilities present challenges in conducting separate validity studies (Mehrens, 1997; Phillips, 1994).

A four-year study of the SAT and the GRE to assess the validity and comparability of those admissions tests administered to persons with disabilities (Willingham et al., 1988) drew several conclusions, including determining that (a) nonstandard tests were in general as reliable or precise measures for individuals with disabilities as they were for individuals without disabilities; (b) nonstandard tests seemed to measure comparable abilities for both groups of examinees; and (c) test content was generally comparable for both groups. However, the study also indicated that predictions of future academic performance for students with disabilities were less accurate, on the basis of either test scores or grades, than for other students. The most common form of accommodation, extended time to take the test, was reported to overpredict first-year college performance in some instances for students with learning disabilities, although the study provides no evidence that it assessed whether those students received appropriate accommodations during their first year of higher education coursework.

Relatively little validity research on modifications to address disabilities has appeared since the Willingham study (see chapters 7 and 13, this volume). A summary of research in the area by Mehrens (1997) reported several studies generally confirming Willingham's conclusions, including a 1991 ETS review of modified SAT administrations that confirmed the potential for overprediction for students with learning disability but also noted that predictions based on a combination of SAT scores and high school performance resulted in little or no overprediction. He also reported ACT studies with similar results. A study of modified administrations of the LSAT also assessed the impact of accommodations for persons with disabilities on that test and reported overpredictions for first-year law school performance (Wightman, 1993).

It is essential that test developers, test administrators, and test users significantly increase their efforts to gather data on the effects of accommodating for disabilities and analyze that data to assess the impact of accommodations on the technical qualities of a test. Without this important social science research, those who administer, interpret, and use tests and assessments for individuals with disabilities are at a serious disadvantage. Good faith efforts to meet professional standards and legal requirements can only succeed if there is a sufficient research base to establish appropriate processes for determining accommodations and for ascertaining the comparability of accommodated administrations.

PROVISIONS IN THE TEST STANDARDS CONCERNING INDIVIDUALS WITH DISABILITIES

Although an understanding of the legal requirements concerning the testing and assessment of individuals with disabilities is essential, it is also important to understand the provisions of the professional standards of practice in this area. As well, it is important to assess the extent to which the professional standards of practice and the legal requirements do, or do not, conflict.

The 1985 version of the *Standards for Educational and Psychological Testing* (AERA/APA/NCME, 1985) was the first edition to separately address the issues concerning testing individuals with disabilities (or, as they were termed then, "handicaps"). In a separate chapter, the 1985 *Standards* set forth some general requirements in this arena. That document states, for example, that "reporting scores from nonstandard test administrations without special identification . . . violates professional principles, misleads test users, and perhaps even harms handicapped test takers whose scores do not accurately reflect their abilities." The 1985 *Standards* further require that "unless it has been demonstrated that the psychometric properties of a test . . . are not altered significantly by some modification, the claims made for the test . . . cannot be generalized to the modified version" (AERA/APA/NCME, 1985, p. 78).

The most recent 1999 version of the *Standards for Educational and Psychological Testing* developed by a Joint Committee of the American Educational Research Association, the American Psychological Association, and the National Council on Measurement in Education offers some new provisions concerning testing and assessing individuals with disabilities (AERA/APA/NCME, 1999). The document recognizes that there is a far from perfect match between the current technical capabilities of the measurement community and the social and legal policy goals that have been embraced concerning the interests of individuals with disabilities. The chapter on testing individuals with disabilities calls for careful attention to the validity of inferences drawn from tests of individuals, careful use of knowledge concerning the impact of disabilities on test performance, and special attention to the development and impact of modifications or accommodations in testing. The chapter also calls for greater emphasis on the collection and analysis of data from modified administrations of tests to study the impact of modification practices, particularly on validity and other technical characteristics of a test. Finally, based on the presumption that adequate data on comparability of modified and nonmodified tests can be more broadly achieved, the chapter creates a presumption that scores from modified administrations of standardized tests should not carry a "flag" or other indicator of a modification in administration.

There will be increased requests for individuals with disabilities to be given a fair opportunity to participate in testing programs and these requests must be appropriately addressed. There is a critical need for further research on the effects of accommodations in testing for individuals with disabilities. In 1979, in an effort to resolve the legal and educational dilemmas confronting those who dealt with ability testing of individuals with disabilities in educational admissions and employment, the U.S. Office for Civil Rights asked the National Research Council of the National Academy of Sciences to undertake a study designed to propose a resolution to the problem. The result was a call for "a continuing research endeavor to make more useful and meaningful the results of tests given to handicapped people" (Sherman & Robinson, 1982). The 1988 study of the SAT and GRE called for still further research (Willingham et al., 1988). Wightman's 1993 study of the LSAT noted the need for still further research. Yet the published literature since contains few reports of such efforts and few real solutions to the problem of how to validly and fairly conduct tests and report results for individuals with disabilities.

CONCLUSION

Our social and legal policy goals and requirements compel greater efforts to address the many challenges associated with the testing of individuals with disabilities. Research efforts to gather data on the nature and effects of accommodations for disabilities must be expanded and those data publicly reported. Validity studies on modified tests should be regularly and systematically implemented and reported. For situations involving low-incidence disabilities and unusual accommodations where quantitative data may be limited, qualitative validity study methodologies should be considered to at least begin the validity inquiry (Heaney & Pullin, 1998).

Those developing, administering, and using tests and assessments need to pay close attention to the issues of involving individuals with disabilities in their programs and practice. The challenges are not insignificant. This volume is an important initial effort to aid that process.

REFERENCES

Albertsons, Inc. v. Kirkingburg. (1999). 527 U.S. 555.

Alexander v. Choate. (1995). 469 U.S. 287.

American Council on Education. (1992). *More disabled students attending college. Special Education Report.* Iowa City: Author.

American Educational Research Association, American Psychological Association, & National Council on Measurement in Education (AERA/APA/NCME). (1985). *Standards for educational and psychological testing.* Washington, DC: American Psychological Association.

American Educational Research Association, American Psychological Association, & National Council on Measurement in Education (AERA/APA/NCME). (1999). *Standards for educational and psychological testing.* Washington, DC: American Educational Research Association.

Americans With Disabilities Act of 1990. 42 U.S.C. § 12101 (1994).

Bartlett v. New York State Board of Law Examiners. (1998). 156 F.3d. 321 (2d Cir.) *(judgment vacated and case remanded to appellate court),* 119 S. Ct. 2388 (1999).

Bergdorf, R. L., Jr. (1995). *Disability discrimination in employment law.* Washington, DC: Bureau of National Affairs.

Board of Educ. of Northport-East Northport Union Free School Dist. v. Ambach. (1983). 60 N.Y.2d 758, 469 N.Y.S.2d 669, 457 N.E.2d 775, *cert. denied,* 465 U.S. 1101 (1984).

Board of Trustees of the University of Alabama v. Garrett. (2001). 531 U.S. 356.

Board on Testing and Assessment, National Research Council/National Academy of Sciences. (1997, Sept.). Test score flagging workshop, Washington, DC.

Brookhart v. Illinois State Board of Education. (1983). 697 F.2d 179, 183 (7th Cir.).

D'Amico v. New York State Board of Law Examiners. (1983). 813 F. Supp. 217 (W.D. N.Y.).

Disability Rights Advocates. (2001, Feb. 7). ETS agrees with disability groups to stop "flagging" on Graduate Admissions Tests [press release]. Oakland, CA: Author. Retrieved February 20, 2001, from www.dralegal.org/publication/ets.htm.

Educational Testing Service (ETS). (2001, Feb. 7). ETS agrees with disability groups to stop "flagging" on Graduate Admissions Tests [press release]. Princeton, NJ: Author. Retrieved February 20, 2001, from www.ets.org/aboutets/news/01020701.htm.

Goals 2000 Educate America Act. (2000). 20 U.S.C. § 5801 et seq.

Heaney, K., & Pullin, D. (1998). Accommodations and flags: Admissions testing and the rights of individuals with disabilities. *Educational Assessment, 5*(2), 71–93.

Heubert, J., & Hauser, R. (1999). *High stakes. Testing for tracking, promotion, and graduation.* Washington, DC: National Academy Press.

Improving America's Schools Act. (1994). 20 U.S.C. § 6301 et seq.

Individuals With Disabilities Education Act (IDEA). (1994). 20 U.S.C. § 1400 et seq.

McDonnell, L., McLaughlin, M., & Morison, P. (Eds.). (1997). *Educating one and all: Students with disabilities and standards-based reform.* Washington, DC: National Academy Press.

Mehrens, W. (1997). *Flagging test sores: Policy, practice, and research.* Unpublished paper submitted to the Board on Testing and Assessment, National Research Council, National Academy of Sciences, Washington, DC.

Messick, S. (1993). Validity. In B. Linn (Ed.), *Educational measurement: Issues and practice* (3rd. ed., pp. 13–103). Phoenix: American Council on Education and Oryx Press.

Milani, A. A. (1996). Disabled students in higher education: Administrative and judicial enforcement of disability law. *Journal of College and University Law, 22,* 989–1043.

Mobile County Bd. of Education. (1997). *Individuals With Disabilities Education Law Reporter, 26,* 695.

Murphy v. United Parcel Service. (1999). 527 U.S. 516.

Nestor, M. A. (1985). Psychometric testing and reasonable accommodation for persons with disabilities. *Rehabilitation Psychology, 38*(2), 75–85.

Phillips, S. E. (1994). High-stakes testing accommodations: Validity versus disabled rights. *Applied Measurement in Education, 7*(2), 93–120.

Pullin, D. C., & Heaney, K. J. (1997). The use of "flagged" test scores in college and university admissions: Issues and implications under Section 504 of the Rehabilitation Act and the Americans With Disabilities Act. *Journal of College and University Law, 23,* 797–828.

Pullin, D., & Zirkel, P. (1988). Testing the handicapped: Legislation, regulations, and litigation. *Education Law Reporter, 44,* 1–17.

Ragosta, M., & Wendler, C. (1992). *Eligibility issues and comparative time limits for disabled and nondisabled students.* Educational Testing Service Report RR-92-35.

Rehabilitation Act of 1973. (1994). 29 U.S.C. § 794.

Sherman, S. W., & Robinson, N. M. (Eds.). (1982). *Ability testing of handicapped people: Dilemma for government, science, and the public.* Washington, DC: National Academy Press.

Silverstein, R., Kamil, B., Delany, B., & Cassidy, J. (1979). *Department of Health, Education, and Welfare handbook for the implementation of Section 504 of the Rehabilitation Act of 1975.* Washington, DC: U.S. Department of Health, Education, and Welfare.

Slobodzian, J. (1997a, April 21). Blind test-takers: LSAC failed to comply with disabilities act. *National Law Journal,* p. A13.

Slobodzian, J. (1997b, Nov. 21). Settlement helps blind with LSAT. *Philadelphia Inquirer,* p. 35.

SUNY Health Science Center at Brooklyn College of Medicine (NY). (1993, Aug. 18). *National Disability Law Reporter, 5,* ¶ 77.

Sutton v. United Air Lines. (1999). 527 U.S. 471.

Thurlow, M., Ysseldyke, J., & Silverstein, B. (1995). Testing accommodations for students with disabilities. *Remedial and Special Education, 16*(5), 260–270.

Tucker, B. (1996). Application of the Americans With Disabilities Act (ADA) and Section 504 to Colleges and Universities. *Journal of College and University Law, 23*(1), 5.

University of Michigan. (1991, Oct. 18). *National Disability Law Reporter, 2,*

U.S. Department of Education, Office for Civil Rights. (1987a, June 26). *State Dep't of Educ. (GA). Education of Handicapped Law Reporter, 352,* 480.

U.S. Department of Education, Office for Civil Rights. (1987b, June 23). *South Carolina Dep't of Education. Education of Handicapped Law Reporter, 352,* 475.

U.S. Department of Education, Office for Civil Rights. (1990, Oct. 11). *Hawaii State Dep't of Education. Education of Handicapped Law Reporter, 17,* 360.

U.S. Department of Education, Office for Civil Rights. (1996, May 23). *Nevada State Department of Education. Individuals With Disabilities Education Law Reporter, 25,* 752.

U.S. Department of Education, Office for Civil Rights. (1997, Sept. 1). *Virginia Department of Education. Individuals With Disabilities Education Law Reporter, 27,* 1148.

U.S. Department of Education, Office for Civil Rights. (1998, Feb. 5). *Florida State Department of Education, Individuals With Disabilities Education Law Reporter, 28,* 1002.

Wightman, L. F. (1993). *Test takers with disabilities: A summary of data from special administrations of the LSAT.* Newtown, PA: Law School Admissions Council.

Willingham, W., Ragosta, M., Bennett, R., Braun, H., Rock, D., & Powers, D. (1988). *Testing handicapped people.* Boston: Allyn and Bacon.

Wynne v. Tufts University School of Medicine. (1991). 932 F.2d 19 (1st Cir.), *aff'd* 976 F.2d 791 (1992).

2

THE PSYCHOMETRICS OF TESTING INDIVIDUALS WITH DISABILITIES

KURT F. GEISINGER, GWYNETH BOODOO, AND JULIE P. NOBLE

Psychometrics is the field that studies the appropriateness and usefulness of test scores. Among the most important concepts studied by psychometricians are the validity of scores, the fairness of scores, and the reliability or consistency of scores. Psychometricians are also involved in the construction of measures to ensure that the tests that are created manifest the qualities (e.g., validity, fairness, reliability) they desire. Many psychometricians would argue that fairness and, perhaps, reliability are subsumed under the concept of validity. For the present discussion, however, we present these concepts separately with the understanding that fairness and reliability are perhaps best understood as contributing to test validity. At the conclusion of the chapter, a fourth psychometric concept, robustness, is introduced.

Tests are of necessity often administered to individuals with disabilities in a manner that differs somewhat from how the same test is administered to the general population. Such changes in test procedures may raise questions. Are the test scores emerging from such accommodated test administrations still meaningful? Do they carry the same meaning as scores from standard or traditional test administrations? These are some of the important questions that psychometrics addresses when facing this issue.

VALIDITY, FAIRNESS, AND RELIABILITY: THREE PSYCHOMETRIC CONCEPTS

Psychometricians study a number of the characteristics of tests to determine how valuable the tests are likely to be. *Validity* refers to the usefulness and appropriateness of scores resulting from a test. Validity is sometimes defined as the agreement between a test score from a particular measure and the quality that the test is intended to assess. Generally speaking, test use is valid if the test provides the kind of information that is sought by a test user. Most psychometricians hold that only test uses shown to be valid are appropriate. Tests are not universally valid or invalid; rather, tests are valid for specific uses and interpretations with specific populations. A given test might be appropriate for use with a given group of people but inappropriate for others. Similarly, a psychological measure that might be quite useful for determining whether an individual should be placed in a psychiatric facility would rarely be useful, for example, in job settings such as in personnel selection.

Validity may be assessed in any of a number of ways; many kinds of evidence may be used to justify and document the valid uses of a test, depending on the intended purpose of the test and the uses of its scores. For example, if test scores from a new test correlate highly with those from a well-established test of the same characteristic, it may be perceived as valid. Similarly, when test scores intentionally predict a criterion variable representative of success in a subsequent venture, the test is often seen as valid. Some kinds of test validity, however, do not involve the kinds of empirical verification heretofore mentioned. A final examination in a course, for example, is generally seen as valid if it covers material that is representative of the material taught in the course. Similarly, a test that samples a representative portion of the skills required in a job is generally perceived as a valid measure to use for selecting employees for that position. All of these rather dissimilar operations may be used to corroborate that a test is valid for a given use because they all provide information that a test does what its users wish it to do. For published tests and measures, manuals written for test users should provide information on the extent to which scores from the measure in question have been validated against the most important uses for which the test is commonly used.

Fairness is a relatively more recent concept in psychometrics, when compared to reliability and validity. It is the extent to which a test is developed and used so as to provide valid results for all groups. Fairness analyses are generally performed to investigate whether tests, a test, or components of a test operate equivalently for members of differing groups —for example, for men and women. There are generally two kinds of psychometric approaches to fairness. In the first, scores are compared for members of the various groups under investigation to determine if the test is equivalently valid for all groups. If a college entrance examination has been validated for use as one component of a college admissions process by virtue of the relationship between the scores emerging from the test and college success (typically grades in college), then the fairness of that same measure might be determined by considering the equivalence of the relationships in each of the groups under investigation. Presumably, if the relationships are equivalent, then the test is fair.

A second type of fairness investigation is performed using the components that make up tests, typically test items. This type of analysis compares the performance of members of different groups with the same levels of ability (or whatever is measured by the test) on individual test items. If members of different groups that have equivalent levels of the characteristic measured by the test answer a question correctly with approximately the same frequency, then the item may be seen as fair. If they do not, then it may not be seen as fair. For this reason, this type of analysis has been called differential item functioning (dif). This procedure has become an increasingly important step in constructing and evaluating many tests in a world that values fairness and equity.

In addition to the fairness analyses presented earlier, individuals often investigate the impact of the use of an examination on specific groups of interest. Imagine a researcher who wishes to investigate the impact of the use of a large-print form of a test. The researcher could, for example, compare the average scores earned on the large-print version of the test by test takers with visual disabilities against the average score earned by the general population using the standard administration of the test. Similarly, if the test was used to make pass–fail or competency decisions, the pass rates earned by the test takers with visual disabilities using the large-print form could be compared with the resulting pass rate occurring from the standard administration.

Another characteristic by which tests are appraised is reliability. In general, reliability refers to several specific varieties of consistency among test scores. Reliability is primarily of importance because the extent to which test scores are reliable generally limits their validity. A test may be seen as a sample of items from the universe of all possible test items measuring the characteristic in question. If a test is reliable, the scores that emerge from the administration of one sample of test questions from that universe will be comparable to those from other samplings from that universe as well. A test that is determined to be reliable will yield similar scores for the same examinees when they take the test on multiple occasions—for example, especially if memory is not involved. If there are multiple versions or forms of a given, reliable test, the scores that emerge from each of these test versions will be highly consistent. To the extent that scores change over time, inferences of validity relating to these changing scores will be affected. Finally, some tests involve the subjective–professional judgment of the examiner (test scorer) to a greater or lesser extent. As with the previous examples, the examiners involved in a test administration are seen as reliable when they administer the same test to the same test takers and generate comparable scores. In general, then, reliability involves consistency of scores across samplings of items, time, and raters (those evaluating performance on the examination). When a test is shown to have consistency across one or more of these dimensions, it is said to be reliable.

One group in our society for whom validity, fairness, and reliability have all been of major consequence includes individuals with disabilities (with virtually all types of disabilities included in this group). This chapter attempts to summarize some of the early research on reliability, validity, and fairness for members of this diverse group. Longer and more extensive reviews may be found in Willingham et al. (1988) and Geisinger (1994).

TESTING UNDER THE AMERICANS WITH DISABILITIES ACT

Two major pieces of legislative action in the United States have governed the use of testing of people with disabilities. Section 504 of the Rehabilitation Act of 1973 "mandated both that admissions tests administered to individuals with diabilities . . . be validated and that scores resulting from such instruments . . . reflect ability and aptitude (whatever the test was intended to measure) rather than any disabilities extraneous to what is assessed" (Geisinger, 1994, p. 123). The Americans With Disabilities Act of 1990 (called ADA) expanded and extended those rights. (Note that much of the material that is presented in this section is provided in more detail in the first chapter of this volume.)

Unlike the Rehabilitation Act of 1973, the primary focus of the ADA was employment testing (Tenopyr, Angoff, Butcher, Geisinger, & Reilly 1993). With regard to testing, the ADA requires that test takers with disabilities be assessed in a manner that demonstrates the extent to which they have the skills and abilities assessed by the measure and that the administration of the measure must not be made unnecessarily more "difficult as a result of their irrelevant disabilities" (Geisinger, 1994, p. 124).

There are many kinds of tests and many types of decisions for which tests are used. Tests used in situations in which major life decisions are made are sometimes referred to as high-stakes tests. Such decisions include college, graduate school, and professional school admissions; placement in special education; high school graduation; personnel hiring and promotion;

and certification or licensing. High-stakes tests are normally administered under controlled conditions. For example, test administrators usually adhere strictly to prespecified time limits for a given test. It is impossible to test many individuals with disabilities in such a manner, however. The extent to which the results of testing individuals with disabilities has the same meaning as the results of standard administrations is unclear. Adaptations in test administration conditions (such as time limits) must be made so that those using the test results receive information that bears on the skills and abilities of a test taker with a disability, rather than on the disability itself. These changes in test administration have been termed *test accommodations*. However, there are a great number of potential disabilities, and within each of these categories there are multiple gradations of disability. As a result, there is a seemingly huge number of potential accommodations.

Most standardized testing programs may offer a relatively finite number of accommodations. They may be offered singly or in combination. Tests may be administered in standard format, with improved type, large-type, Braille, audiocassette forms, or with a reader. Time limits can be enforced, extended in varying amounts, or waived altogether. Responses may be made on a test form, on an alternate form, on a tape recorder, or given to an amanuensis (human recorder). Test takers may also be provided with rest pauses, more convenient test-taking locations and times, full accessibility of test-taking locations, and other accommodations as are needed. Many testing programs report that the vast majority of test accommodations are for time extensions. (Chapter 3 in this volume provides more detailed information on test accommodations.)

Effects on Test Results From Accommodated Test Administrations

A key issue related to the usefulness of the results of testing from accommodated test administrations requires empirical evaluations of such assessments. It is not possible to evaluate such assessments without having them taken in the actual context of testing. Experimental testings do not ensure the requisite levels of test taker motivation. Such research is also quite difficult to perform, primarily because the numbers of individuals taking the tests with accommodated test administrations is quite low. Following we present a summarization of the validity, fairness, reliability, and robustness of test administrations.

Validity Evidence for Accommodated Test Results

To attempt to study the testing of individuals with disabilities, Willingham (1988, 1991) and his associates (1988) grouped individuals into four categories based on the type of disability for which they had received an accommodated test administration: visual disabilities, hearing disabilities, physical limitations, and learning disabilities. These individuals had taken one or more educational tests, primarily one of several tests for admission into higher education programs (e.g., Scholastic Assessment Test or the Graduate Record Examination). As summarized by Braun, Ragosta, and Kaplan (1988), for the most part accommodated assessments were as valid in predicting the criteria of first-year college or graduate school grades as they were for test takers who did not receive such accommodations (those who were administered the examinations under the normal, standardized test administrations). The only significant exception to this conclusion was for the test takers identified as learning disabled. Such individuals typically took the standard test form but received extended and, in some instances, unlimited time to answer questions on the test. For this group, test scores overpredicted their college grades. That is, these students did not do as well in college as their test scores would have predicted.

Ziomek and Andrews (1996) performed a study using three groups of college applicants, all of whom were classified into one of three subcategories of what Willingham and his associates called learning disabilities. The three groups were attention deficit disorder, dyslexia, and the learning disabled. These researchers used data from ACT assessment scores and the test takers' self-reported high school grades. The predictions indicated that the college grades for the attention deficit disorder and the learning disabled groups were slightly overpredicted relative to those receiving standard test administrations of the ACT assessment with little difference for the dyslexic group. Barton and McDaniel (1999) have compared reading test results for students who needed an oral administration and those using the standard administration. Students receiving an oral administration did not perform differently from their standard administration comparison group.

A more recent study by Ziomek and Andrews (1998) investigated the ACT assessment scores of students with disabilities who took the test at least twice, and at least once under extended-time conditions. Groups of students included those who took the test under extended time at least twice (Group 1), those who took the test initially under standard time limits and subsequently took the test under extended-time conditions (Group II), and those who took the test initially under extended-time conditions and subsequently tested again under standard time limits (Group III). Though Group II had lower initial average ACT composite scores, this group also had the highest overall average gain and final average ACT composite score. Overall average changes in ACT composite scores for the three groups were 0.9, 3.2, and -0.6 scale score units, respectively. The average ACT composite score gain for students testing twice under standard conditions is 0.7 scale score units (Andrews & Ziomek, 1998).

The factor structure of admissions measures was studied by Rock, Bennett, and Kaplan (1987) and Rock, Bennett, and Jirele (1988). Six years of data were assembled to develop a data set large enough to apply factor analysis. The researchers found a factor structure that was highly similar to those found with standard test administrations. Rock and his colleagues concluded that the test scores from accommodated administrations could be interpreted as comparable to those administered under standard conditions. Nevertheless, some questions were raised about whether the factors that resulted from the analyses (and hence the characteristics measured) were always identical when assessed in an accommodated test administration format. For example, mathematical items that are administered in a large-type format may extend over two pages, where the original item appeared on a single page. Memory thus becomes a more important factor than it was in the original version.

Most of the validation studies that have considered nonstandard test administrations suffer from similar methodological problems. The primary problem relates to the relatively small number of test takers who receive nonstandard test administrations. For example, Rock et al. (1988) reviewed data from three years of GRE administrations—approximately 60,000 testings. "After three years, only 118 individuals with visual impairment took the standard GRE in a typical, timed fashion, and another 151 took the large-type extended time administration" (Geisinger, 1994, p. 131). Most statistical procedures require numbers larger than these. Yet testing programs such as the GRE are among the largest testing programs in the country. If such programs cannot generate appropriate numbers to permit the proper statistical analyses, serious issues exist. Clearly, validation efforts are difficult for most testing programs that are not as large.

Fairness

Test fairness under nonstandard test conditions has been studied primarily using predictive validity studies linking college admissions tests with success in college. As noted earlier, such test conditions have been found to be fair, with the possible exception of the impact of additional time for those with learning disabilities and other similar cognitive conditions. Bennett, Rock, and Kaplan (1987) and Willingham et al. (1988) performed differential item functioning analyses using data from standard and nonstandard test administrations. They concluded that items were generally equally difficult for test takers of comparable ability levels. That is, items were approximately equally difficult across standard and nonstandard test conditions. However, Bennett, Rock, and Novatkoski (1989) found that some mathematical items were significantly more difficult when presented in a Braille format. Lengthy word problems, for example, were more difficult.

Reliability of Test Results

Few studies of the reliability of accommodated test administrations have been performed. Bennett, Ragosta, and Stricker (1988) studied the reliability of educational achievement tests used with elementary schoolchildren and found that test scores obtained under nonstandard test conditions were approximately as reliable as those obtained under standard test conditions. Bennett, Rock, Kaplan, and Jirele (1988) studied the reliability of scores from the SAT and the GRE and found that the measurement precision of scores earned under the nonstandard testing conditions of these instruments were as reliable as those under standard administrations.

Robustness

Klimoski and his colleagues (1993; Klimoski & Palmer, 1993) have suggested the use of the term *robustness* for psychological testing. In this chapter, this term refers to the ability of a test to be adapted across the modalities needed for proper test accommodations. A test that can be adapted and that continues to provide valid results would be considered a robust test. As test developers gain experience in building tests that will need to be adapted, they will learn more about those factors needed to help to make tests robust and ultimately build these qualities into future tests. We are at the earliest stage of such work and much effort of this type is needed.

CONCLUSION

Testing and assessment have become prevalent in the United States primarily because valid test use improves the quality of decision making. It is nevertheless true that the validity of a test as an aid to decision making may be population-specific, and such specificity may be especially true when comparing populations that differ in regard to disability status. When using a psychological assessment to make decisions about test takers with particular disabilities, the test user should investigate the usefulness of the instrument with members of such populations. Such information is likely to come from empirical validation research and should generally be summarized in the test manual or a similar document produced by the test publisher. When using tests for which no psychometric (e.g., validity, fairness, and reliability) data are available, extreme caution must be used, and perhaps their very use must be questioned. Without supportive data, it is not necessarily clear that the instrument measures the same psychological constructs in populations with and without specific disabilities. If it does, its scoring may not be equivalent for all groups. Without validity and fairness evidence, the interpretation of scores for those with certain disabilities must be queried. Thus, test users must engage in investigative research to consider whether it is appropriate to use particular instruments with particular test users. In so doing, test users affirm the underlying principles applicable to all appropriate test use. Use must be consistent with validity evidence. Validity may not be assumed. Reliability and fairness evidence may offer certain support for some test uses, but ultimately validity must be ensured.

REFERENCES

Americans With Disabilities Act. (1990). 42 U.S.C. § 12111–12213, Pub. L. No. 101–336.

Andrews, K. M., & Ziomek, R. L. (1998). *Score gains on retesting with the ACT Assessment* (ACT Research Report No. 98–7). Iowa City, IA: ACT.

Barton, K., & McDaniel, F. (1999). *Variance attributable to modifications for students with disabilities in statewide testing: An investigation of score validity.* Unpublished manuscript, University of South Carolina.

Bennett, R. E., Ragosta, M., & Stricker, L. J. (1988). Test results. In W. W. Willingham, M. Ragosta, R. E. Bennett, H. Braun, D. A. Rock, & D. E. Powers (Eds.), *Testing handicapped people* (pp. 37–46). Needham Heights, MA: Allyn and Bacon.

Bennett, R. E., Rock, D. A., & Kaplan, B. A. (1987). SAT differential item performance for nine handicapped groups. *Journal of Educational Measurement, 24,* 41–55.

Bennett, R. E., Rock, D. A., Kaplan, B. A., & Jirele, T. (1988). Psychometric characteristics. In W. W. Willingham, M. Ragosta, R. E. Bennett, H. Braun, D. A. Rock, & D. E. Powers (Eds.), *Testing handicapped people* (pp. 84–97). Needham Heights, MA: Allyn and Bacon.

Bennett, R. A., Rock, D. A., & Novatkoski, I. (1989). Differential item functioning on the SAT-M Braille Edition. *Journal of Educational Measurement, 26,* 67–79.

Braun, H. Ragosta, M., & Kaplan, B. (1988). Predictive validity. In W. W. Willingham, M. Ragosta, R. E. Bennett, H. Braun, D. A. Rock, & D. E. Powers (Eds.), *Testing handicapped people* (pp. 109–132). Needham Heights, MA: Allyn and Bacon.

Geisinger, K. F. (1994). Psychometric issues in testing students with disabilities. *Applied Measurement in Education, 7,* 121–140.

Klimoski, R. J. (1993, Aug. 22). Implications of the ADA of 1990 for the practice of psychology. In S. M. Bruyere (Chr.), *Americans With Disabilities Act and related Canadian legislation—Implications for psychologists.* Symposium presented at the annual meeting of the American Psychological Association, Toronto.

Klimoski, R., & Palmer, S. (1993). The ADA and the hiring process in organizations. *Consulting Psychology Journal, 45,* 10–36.

Rehabilitation Act of 1973. (1973, Sept. 26). Pub. L. No. 93–112, 87 Stat. 355.

Rock, D. A., Bennett, R. E., & Jirele, T. (1988). Factor structure of the Graduate Record Examination's general test in handicapped and nonhandicapped groups. *Journal of Applied Psychology, 73,* 382–392.

Rock, D. A., Bennett, R. E., & Kaplan, B. A. (1987). Internal construct validity of a college admissions test across handicapped and non-handicapped groups. *Educational and Psychological Measurement, 47,* 193–205.

Tenopyr, M. L., Angoff, W. H., Butcher, J. N., Geisinger, K. F., & Reilly, R. R. (American Psychological Association Division of Evaluation, Measurement, and Statistics). (1993). Psychometric and assessment issues raised by the Americans With Disabilities Act (ADA). *The Score, 15*(4), 1–2, 7–15.

Willingham, W. W. (1988). Testing handicapped people—The validity question. In H. Wainer & H. Braun (Eds.), *Test validity* (pp. 89–103). Hillsdale, NJ: Erlbaum.

Willingham, W. W. (1991). Standard testing conditions and standard score meaning for handicapped examinees. *Applied Measurement in Education, 2,* 97–103.

Willingham, W. W., Ragosta, M., Bennett, R. E., Braun, H., Rock, D. A., & Powers, D. E. (1988). *Testing handicapped people.* Needham Heights, MA: Allyn and Bacon.

Ziomek, R. L., & Andrews, K. M. (1996). *Predicting the college grade point averages of special-tested students from their ACT assessment scores and high school grades* (ACT Research Report No. 96-7). Iowa City, IA: ACT.

Ziomek, R. L., & Andrews, K. M. (1998). *ACT assessment score gains of special-tested students who tested at least twice* (ACT Research Report No. 98-8). Iowa City, IA: ACT.

II

TESTING ACCOMMODATIONS AND SCORE REPORTING

3

TYPES OF COMMONLY REQUESTED ACCOMMODATIONS

PETER BEHUNIAK

This chapter describes some of the many possible types of testing accommodations that can increase access to test participation by test takers with disabilities. There are several distinctions and points that require elaboration to set the appropriate context for the discussion of specific accommodations that follows.

The terms *modification* and *accommodation* can sometimes cause confusion. Although some organizations and publications treat these terms as synonyms, others draw distinctions between them, though not always in the same way. The National Center on Educational Outcomes and the Parents Engaged in Education Reform Project (1997, p. 14) concluded, "Distinctions between the meanings of the terms are not worthy of discussion because they are used to mean the same thing as often as they are to mean different things." Therefore, in the interest of clarity and simplicity, all possible test alterations discussed will be referred to as "accommodations."

A general reason for providing accommodations is that such accommodations improve the access of individuals to assessments by allowing examinees a fair opportunity to respond to the test questions and tasks.

However, because tests have many different purposes, a more complete statement would be that test accommodations are necessary to extend to every potential examinee the benefits that can result from the examinee receiving a test score. These benefits may be an action (e.g., college admission), establishment of a given status (e.g., certification, graduation), or the identification of a problem that can then be addressed (e.g., remedial instruction). The failure to provide reasonable accommodations could result in an individual being unfairly denied one or more of these benefits.

Test accommodations also help to ensure that all individuals have a fair opportunity to participate in assessments that may be presented in many different settings and formats. Tests can be administered individually or in groups. Tests may be presented orally, in print, or by using a computer. A test may be designed to be completed in a few minutes, hours, or even days. Each of these circumstances may pose to an examinee challenges that are unrelated to what is being measured. That is, one or more features of the test format or test administration may unintentionally interfere with an examinee's capacity to demonstrate his or her ability or proficiency. Many of the test accommodations described in this chapter are appropriate for consideration in various settings, whether large group or individual administrations. Other accommodations are most useful when applied to a particular setting or format. All of the test accommodations presented, however, are intended to help eliminate unintentional obstructions to examinee performance caused by the test environment or the format.

The issue of test validity is addressed in detail elsewhere in this book (see chapter 2, this volume). However, it is important to note that each of the accommodations discussed in this chapter may affect the validity of the resulting test scores in either positive or negative ways. The effects of testing accommodations on validity depends on many factors, including test content, test construct, purpose of the test, and the format of the test questions and examinee responses (Phillips, 1993). It is not possible to discuss each individual accommodation in every context. Therefore, the reader must be aware that the comments regarding each accommodation are generally true but must always be considered in relation to the specific details of each assessment.

A generally allowable accommodation might invalidate the scores for one test even though that accommodation would be fine for many other tests. Thus, extending the time limits on a reading, writing, or other academic achievement test would be generally acceptable, but extending the time on a typing test alters one of the factors important to the assessment. Conversely, an accommodation that is generally not recommended might not adversely affect the validity for a given test.

The applicable principle is that the accommodation should increase examinee access while maintaining or enhancing the validity of the resulting test scores. Accommodations that have adverse effects on test score validity should not be allowed. Decisions regarding the probable effect of any accommodation on validity, therefore, should take into account the specific nature and context of each test.

Validity issues also require some consideration of the differences between criterion-referenced tests (CRT) and norm-referenced tests (NRT). A CRT evaluates performance on specific skills or areas and the results are interpreted in relation to established criteria (e.g., the examinee correctly answered at least 8 of 10 two-digit multiplication problems). An NRT describes performance in relation to other examinees in a defined group— for example, the examinee can read as well or better than 62% of 11-year-old public school students (Gronlund, 1981). Any decision to provide accommodations for an examinee would require that attention be given to whether the test scores are intended to be interpreted in a criterion-referenced manner, norm-referenced manner, or both. The potential effect of an accommodation on a norm-referenced interpretation must consider the degree to which the score for the examinee receiving the accommodation remains comparable to the results of the other examinees in the norm group. In the typing example, an accommodation such as use of a word processor might give the examinee an unfair advantage (e.g., easing corrections) compared to other examinees. The same accommodation, however, might be reasonable if the criterion of interest was the specific speed and accuracy of the examinee and the word processor was judged an acceptable workplace tool. The implication for interpreting test scores will need to be similarly evaluated for each accommodation under consideration.

A final point regarding interpreting test scores resulting from an accommodated administration concerns the need for documentation. Documenting decisions about test accommodations is an important component in the process of ensuring valid assessments. This subject is discussed in detail in chapter 4. Readers are urged to consider that each of the accommodations discussed in this chapter carry with them particular implications for test takers and the interpretation of their scores, which may bear directly on documentation requirements.

PHYSICAL ENVIRONMENT CHANGES AS ACCOMMODATIONS

The setting and physical environment in which the test is administered is a factor that may affect test validity. Typical test settings include, but are not limited to, schools, businesses, counseling centers, and separate locations within these places. The test setting can be affected by environmental aspects such as lighting, equipment, furniture, noise, and whether the test is administered individually or within a group setting (AERA/APA/NCME, 1999).

Many assessments are administered in a classroom or large-group setting. There is usually no problem associated with allowing an individual or small-group administration as an accommodation. The primary advantage to the test taker is a reduction in distractions. However, a complication could arise if the test includes a group activity. In this case it might be possible to allow the test taker to participate in the normal group activity and then move to a small-group or individual setting.

Providing a separate location is usually a reasonable means of reducing the distractions to the test taker with special needs and, possibly, to other test takers. If the alternative location is a facility (e.g., private school, institute), it should be feasible to maintain adequate test security and standardized administrative conditions as long as the test proctor is well-experienced and familiar with the appropriate test administration procedures. In other settings, however, care must be given to offer a standardized, secure test administration (Educational Testing Service, 2000). One strategy would be to arrange for a proctor with experience to go to the test taker's setting and conduct the administration. Determining whether a particular setting is adequate and suitable for a given assessment would need to be made on a case by case basis.

A separate administrator provided to the test taker is generally acceptable if the administrator is familiar with testing procedures and accepts the responsibility for ensuring a standardized administration. For example, 44 states allow individual test administration on what would normally be group-administered statewide assessments (Olson, Bond, & Andrews, 1999). However, the administrator should not view the task as one of helping the test taker to perform better or "bending the rules" in the test taker's favor (i.e., making changes in addition to the predetermined, approved accommodations).

Special lighting or special furniture also may be useful for some test takers. These should not present a problem as long as other test takers are not distracted.

CHANGES IN TESTING TIME AS ACCOMMODATIONS

The amount of time given to test takers to complete the assessment also affects test validity. Ziomek and Andrews (1996) reported modest overprediction of college grades for students allowed extra testing time on the ACT. Accommodations related to this aspect of test administration include limited time extensions, abbreviated test sessions, and frequent rest periods.

An achievement test may be a power test, a speed test, or a combination (Mehrens & Lehman, 1984). A power test is one in which all examinees are expected to have sufficient time to address all questions and tasks, in contrast to a speed test where time is limited and many or most examinees will not finish by design. The practice of identifying time limits for power tests is based on the idea that time limits are administratively practical (Camara, 1995) and of little consequence if set generously to allow the vast majority of examinees sufficient time to complete the assessment (Ahmann & Glock, 1981). It is, therefore, possible to be fairly flexible with time limits. State policies regarding statewide achievement testing include allowing extended testing time (46 states), more breaks (48), and extending sessions over multiple days (42; Olson et al., 1999). Allowing greater time, whether within limits (e.g., up to an extra hour) or unlimited time, should be guided by the principle of providing the test taker ample opportunity to respond to test questions without fatigue becoming a factor. Some consideration should be given to each test taker's attention span in setting or extending time limits.

Speeded assessments present a different challenge. In certain situations, it is important to know how quickly a test taker can perform. For example, speed is a critical element in tests of typing or shorthand proficiency. In these cases, time extensions either should not be permitted or should be allowed only if an appropriate explanation of the accommodation accompanies the test score. Time extensions that make test score interpretations misleading should not be allowed. For instance, in the typing example, it is common to report results such as, "The examinee typed 50 words per minute." If time limits were relaxed or eliminated during the assessment, the results would not be interpretable.

Many tests share the attributes of power and speed tests. These tests are not designed to be speeded, though many examinees fail to reach the last item because, at least in part, of time limits. These tests must be individually considered. It will generally be true that accommodations of extended time will more profoundly affect test validity as the speededness factor increases.

Abbreviated test sessions or frequent rest periods are usually acceptable accommodations that can be provided as needed by any test taker. However, it is necessary to ensure that the test taker will not obtain test-relevant information or assistance during any breaks. In-room breaks with the test takers completing the assessment after a rest would be acceptable. Allowing test takers to begin a test session one day and then continue with that session the next would not be acceptable on a test designed for a single-session administration. This concern would not apply to an assessment designed to be administered over two or more days, such as the American Bar Association exam. If a test is normally presented in separate sessions, it should be acceptable to complete one session per day even if a typical administration included two or more sessions each day.

CHANGES IN TEST DIRECTIONS AS ACCOMMODATIONS

The way in which test directions are given to test takers may affect test validity. Accommodations regarding this aspect of testing may entail reading directions aloud, repeating directions, signing, giving separate directions, and highlighting directions. The effect of specific accommodations on test validity appears to depend on the degree to which the accommodation is related to what is being tested. "Although it may be valid to read the questions on a mathematics test to a student who has dyslexia or some other reading disability, it may not be valid to have someone read a test of reading to the same student. The problem arises when the accommodation is closely related to the skill being assessed" (Olson & Goldstein. 1997, p. 18). Recently there has been increased research attention to collecting evidence on the particular ways in which these accommodations affect validity (Olson & Goldstein, 1997; Tindal, 1996).

Directions may be presented orally to the test takers, either as they read along or in place of a written presentation. In many standardized testing situations, directions are read aloud by the proctor as a matter of regular procedure, so this may not even qualify as an accommodation. Similarly, it may be beneficial for some students to have the directions presented on a separate sheet of paper. The use of sign language as a presentation option is usually a reasonable alternative for hearing-impaired examinees.

The strategy of highlighting or providing other emphasis of parts of the directions (e.g., verbs) is potentially problematic. Standardized assessments incorporate carefully developed directions that may or may not include certain emphases. Allowing test administrators the right to emphasize selected words, phrases, or sections of the directions at their discretion presents a problem in that such emphasis might unintentionally mislead examinees as they proceed to complete the test. Further complicating this scenario, there likely would be no evidence available to confirm if a test taker was confused or misdirected by such an accommodation. The result would be an invalid test score.

A possible alternative to editing the directions would be to provide additional preparation before the test administration. For example, if a test administrator believed it would be helpful to emphasize the part of the directions that tell the test taker to "choose the best answer" from among the options presented, rather than highlighting the formal test directions, the test administrator could discuss the meaning of this type of direction and provide a few practice exercises before the test administration.

Often it is possible for a proctor to review the test directions and sample-item formats well in advance of the actual test administration. If the proctor anticipates that an examinee may experience confusion caused by unfamiliar directions or formats, the proctor may suggest the examinee complete sample items or practice tests before the actual test administration. Test publishers and many other test developers routinely provide sample items and practice tests.

TEST ACCOMMODATIONS INVOLVING CHANGES IN TEST FORMAT AND RESPONSE MECHANISMS

Testing accommodations are often related to the format in which the test material is presented and how test takers respond to the assessment. The test may be presented in large print with increased space between items or fewer items per page, or it may be presented in Braille, sign language, orally by test administrator or reader, or by audiotape. Concomitantly, the test taker may respond on enlarged answer sheets, in Braille, in sign language, by dictation to a scribe or to audiotape, or with a typewriter or word processing program. Test format accommodations that may have an effect on test validity include having the test administrator omit problematic questions and reading aloud test passages and items for tests that measure reading comprehension.

Large print, Braille, and sign language are all reasonable accommodations that can be used if certain constraints are considered. Resources would need to be available to the test developer or another party to create large print and Braille copies of the tests. If signing is needed, the test administrator must be capable of signing. Test administrators who will be signing or reading test materials must possess experience in communicating accurately the specific information included on the test. This may include technical terms or special symbols (e.g., mathematical, scientific). In addition, all information must be presented to the examinee without providing clues through such means as intonation, emphasis, or pausing.

Some test items, such as ones involving complicated drawings or pictures, do not lend themselves to translation into Braille. This means the test taker may not have the opportunity to respond to all of the regular test items. In assessments intended primarily for diagnostic purposes, this presents only a minor problem because only the validity of the section or objective directly incorporating the excluded test item(s) is affected. However, in tests with overall standards (e.g., proficiency level, certificate of mastery, licensure) the interpretation of the total test score is a more serious problem. Consider, for example, a 100-point test on which an examinee needs a minimum score of 60 to meet the standard. If the test taker cannot attempt 10% of the test questions because they could not be translated to Braille (or expanded or signed), how would this test taker's score of 53 consequently be interpreted? It is below the standard on an absolute basis, but the test taker might have reached or surpassed the standard if provided the same opportunity as everyone else to try all test questions.

Test takers who take a test with one of the accommodations described may also benefit from responding on an enlarged document, in Braille, or sign language. The translation of Braille response may be done either on-site or at a central location such as a test-scoring center. The on-site translator may know the test taker better, which may enhance the accuracy of the translation. However, it may be more difficult for the on-site translator to remain objective and to avoid giving the test taker the benefit of any doubt. A similar concern exists for the use of an on-site translator for test takers who are signing their responses. A possible option would be to videotape the test taker's response for translation at a central site.

A test administrator may read test passages and items to the test taker provided (a) the test administrator reads verbatim and (b) the test is *not* a measure of reading comprehension. An alternative to this is to play a prerecorded (standardized) audiotape. The use of the tape eliminates potential problems of individual differences among test administrators regarding speed, inflection, pronunciation, and intelligibility. Sign language videotape presentation is also an option. However, the tape presentation still must be monitored for appropriate pace, volume, and equipment malfunction. It should also be noted that auditory presentations could place a greater demand on memory than print formats. A routine test-taking activity with a printed version of the test, such as going back to check a portion of the text, can be much more difficult and time consuming with an auditory presentation.

An enlarged answer document may be used in many circumstances. For multiple-choice tests, this consists of merely providing larger sets of bubbles. The test taker's responses can then be transcribed to a normal answer document for scanning or the enlarged document can be hand scored. For tests involving written responses, larger spaces between lines or larger response areas can be provided. Certain specific content may be inappropriate for this accommodation, such as responses to geometry questions that require particular dimensions for a proper response.

Accommodations for which caution is advised include allowing test administrators to (a) omit questions they consider problematic and (b) read to the test takers test passages and items on reading comprehension tests. Allowing test administrators the discretion to omit questions introduces a degree of nonstandardization, because the test taker would not have the opportunity to respond to some number of test questions. This also seems to be an unnecessary modification because if the test taker is unable to respond to a particular question, the test taker only needs to skip that item. This is consistent with how most test takers deal with questions that are too difficult or confusing. The accommodation of having a test administrator read aloud the reading comprehension passages and items is very likely to alter significantly the construct being assessed, therefore interfering with test validity. A reading comprehension score generated without the test taker having read the material must necessarily reflect a different ability than if the test taker had read the material. It is strongly advised that other methods be considered, such as the use of alternative measures (discussed later in this chapter).

Test takers who experience difficulty with gross or fine motor control may benefit by being able to dictate their responses. If a test taker dictates to a scribe, there should be little difficulty when the test consists of multiple-choice questions. Other types of questions that elicit very specific responses (e.g., numerical answers, true/false, one-word answers) may be dictated as well. However, it can be potentially problematic to allow dictation and transcription on questions intended to elicit open-ended, extended written responses. To the extent that the test taker's writing proficiency is the primary factor, or even one of several important factors being assessed, a change of the response mode to dictation can introduce a substantive and unpredictable variation in the difficulty and nature of the task presented to the test taker. Depending on the purpose of the assessment, this may have an adverse impact on test score validity.

Similar issues would apply to allowing a test taker to dictate answers on audiotape. One benefit of using audiotape is the possibility of transcribing and scoring the student responses at a central location where individuals trained in the scoring process might provide greater objectivity. Limitations of audiotape include the possibility of recorder malfunction and the fact that the transcriber/scorer may misunderstand some of the taped responses. One possible solution would be to use both an on-site scribe and taperecorder backup.

Test takers who cannot write or write with great difficulty may be able to use a typewriter or personal computer. This accommodation might be appropriate in many circumstances, depending on the nature and purpose of the test. The widespread use of computers offers word processing as an additional alternative that may be suitable. It is usually necessary to deactivate spell-checking, grammar checking, internal thesaurus, and similar aids to avoid providing an unintended advantage to test takers granted this accommodation.

Many of these accommodations require more than the standard amount of time allowed on a timed test. Test formats using cassettes, oral presentations, or Braille often will require extended time. Similarly, allowing an examinee to respond orally or use a scribe or personal computer may require more time. The extension of time should be anticipated and balanced with the possibility of introducing fatigue as a factor.

RESPONSE AIDS AS ACCOMMODATIONS

Test takers requesting special accommodations may increase their access to fair testing situations by being allowed to use certain response aids.

Response aids include items such as an abacus, calculator, voice-activated word processor, magnifying lens, electronic reader, and an optacon.

Each of these aids can increase the access of certain test takers to the tests. However, as indicated previously, each aid poses some threat to the validity of the resulting test scores. For instance, the advisability of allowing an abacus or calculator is very sensitive to the content and constructs being assessed. Some standardized achievement tests are designed for *all* examinees to have a calculator available. Clearly, in these cases calculators are an integral part of the constructs being measured. But consider an elementary-level mathematics test of basic computation skills. The absence or availability of a calculator may partially or completely alter the skill being measured. For any particular assessment, a judgment is necessary regarding the degree to which a calculator might change each individual task in the test.

Similar concerns would apply in varying degrees to the other aids. The use of magnification would be the easiest to justify under most circumstances. The use of the voice-activated word processor may be quite likely to alter the construct being assessed, at least when certain skills are being measured. For example, if a test taker responds orally using a voice-activated word processor to a test of writing proficiency, it may be the test taker's oral proficiency that is assessed. Nevertheless, each of these aids could be effectively used in some contexts, depending on the purpose, content, and format of the test.

COMPUTER-BASED TESTING

The increased availability of computer-based tests offers a number of opportunities and challenges for test developers and administrators trying to provide access to as many examinees as possible. When a computer-based version of a test exists, all of the potential benefits of keyboard access are immediately available. In addition, there may be an improved capacity to provide some of the previously described accommodations, such as extended time, frequent rest periods, individual test administration, and oral presentation to accompany a visual presentation. If computer-adaptive testing is available, an added benefit is the potential decrease in overall testing time with no sacrifice in test validity. This saving in testing time is a result of the fact that test takers may not need to respond to as many test items as they would have to answer on a nonadaptive test.

Computer-based testing presents some potential difficulties. Certain test content may not lend itself to be presented on a computer. For example, early elementary grade mathematics questions regarding the use of rulers and other measuring devices may be better suited to a paper presentation. A more general concern would apply anytime both paper and computer-based versions of the same assessment are presented. In this case, it is necessary to examine the comparability of the two measures. Unintended differences caused by the mode of presentation could adversely affect the validity of the resulting test scores. In high-stakes assessments, it would be advisable to investigate any potential differences between the two methods of presentation by conducting controlled studies with comparable or equivalent groups of examinees.

Examinee familiarity with computer-based testing can pose a potential problem because examinees are likely to differ in their previous exposure. Examinees need to have a reasonable amount of experience with computers before beginning the test administration. Tutorials, sample items, and computer-based practice tests are usually available and may be helpful with students who have limited computer experience.

ALTERNATIVE MEASURES

One option to consider for any assessment is the use of alternative measures. In any given instance the accommodations previously described might allow access to some examinees, whereas others remain excluded. Similarly, for any one examinee, these accommodations might allow access to certain parts of an assessment but not to the entire assessment. In these cases, it may be feasible to offer an alternative measure in a format that would accommodate additional special-examinee needs.

The need to consider the use of alternative measures was heightened with the recent authorization of programs such as Goals 2000: Educate America Act, Improving America's Schools Act, and the Individuals With Disabilities Education Act (IDEA), all of which call for "assessments that are meaningful, challenging and appropriate for *all* students" (NCES, 1996, p. 1). The 1997 reauthorization of IDEA called for states to have in place, by July 1, 2000, alternative assessments to be used to assess students with disabilities who would otherwise be unable to participate in large-scale state and district assessments. Alternative measures may prove an option for individuals who might not otherwise be assessable. For example, test takers who are unable to write or use allowable accommodations to respond to a writing test (e.g., typewriter or word processor) may be candidates for an alternative measure. If the writing assessment was developed to determine an examinee's ability to compose a narrative work, an alternative assessment might be developed to determine whether an examinee could dictate the narrative. During test development, care must be taken to frame the task for the oral response in such a way as to minimize the differences from the original writing task. However, the resulting test score and interpretation would need to take into account that a different, though related, construct has been assessed.

Guided by the IDEA legislation, more attention is being given to developing alternative measures. The trend toward increasing the number and types of alternative measures is likely to continue. However, all attempts to develop alternate measures need to recognize and address the likelihood that the construct and difficulty of the alternative measure will likely differ from the original. Overcoming the difficulties inherent in trying to provide suitable and valid alternative measures is considered a major challenge at this time (Ysseldyke, Olson, & Thurlow, 1997). Possible methods of addressing this would include the collection of comparative data during test development, thoughtful standard setting (if appropriate), and modified reporting procedures.

CURRENT ACCOMMODATIONS ON MAJOR ASSESSMENT PROGRAMS

It might be instructive to consider the scope and extent to which major testing programs and large-scale state assessments are currently offering accommodations like the ones described in this chapter. However, most testing programs and states are regularly revisiting the issue of accommodations and often revise their policies. This occurs because of changing political climates, legal developments, and information gained from new research on the effects and implications of various accommodations. Therefore, it is not very useful to provide a summary of policies that were in effect as this book goes to press, knowing that they will soon be modified. Readers are encouraged to contact the testing programs directly. The Council of Chief State School Officers publishes information on state student assessment programs. The National Center on Educational Outcomes also has state reports. The National Center on Educational Statistics can provide information about accommodations used in the National Assessment of Educational Progress (NAEP). The addresses and websites for these and other useful resources can be found in chapter 16.

CONCLUSION

This chapter has provided an overview of frequently used testing accommodations. The type of accommodation varies with the setting in which the testing occurs and is further addressed in the sections of this book dealing with clinical and counseling settings, educational settings, and testing for employment, certification, and licensing. For a discussion of the issues associated with accommodations, see Pitonick and Royer (2001).

REFERENCES

Ahmann, J. S., & Glock, M. D. (1981). *Evaluating student progress: Principles of tests and measurements* (6th ed.) Boston: Allyn and Bacon.

American Educational Research Association, American Psychological Association, National Council on Measurement in Education (AERA/APA/NCME). (1999). *Standards for educational and psychological testing.* Washington, DC: American Educational Research Association.

Camara, W. J. (1995). Speededness, flagging and other issues in testing candidates with disabilities in large testing programs. *Personnel Testing Council Newsletter, 18*(10), 1–3.

Educational Testing Service. (2000). *ETS standards for quality and fairness.* Princeton, NJ: Author.

Gronlund, N. E. (1981). *Measurement and evaluation in teaching* (4th ed.) New York: Macmillan.

Mehrens, W. A., & Lehman, I. J. (1984). *Measurement and evaluation in education and psychology* (3rd ed.) New York: Holt, Rinehart and Winston.

National Center on Educational Outcomes and the Parents Engaged in Education Reform Project. (1997). *Opening the door to educational reform: Understanding educational assessment and accountability.* Boston: Author.

National Center for Educational Statistics (NCES). (1996). *Focus on NAEP: Increasing the inclusion of students with disabilities and limited English proficient students in NAEP.* Washington, DC: U.S. Department of Education.

Olson, J. F., Bond, L., & Andrews, C. (1999). *Annual survey of state student assessment programs. Volume II.* Washington, DC: Council of Chief State School Officers.

Olson, J. F., & Goldstein, A. A. (1997). *The inclusion of students with disabilities and limited English proficient students in large-scale assessments: A summary of recent progress National Center for Education Statistics Research and Development Report.* Washington, DC: Office of Educational Research and Improvement, U.S. Department of Education.

Phillips, S. E. (1993). Testing condition accommodations for disabled students. *Education Law Reporter, 80,* 9–32.

Pitonick, M., & Royer, J. (2001). Testing accommodations for examinees with disabilities: A review of psydrometric, legal and social policy issues. *Review of Educational Research, 71,* 53–104.

Tindal, G. (1996, June). *Conducting research on accommodations in performance assessments: Issues and options.* Proposal submitted to State Collaborative on Assessment and Student Standards Technical Guidelines for Performance Assessment Consortium, Eugene, University of Oregon.

Ysseldyke, J., Olson, K., & Thurlow, M. (1997). *Issues and considerations in alternative assessments* (Synthesis Report 27). Minneapolis, MN: National Center on Educational Outcomes.

Ziomek, R. L., & Andrews, K. M. (1996). *Predicting the college grade point averages of special tested students for their ACT assessment scores and high school grades* (Research Report Series 96–7). Iowa City: ACT.

4

DOCUMENTATION

NICHOLAS A. VACC AND NANCY TIPPINS

Psychologists, counselors, and other testing professionals are sometimes asked to assist in the documentation of a disability. The most common uses of such documentation include (a) planning services and educational programs for the individual whose disability has been documented and (b) making decisions about appropriate accommodations for the individual in educational settings. Documentation is also used by testing professionals when making decisions about appropriate accommodations in most types of testing and assessment.

DOCUMENTING A DISABILITY

The exact content of the documentation depends on the reason it is being prepared. The content may also be determined by laws or by the guidelines of the organization or educational institution that will be using the information. In addition, different types of disabilities may require different types of documentation. Individuals preparing documentation should have appropriate knowledge and experience regarding both the disability and the situation in which the documentation will be used.

As indicated in chapter 1, the Americans With Disabilities Act

(ADA) and Section 504 of the Rehabilitation Act of 1973 are broad pieces of legislation that protect the rights of individuals with disabilities. Section 504 applies to almost all educational testing and to testing for professional licensing and certification. The ADA also applies to employment. Another important piece of legislation, the Individuals With Education Act (IDEA), deals with the provision of special education and services for students with disabilities. In each piece of legislation, there are guides for documenting a disability.

The Americans With Disabilities Act

Guides for documentation requirements under the ADA are contained in the Equal Employment Opportunity Commission (EEOC) Enforcement Guidance documents (1994, 1999, 2000). The enforcement documents explain that an employer may ask an individual to provide documentation that substantiates a disability covered under the ADA and the need for a reasonable accommodation. The documentation is deemed sufficient if it describes the nature, severity, and duration of the impairment, the activity(s) that are limited, the extent to which these activities are limited, and the reason(s) why an accommodation is needed.

Testing professionals in organizations using tests and assessments for employment should note that documentation is not always required in employment situations. The EEOC, in its 1993 publication, *Technical Assistance Manual on the Employment Provisions of the ADA*, and in subsequent enforcement guidance documents, stated that documentation is not necessary in employment testing when the test taker has observable, physical disabilities but may be requested for nonobservable disabilities such as learning or psychiatric disorders or other situations when the need for accommodation is not obvious.

Unless the disability is observable, employers usually follow the practice of requiring documentation for a request for accommodation on any test if the accommodation changes the standardized administration of the test or would affect the interpretation of the test score. Thus, accommodation requests such as special lighting or higher tables are typically granted in employment testing without any documentation of the disability. In contrast, requests for accommodations like additional time or the use of a reader would require appropriate documentation (Mahaffey, 1992). Some employers document all requests for accommodation regardless of the nature of the disability or the impact of the accommodation of the disability to treat all applicants with a disability in a consistent manner and to ensure appropriate documentation in the event of future litigation.

The IDEA and Section 504

The documentation process for the IDEA specifies that one or more testing professionals serve as part of a child study team that will document the disability. These teams are formed when special education referrals are received. The IDEA specifies the composition of the team, which includes the referring teacher, a special education representative for the suspected disability area, an assessment professional, the parents, a special education administrator, and others that the team may deem appropriate. The team determines the assessment plan. After this assessment has been completed, the team meets to determine if there is a disability and, if one is determined, whether special education services are needed. If the team receives a diagnosis from a physician, such as an attention deficit hyperactivity disorder (ADHD), the same process would apply. The team documents the nature and extent of the disability.

Section 504 also specifies teams that operate in a similar manner, but this legislation uses a less restrictive definition of disability than is contained in the IDEA regulation. Section 504 provides guidance for documenting a disability and a request for accommodation.

Documenting Physical and Sensory Disabilities

Documenting physical and sensory disabilities is fairly straightforward. For example, if an individual has a vision impairment, an ophthalmologist or optometrist can provide information about the nature of the vision loss and a special education teacher or an orientation and mobility specialist can provide a functional vision assessment describing how the individual uses his or her vision and the kinds of lighting, print size, and special equipment that the individual needs. The functional vision assessment is especially helpful in planning any psychological assessment as well as in planning the educational or rehabilitation program. Typical criteria for documentation of a physical or sensory disability include a statement of the diagnosis, a description of procedures used to diagnosis the disability, a description of the functional limitations of the disability, and recommendations for accommodations. Except in the case of physical or sensory disabilities of a permanent or unchanging nature, most documentation guidelines specify that the information provided be recent.

Documenting Psychological Disabilities, Learning Disabilities, and ADHD

Documentation guidelines are more specific for psychological and learning disabilities and for ADHD. Often specific tests are required as part of the documentation. For example, guidelines for the documentation of a specific learning disability often specify that information must be gathered from aptitude, achievement, and information processing tests as well as a diagnostic report similar to the type used for physical and sensory disabilities.

In the late 1990s, the Association for Higher Education and Disabilities (AHEAD) issued guidelines for the documentation of a learning disability (AHEAD, 1997). AHEAD is an organization of professionals who help college students with disabilities. The AHEAD guidelines became the model for other, similar guidelines, used by testing organizations and employers. The AHEAD guidelines covered the qualifications of the evaluator, the nature of the documentation, the kinds of information needed to substantiate the existence of a learning disability, as well as provided recommendations for accommodations. It was suggested that the documentation provide information from a diagnostic interview; scores from aptitude, academic achievement, and information processing tests; and a specific diagnosis and clinical summary. The AHEAD guidelines recommended that scores on normed tests be presented as standard scores or percentiles and that all tests used be reliable, valid, and standardized for use with an adolescent–adult population. An appendix provided, as examples, the names of specific tests that might be useful in documenting a learning disability. Another appendix provided recommendations for consumers seeking to find an appropriate assessment professional to document a learning disability.

Guidelines for documenting learning disabilities and ADHD have been somewhat controversial. Some individuals feel that they are being too strictly implemented, thus making it difficult for people with learning disabilities to obtain testing accommodations. Others feel that even stricter guidelines might be needed to prevent individuals without learning disabilities from alleging such disabilities to gain extra time on a test or examination.

Who Is Qualified to Provide Documentation of a Disability? The ADA guidelines require a "qualified professional" and provide clarification by stating,

> The appropriate professional in any particular situation will depend on the disability and the type of functional limitation it imposes. Appropriate professionals include, but are not limited to, doctors (including psychiatrists), psychologists, nurses, physical therapists, occupational therapists, speech therapists, vocational rehabilitation specialists, and licensed mental health professionals. (EEOC, 1999)

The AHEAD guidelines stated that professionals documenting learning disabilities should be qualified to do so, emphasizing that comprehensive training and direct experience with adolescents and adults with learning disabilities is essential.

The following professionals would generally be considered to be qualified to evaluate specific learning disabilities provided that they have additional training and experience in the assessment of learning problems in adolescents and adults: clinical or educational psychologists, school psychologists, neuropsychologists, learning disability specialists, medical doctors, and other professionals. (AHEAD, 1997, p. 2)

Professional Ethics

Testing professionals asked to provide documentation of a disability should adhere to their professional code of ethics. This includes having the appropriate training and experience, both in using the assessment instruments and in working with individuals with the type of disability involved. It also includes avoiding dual relationships and conflicts of interest. If the testing professional has concerns about his or her qualifications for documenting the disability, or about his or her relationship to the individual requesting the documentation, a referral should be made to another testing professional.

Family members and close personal friends generally should not be documenters of the need for test accommodation, regardless of their credentials or knowledge of the individual. Many ethical codes of professional groups define such behaviors as ethics violations. Test users again must use their judgment to determine if the relationship of the qualified professional to the test taker impedes a fair and objective assessment of the individual's disability and associated limitations.

THE ROLE OF DOCUMENTATION IN TEST ACCOMMODATIONS

When individuals with a disability request that a test be administered under nonstandard conditions to accommodate their needs, they are often asked to provide information about or documentation of their disability. This documentation is part of providing reasonable and appropriate accommodations to individuals with disabilities, as required by the ADA and Section 504 of the Rehabilitation Act of 1973. Developing procedures for documentation of disabilities and for handling requests for accommodation are major tasks for organizations that administer tests.

Informing Test Takers

Test takers should be informed about (a) the process used to request an accommodation and (b) the activities the test requires, so that they can determine whether they are able to demonstrate the tasks without accommodations. Multiple opportunities to request an accommodation should be given to the test taker to ensure the test taker is aware of the opportunity to request an accommodation and be done in a manner that protects the privacy of the individual and minimizes embarrassment. Under no circumstances should a test taker be given a test before having an opportunity to request an accommodation. Because documentation is required for many kinds of accommodations, the actual testing session may be postponed so that appropriate documentation can be provided. The testing session may also need to be delayed to implement the requested accommodation. The individual should not be penalized for requesting an accommodation at any time during the test application process.

In employment settings, several methods of informing applicants that they can request an accommodation are typically used, including (a) informing an applicant orally or in writing how to request an accommodation; (b) providing a test brochure describing the test that includes the process to be followed for requesting an accommodation; (c) reading aloud the instructions to the applicant before beginning the test, including a statement that the organization complies with the ADA legislation and that test takers who need an accommodation should inform the test administrator. Normally, once a test is taken, the applicant may not be retested with or without accommodations until the required retest interval has expired.

Testing accommodations for students in elementary and secondary school are usually determined by information in the student's individual educational plan (IEP) and by the types of accommodations the student uses in everyday schoolwork. As indicated previously, the IEP is based on the disability documentation information specified under the IDEA. (See chapter 13 for a discussion of large-scale testing programs of local school districts and state education departments.)

Most testing organizations that administer tests for admission to colleges or to graduate and professional schools include information about how to request a testing accommodation in their test registration materials and provide a description of the documentation requirements. This information is also typically posted on the testing program website. (See chapter 16, this volume.) For example, the administrators of the ACT provide a detailed discussion of their policy for documentation to support requests for testing accommodations; this covers guiding principles, procedures for implementation, qualifications of diagnosticians, currency of documentation, the use of clinical results to substantiate the diagnosis, recommendations and rationale to support the requested accommodations, and confidentiality policies. The ACT provides specific details about the information that must be submitted to document learning disabilities, ADHD, visual impairment, hearing impairment, and other physical disorders.

Uniqueness of Accommodation

An accommodation to a testing situation usually is granted for a particular test at a given time. For example, it may be appropriate to extend the time limits on a reading comprehension test for an individual with a learning disability who is seeking admission to college. However, the same accommodation may not be appropriate for the same individual on a clerical speed and accuracy test used for employee selection. Similarly, a hearing-impaired individual may need an interpreter for tests on which the instructions are given orally but not need such assistance on a paper-and-pencil test with written instructions.

Counselors and other professionals who are assisting students seeking admission test accommodations should be aware that each test or testing program will have its own requirements. Thus, the individual preparing the documentation must include the information requested by each testing program and be aware that subsequent testing may require a new set of documentation materials (although recently the College Board announced that students may submit one set of documentation information for the PSAT, SAT, and Advanced Placement tests). In addition, the student may need to submit documentation of a disability to the college or university they will be attending so that accommodations can be provided on campus. Each institution will have its own documentation requirements, again raising the need to provide all of the specified information. AHEAD has recently published an *Exam Accommodations Reference Manual* that contains detailed information about testing accommodations at the postsecondary level.

The documentation needed for certification and licensing examinations is typically similar to that required for admissions tests (see chapter 15, this volume).

Recommendations for accommodation must be specific, indicating why the accommodation is needed and how it will reduce the impact of the disability in the testing situation. Although a history of previous test accommodations is often helpful, it is important to remember that disabilities can change over time. If the individual has not previously received a testing accommodation, it is especially important for the documenter to indicate why the request is being made at this time and why accommodations were not needed in the past.

The ADA and IDEA legislation require that each request for an accommodation from an individual with a disability be considered independently. In addition, the interpretive guidelines for the ADA imply that persons with disabilities must be considered on an individual basis to prevent segregation or stereotyping. The IDEA Amendments of 1995 state that each kindergarten through twelfth-grade student's needed accommodations are to be explained in his or her IEP and if participation in general assessments even with modifications is not feasible, alternative assessments are to be offered. Therefore, testing professionals are required to base decisions on "facts applicable to individual applicants" and not on the basis of presumptions about what a group of individuals with disabilities can or cannot do. Thus, the test user should take into account such individualized elements as the nature and extent of the disability and the kinds of accommodations the test taker has received in other aspects of life.

The ADA guidance documents are clear that requests for accommodation in testing situations need not be made in writing. An individual may make an oral request or use another mode of communication. The employer in turn may document the verbal request or ask the individual to complete a form or submit the request in written form (see EEOC, 1999).

Types of Accommodations

The preceding chapter provides more detail on the types of test accommodations typically available. For convenience, many test users classify accommodations into three groups: physical or basic accommodations, special accommodations, and test exemptions.

Physical or basic accommodations involve changes to (a) the physical setting in which a test is administered or (b) the testing materials themselves as long as they have no impact on the interpretation of the test score. Examples of such accommodations include brighter lighting, separate testing rooms, ramps to the testing room, an elevated desk to accommodate a wheel chair, a large-print version of the test, longer breaks between sections of the test, and high contrast ink and paper. Although these kinds of accommodations are routinely granted without extensive documentation of the request, good testing practices dictate that the conditions under which the test was administered be documented.

Special accommodations involve changes to the test that could affect interpretation of test results. Examples of special accommodations include extra time and oral presentation of written materials. Documentation of the request for accommodation as well as the nature of the accommodation is normally maintained.

Test exemptions are provided by some employers, organizations, and agencies for cases in which there is no reasonable accommodation that permits the measurement of the skills and abilities assessed by the test. Thus, testing professionals must consider alternate assessments of the skills and abilities or waive the test and rely on other sources of information about the skill or ability assessed by the test. Again, documentation of the request for accommodation as well as the accommodation is normally maintained.

EVALUATING DOCUMENTATION INFORMATION

Accommodations need not be granted if the documentation is insufficient. Clearly, the testing professional must use judgment regarding the adequacy of the professional's knowledge and background to document a disability and the resulting functional limitations and then prescribe a reasonable accommodation.

Documenter Qualifications

The minimum information needed from professional "documenters" to verify their qualifications as professionals is not clearly specified in either the ADA or the IDEA. When guidelines are not available, test users must determine the qualifications of another professional and use their own judgment to decide whether that individual is able to document the need for the required test accommodation.

The IDEA establishes that professionals must provide testing accommodations for kindergarten through twelfth-grade students according to students' IEPs, but test users are told little about the specific criteria to be used to define who is a professional. Questions to consider when evaluating whether another professional has appropriate credentials for documenting a disability include the following.

How Are the Preparation and Credentials of the Documenter Related to the Disability of the Test Taker? The educational background and experience of a professional who is documenting the need for test accommodation for an individual with a disability should be in the field related to the disability. *Enforcement Guidance: Disability-Related Inquiries and Medical Examinations of Employees Under the Americans With Disabilities Act (ADA)* stated that documentation may be insufficient when "the health care professional does not have the expertise to give an opinion about the employee's medical condition and the limitations imposed by it" (EEOC, 2000, p. 13). Thus, the user might reasonably assume that it would not be appropriate for a medical doctor to evaluate a learning disability unless the physician has specific training and experience in that area. The same principle would apply to classroom teachers or other professionals providing documentation for an individual with a disability. Thus, a school psychologist may not be sufficiently trained in visual disabilities to assess the functional limitations caused by the visual impairment and determine the accommodations needed. A test user must review the professional documenter's credentials and make a decision about the appropriateness of the documenter's qualifications.

What Information Does the Documenter Make Available Concerning His or Her Qualifications? The ADA guidance documents do not specify what information about qualifications must be collected; rather, these documents emphasize that the professional must be qualified to assess the individual's disability and the limitations that disability imposes. In contrast, AHEAD, in its 1997 *Guidelines for Documentation of a Learning Disability in Adolescents and Adults*, asserted that the name, title, professional credentials, information about the license or certification, area of specialization, employment, and state in which the individual works ought to be clearly stated on documentation forms. This information would seem to be the minimum that a test user should reasonably expect to request from professional documenters for all disabilities.

Is the Documenter Licensed or Certified? There is no legal requirement for licensure or certification except in the *Enforcement Guidance: Reasonable Accommodation and Undue Hardship Under the Americans With Disabilities Act* (EEOC, 1999), which references "licensed mental health professionals." Again, the key question for test users is whether the person documenting the need for accommodation is a qualified professional trained to diagnose the particular disability evidenced or reported. Licenses or certificates attest to the credentials of an individual in many but not all fields. Therefore, the test user should use sound judgment in deciding whether to require the documenter to be licensed or certified.

Currentness of Documentation

Questions to be asked about the currency of documentation include the following:

How Current Is the Documenter's Evaluation of the Test Taker's Disability? Most guidelines suggest that documentation be recent, often specifying no older than three years when documenting disabilities in children and adolescents. But the need for recent documentation must be considered in relation to the nature of the disability and the likelihood that the disability and the individual's adaptation to the disability have changed significantly over time. The kind of accommodations needed may change from setting to setting (or test type to test type). In addition, the individual may have acquired new skills or use new technology that assists in managing the disability. For example, a childhood evaluation of a stable, congenital visual disability would most likely be acceptable documentation for test accommodations needed by the individual in later life. However, a childhood evaluation of an attention deficit disorder is not acceptable documentation if a person applies for testing accommodations as an adult.

For How Long Should the Documentation Be Considered Valid? The ADA, IDEA, and Section 504 legislation and case law do not specifically address the length of time for which the documentation of a disability is valid. Again, it is recommended that the test user consider the nature of the disability, the nature of the tests to be accommodated, the kind of accommodation requested, and the period of elapsed time since the previous test accommodation was made.

Because some disabilities change over time, the need for accommodations may require periodic reevaluations. Within the context of "normal" developmental changes and depending on the disability, schoolage children may need to be evaluated frequently. With adults, it may not be necessary to conduct reevaluations as often. In addition, test accommodations for some disabling conditions are temporary (e.g., being unable to provide written responses to test items because of a broken wrist), but temporary disabilities are not covered under the ADA. In these situations, future test accommodations are unwarranted if the individual has undergone treatment and had a successful recovery.

Testing professionals should be aware that some disabilities worsen with time. For other disabilities, individuals may learn how to adapt to the disability, and the kind of accommodation previously needed may change. Finally, options for accommodations also change over time. For example, technological innovations provide means for completing tests that previously were not available to individuals with visual impairments.

Reasonableness of Accommodation Request

Sometimes in employment, certification, licensure, and educational contexts, a recommendation for accommodation that is documented by a professional is deemed unreasonable. Accommodations may be considered unreasonable when the recommendation for the requested accommodation is not linked to an identified functional impairment. For example, requesting a large-print copy of a test may not be a reasonable accommodation for an individual with a back problem.

An accommodation may also be considered unreasonable when the accommodation places too great a burden on the test user. Test users should note that the ADA provides guidance on what factors should be considered in determining what accommodations would impose an undue hardship. These include (a) the nature and the cost of the accommodation requested, (b) the overall financial resources of the facility and the entire organization, (c) the number of people employed at the facility, (d) the effect on expenses and resources, and (e) the effect of the accommodation on the operation of the facility.

The accommodation requested should be logically related to the specific functional limitations of the disability as described in the documentation material.

CONCLUSION

Considerable variation exists among the criteria used or suggested for documenting disabilities. In employment testing, many testing professionals and their legal counsels find the ADA legislation and its interpretive guide unclear on some aspects of documentation requirements. Case law continues to define the specific requirements of the ADA. Similarly, the IDEA is being modified by interpretations and case law. Regardless of one's field, the testing professional who works with testing accommodations must stay current on the requirements for accommodations and the documentation of disabilities.

Documentation is an essential step in providing reasonable accommodations to individuals with disabilities in education and employment, as well as in assessment. To ensure that the individual requesting an accommodation has a disability covered under the ADA or the IDEA and that the organization itself understands the extent of the disability and how the accommodation is related, many employers and educational institutions request documentation. Although some of the requirements of documents are clearly stated in the laws and guidance documents are also clear, other practices are based on good testing practices established by professionals and common sense of the test user.

REFERENCES

Americans With Disabilities Act of 1990. (1993). 42 U.S.C.S. § 12101 et seq.

Association on Higher Education and Disability (AHEAD). (1997, July). *Guidelines for Documentation of Learning Disabilities in Adolescents and Adults.* Columbus, OH: Author. (Also available at www.ahead.org/ldguide.htm)

EEOC. (1994). *ADA enforcement guidance: Preemployment disability-related questions and medical examinations.* Washington, DC: Author.

EEOC. (1999, March 2). *Enforcement guidance: Reasonable accommodation and undue hardship under the Americans With Disabilities Act.* Available at www.eeoc.gov/docs/accomodation.html.

EEOC. (2000, July 27). *Enforcement guidance: Disability-related inquiries and medical examinations of employees under the Americans With Disabilities Act (ADA).* Available at www.eeoc.gov/docs/guidance-inquiries.html.

IDEA Amendments of 1995. ERIC Document. (ERIC Reproduction Service No. ED 399739).

The Individuals With Disabilities Education Act of 1975. (1977). Pub. L. No. 94–142, 89 Stat. 773.

Mahaffey, C. (1992). Request for accommodation. In *Accommodating employment testing to the needs of individuals with disabilities.* Glendale, CA: Psychological Services.

The Rehabilitation Act of 1973. (1974). Pub. L. No. 93-112, 504 Stat. 87.

5

THE DECISION-MAKING PROCESS FOR DEVELOPING TESTING ACCOMMODATIONS

DOUGLAS K. SMITH

Providing testing accommodations for individuals with disabilities is not a new concept. Within the educational setting, accommodations have been required since the 1970s with the passage of the Education of All Handicapped Children's Act (EAHCA; 1977) and, within the public setting, since passage of the Rehabilitation Act of 1973. Many accommodations, such as Braille, large print, and extra time, have become common. The Americans With Disabilities Act (ADA) and the 1997 Individuals With Disabilities Act (IDEA) Amendments have expanded our definitions of both disabilities and testing accommodations. Not all individuals with disabilities need testing accommodations, and accommodations may not be needed for all assessments. The need for accommodations must be made on a case by case basis, considering the individual involved and the specific nature and purpose of assessment.

The reasons for assessing individuals with disabilities continue to expand. Within the educational setting, assessment is mandated for placement in special education programs, and periodic reevaluations are required in developing individual educational plans. Assessment is also used in planning transitional services for students with disabilities and in rehabilitation program planning. More and more emphasis is being placed on assessment in a variety of settings, including admission to educational programs, evaluating academic progress, career planning, meeting graduation standards, meeting employment standards, and demonstrating proficiency in a profession, to name a few. For all of these, accommodations for individuals with disabilities are now required.

The focus of this chapter is the process for making decisions about testing accommodations. Although the emphasis is on individually administered standardized tests, the process is also applicable in other situations. It is assumed that testing will occur in an appropriate environment accessible to the examinee.

Accommodations are changes in the standard way in which a test is administered (see chapter 3, this volume). Testing accommodations may involve changes in the setting, the timing, the scheduling, the presentation, or the response (Thurlow, Elliott, & Ysseldyke, 1998). Modifications to timing may include providing the individual with additional time to complete the testing, eliminating bonus points for rapid performance, allowing additional exposure time for test stimuli, or providing frequent breaks. Scheduling modifications may include changing the order in which subtests are administered or testing over an extended period of time rather than in one sitting. Changes in presentation mode may involve the use of sign language, large print, Braille, or repeating directions, whereas response modifications may involve writing responses instead of verbally responding or using a word processor instead of writing. In general, accommodations for physical or sensory disabilities are more readily understood and accepted than accommodations for cognitive or affective disabilities that may be less apparent but of equal importance (Olson & Goldstein, 1997).

Accommodations may have a substantial impact on examinee scores and may affect the validity of those scores. Accommodations may be appropriate in some situations and inappropriate in others. How can a testing professional decide if an accommodation is appropriate? What factors should be considered in developing appropriate accommodations? Does the purpose of the testing affect the appropriateness of specific accommodations? These are some of the questions examined in this chapter.

The purpose of this chapter is to provide the reader with a process for making testing accommodations in individual, norm-referenced testing. Although each request for a testing accommodation represents a unique situation and should be treated individually, there are some universal principles or guidelines that form the basis for the decisions that we make.

As testing professionals we are guided by the standards of our professional organizations as well as relevant state and federal laws. Perhaps none is more influential than the 1999 *Standards for Educational and Psychological Testing* (AERA/APA/NCME, 1999). In the latest edition of *Standards*, an entire chapter is devoted to the assessment of individuals with disabilities. This chapter addresses some of the more common types of accommodations, situations in which accommodations may be appropriate, situations in which accommodations may not be appropriate, and possible effects of accommodations on test scores. From this chapter it is clear that testing accommodations should be carefully developed and their impact on the resulting scores closely examined.

There is, however, a lack of research examining the process by which testing professionals develop appropriate testing accommodations. Although several authors (e.g., Berg, Wacker, & Steege, 1995; Braden & Hannah, 1998; Bradley-Johnson, 1994; Reschly & Grimes, 1995) and test authors or manuals indicate the types of accommodations that may be appropriate or inappropriate with selected disabilities, the practitioner is not presented with a process to use in making such determinations.

PREREQUISITES IN DEVELOPING ACCOMMODATIONS

Examiner prerequisites for testing students with disabilities are knowledge and understanding of the disability as well as experience in working with individuals with that disability. Special education textbooks (e.g., Hallahan & Kauffman, 1997; Haring, McCormick, & Haring, 1994; Heward, 1996) and *Best Practices in School Psychology III* (Thomas & Grimes, 1995) are sources for information and knowledge about disabilities. Direct experience with a disability is equally important. It is essential that the examiner be familiar with the disability and feel comfortable in working with individuals with the disability. This type of experience is usually obtained during professional training but can also be gained by spending time in classrooms with students with disabilities, working with special education teachers and their students, and working with testing professionals with specialties in assessing students with disabilities, particularly low-incidence disabilities.

When an accommodation is developed, it is essential that the examinee feels comfortable with the accommodation and has direct experience with it. For example, allowing an individual to use a word processor instead of writing a response by hand would not be appropriate if the examinee has never used a word processor.

Information on the individual's medical condition is important in making a decision about an accommodation. In the case of sensory impairment, this information may include functional visual assessments and hearing acuity results. Guidelines for documenting a learning disability or an attention-deficit/hyperactivity disorder (ADHD) cover the type of information needed in such cases (see chapter 4, this volume). The testing professional should be aware of any accommodations that may have been used by the individual in previous evaluations or that are regularly used in the classroom or work setting. This information should be obtained before determining if testing accommodations will be needed and, if they are determined to be needed, the appropriate type of accommodation.

DEVELOPING TESTING ACCOMMODATIONS

This is a step-by-step guide to making decisions on accommodations and should be used before setting up examinee testing accommodations.

Step 1: Determine the Examinee's Receptive Skills

The examiner must determine if the examinee's disability places limitations on the person's ability to understand visual or auditory material. Will the examinee be able to see the test materials, test questions, or any visual stimuli that are used? Will the examinee be able to hear the test directions or any verbal stimuli that are used? Any limitations in these receptive skills should be noted.

Step 2: Determine the Examinee's Expressive Skills

The examiner must determine if the examinee's disability places limitations on the individual's ability to respond verbally or motorically to test items. Because many test items require a verbal response, the examiner must determine if there are any limitations in this area. Some test items require motor responses that may range from pointing to a response, to manipulating puzzle pieces and blocks, to copying marks or symbols with a pencil, to writing responses ranging from one word to a sentence or paragraph or more.

Step 3: Determine the Construct Being Measured

Some test accommodations may have the effect of altering the construct being measured. What are the specific skills that are to be measured? In the area of ability or intellectual testing, skills may include general level of intelligence, crystallized intelligence, fluid intelligence, visual intelligence, auditory intelligence, short-term memory, long-term retrieval, and processing speed as described by Carroll (1993), Horn (1991), and Woodcock (1998). In the area of academic achievement, skills may include word recognition, reading comprehension, spelling, listening comprehension, mathematics reasoning, mathematics computation, oral expression, written expression, general information, and many others. In employment testing, the skills measured are related to the essential functions of the job, and thus vary considerably from situation to situation. Such skills may involve keyboard skills (speed and accuracy), skill in using specific word processing programs, and knowledge specifically related to the job. In licensure exams, knowledge related to specific disciplines is measured. The examiner needs to determine what is to be measured so that an appropriate test can be used. An appropriate test is one that reliably and validly measures the construct and does not require receptive or expressive skills that the examinee lacks because of the disability.

Step 4: Determine the Purpose(s) of Assessment

Is the purpose of the assessment to make norm-based comparisons? Is it to determine if the individual has mastered a particular skill or set of skills? Is it to demonstrate mastery of an area, as in licensing exams? Is it for program planning purposes? Is it for developing academic interventions? Is it a combination of purposes? This distinction is of utmost importance, because the degree to which a test can be modified to accommodate individuals with disabilities and continue to produce valid scores is dependent, in part, on the purpose of the test.

Norm-referenced tests are used to make comparisons between an individual's performance and the performance of individuals in the normative sample. The purpose of testing is to determine relative standing. Modifications in test stimuli, test procedures, or response format may reduce the meaningfulness of the test norms, because norm-referenced tests are based on the assumption that the same stimuli were administered in the same way to all examinees. Thus, normative comparisons under conditions of accommodation need to be interpreted cautiously.

Criterion-referenced tests are designed to determine the level of skill development and whether specific skills are possessed by the examinee rather than to make comparisons. Thus, accommodations in testing, although important, do not have the same impact on the interpretation of scores as with norm-referenced tests.

Step 5: Determine the Test or Tests to Be Used

This decision "must be based on the characteristics of the student . . . such as age, sensory status, language competencies, and acculturation" (Reshly & Grimes, 1995, p. 769). Best practice dictates that a standard or mandatory test not be used. "Familiarity with a variety of instruments and knowledge of various disabling conditions is essential to choice of measures and interpretation of results" (Reschly & Grimes, 1995, p. 769).

Step 6: Determine the Receptive Skills and Expressive Skills Required by the Selected Test or Tests

This step involves an analysis of how the test stimuli are presented (visually, verbally, or a combination of the two) and the response format of the test. How are examinees expected to express their responses? Although many tests require verbal responses, others may require the manipulation of blocks or puzzles or a written response or pointing to the correct response or copying a design or symbols or using a keyboard and other specialized tools.

Step 7: Determine If the Examinee Has the Receptive Skills and the Expressive Skills to Understand the Test Items and to Respond Appropriately

This determination is completed by comparing the answers to steps 1, 2, and 7.

Step 8: Use Professional Judgment About Whether the "Match" Between the Set of Skills Needed for Completing the Test and the Set of Skills Possessed by the Examinee Are Sufficiently Close to Permit Use of the Test or Tests

If this requirement is met, then testing can proceed. If not, the examiner must determine the type of accommodations that will be needed. The guiding principle in determining needed accommodations is that the accommodations should allow the examinee with disabilities to be assessed fairly and not be penalized as a result of the disability.

Step 9: Determine If the Needed Accommodations Will Compromise the Test Results

This decision rests heavily with the purpose of the assessment. If the purpose of assessment involves norm-based comparisons, several issues must be considered:

- Were individuals with disabilities included in the standardization sample? If so, were any of them provided with testing accommodations? If the answers to both parts of this question are yes, then we can have greater confidence in making normative comparisons because our examinee would not have been specifically excluded from the standardization sample. If the answer to both parts of this question are no or if accommodations were not made for individuals with disabilities in the standardization sample, then we must be more cautious in making normative comparisons.

- Are there any accommodations that have been specifically developed for the particular test? Consulting the test manual and contacting the publisher of the test are some means to obtain this information.
- Does the testing modification alter the construct that is being measured? In other words, does the test measure the same construct with the accommodation? If the constructs being measured are not the same, then the accommodation is not appropriate. For example, a reading comprehension test that requires the individual to read a passage and verbally answer questions about it would be fundamentally altered by reading the passage to the examinee and having the examinee verbally answer questions about it. In this case the original construct, reading comprehension, is not being measured in the altered format; rather listening comprehension is being measured. Therefore, the testing accommodation, although well-intentioned, is not appropriate.

After answering these questions, the examiner must look at each proposed testing accommodation and determine if the accommodation is appropriate to the purpose of the test and if such an accommodation can be made. This step involves answering two questions: Does the accommodation alter the construct being measured by the test? Is the accommodation of sufficient magnitude that a comparison of scores between examinees with and without the accommodation is not appropriate? This decision should be made carefully based on author and publisher recommendations, previous research, and professional judgment as described in the 1999 *Standards* (AERA/APA/NCME, 1999).

Step 10: If Sufficient Accommodations Cannot Be Made, the Examiner Must Look for Other Ways to Assess the Skill or Construct in Question

To accomplish this, the examiner must be familiar with as many instruments as possible (Reschly & Grimes, 1995).

Step 11: Describe Any Cautions or Limitations in Interpreting Test Results

It is at this point that the examiner must decide (based on legal and ethical standards) if the test results can be interpreted in a valid way. A cautious stance is recommended in interpreting norm-referenced tests because any modification of the standardized administration format alters the meaning of the test results. The examiner must be as specific as possible about the appropriate use of the results and the limitations of the results. In evaluations involving students being considered for special education services, the examiner must describe the modifications to standardized procedures that were used as outlined in the IDEA 1997 Amendments.

Using the Worksheet

The eleven steps above have been operationalized in the worksheet for developing testing accommodations, presented in appendix A of this chapter. The skills to be assessed (Step 3) will vary depending on the setting in which the worksheet is used. For illustrative purposes only cognitive and academic skills are listed.

Use of the worksheet is illustrated in the following example: The child study team has decided that Pat's reading comprehension skills need to be assessed. Pat is a high school student with a severe expressive language problem. In fact, Pat's speech is not understandable to most people. Jan, the school psychologist at the high school, has been asked to determine how Pat compares with other students in reading comprehension. Jan usually uses the reading comprehension subtest of the Kaufman Test of Educational Achievement NU (KTEA NU; Kaufman & Kaufman, 1998), a norm-referenced test, to measure reading comprehension skills in high school students. This subtest requires the examinee to read a passage and then respond orally to questions about each passage. In this situation the subtest, as standardized, is not appropriate because of the need for oral expressive language skills that are deficient in Pat's case. Pat could be asked to write the responses to the questions, but the normative comparison would be questionable. Often oral responses are more detailed and complex than are written responses. In addition, it takes longer to write responses than to verbalize responses, thus introducing a possible fatigue factor. Therefore, Jan should find a more appropriate test. The reading comprehension subtest of the Peabody Individual Achievement Test-Revised NU (PIAT-R NU; Markwardt, 1998), another norm-referenced test, measures reading comprehension by having the examinee choose one of four pictures that best illustrates a sentence. This response format does not involve oral expressive skills and is a format that Pat can handle. Because both tests were co-normed as part of the Normative Update Project, as described in the respective test manuals, and have current norms including students with disabilities, the reading comprehension subtest of the PIAT-R is the more appropriate test for Pat. The completed worksheet for developing testing accommodations for Pat is presented in appendix B of this chapter.

SPECIAL SITUATIONS

Intelligence Testing

Among the most complex issues in testing is ability or intelligence testing. School psychologists are most affected by this issue because they often use intelligence tests in establishing eligibility for certain special education programs and yet they must also accommodate individuals with disabilities in the testing process. The past few years have brought a number of new tests of intelligence, each with a different definition of intelligence and requiring different sets of test-taking skills.

Test selection is the most important step in intelligence testing. Similar to other situations, this involves matching the examinee's skills with those required by the test. Difficulties are most likely to occur with subtests that require motor skills (especially for examinees with orthopedic impairments), provide time bonuses for rapid performance (especially for examinees with motor impairments, learning disabilities, processing difficulties), involve exclusively auditory or visual input, require lengthy attention spans, or require verbal expressive skills. Rather than modify test procedures, examiners should search for alternative measures that minimize the impaired skills.

The Universal Nonverbal Intelligence Test (Bracken & McCallum, 1998), a nonverbal test of intelligence, measures intelligence by having the examiner present instructions through pantomime. No words are exchanged between examiner and examinee and all responses are nonverbal. Similarly, many more traditional measures of intelligence have nonverbal scales that have been standardized. Examples include the Differential Ability Scales (Elliott, 1990) and the Kaufman Assessment Battery for Children (Kaufman & Kaufman, 1983). Both examiner and examinee are best served by using alternative measures (when they exist) rather than modifying tests and using norms that are not based on those modifications.

When alternative measures do not exist, the examiner must determine if available measures can be modified to meet the needs of the examinee and still result in valid interpretations, as previously discussed. The examiner must remain cautious and continually ask if the modifications fundamentally alter the test. For example, providing the examinee with the printed word in addition to the pronounced word does not fundamentally alter a vocabulary test that asks the examinee to define specific words. The same test is fundamentally altered if the examiner creates four definitions and asks the examinee to choose the correct definition or presents four pictures and asks the examinee to choose the picture that best depicts the stimulus word.

High-Stakes Testing

High-stakes testing includes the use of tests for decisions such as graduation from high school or acceptance into a special program. State and district assessments of public school students that require students to achieve a passing score to advance to the next grade level or to graduate from high school are also examples of high-stakes tests (see chapter 9, this volume). Such tests have a profound impact on the future of the individual. As a consequence, special attention must be focused on whether the test discriminates against the individual with disabilities by measuring the disabilities rather than the abilities of the individual.

The purpose of high-stakes testing is to ensure that the individual meets the standards in the area being measured. The emphasis is on demonstrated proficiency or level of skill development, and specific cut-off scores or minimum scores are required. Many high-stakes tests are presented in a written format involving multiple-choice responses, and others may be performance-based. The process for developing appropriate test accommodations for these kinds of tests is the same as described previously. The guiding principle is whether the accommodation compromises the construct being measured. If it does not, the accommodation is probably appropriate. An additional consideration in providing accommodations for high-stakes testing is to ensure that the accommodations provide the examinee with equal access to the benefits of testing.

Employment Testing

The purpose of most employment testing is to determine whether the employee or applicant has the required skills for the particular job. (See chapters 12, 13, and 14, this volume, for more detailed information about employment testing.)

In employment testing the first step in the accommodations process is to determine the essential skills needed for the job. This usually begins with a detailed job description and analysis of the duties and abilities related to the job. Once a list of specific skills is generated, then the employer must decide how to measure the skills in a reliable and valid way. Caution should be exercised to ensure that the specified skills are being measured and not supplementary skills that are not required by the job in question. This requires distinguishing between essential and nonessential skills. Some flexibility is often needed to examine the nature of the job and the different ways in which it can be carried out. The screening procedure should be the same for all applicants with necessary accommodations as needed for individuals with a disability. A disability should not prevent an individual from being offered the job if they can successfully discharge the essential functions of that job.

CONCLUSION

Modifying standardized tests for individuals with disabilities is a complex issue. Tests should be modified only when alternative measures do not exist. Testing professionals should be aware that whenever modifications are made, normative interpretations should be made cautiously. The examiner should consider if the accommodation significantly alters the format of the test and thus changes the nature of the test.

REFERENCES

American Educational Research Association, American Psychological Association, & National Council on Measurement in Education (AERA/APA/NCME). (1999). *Standards for educational and psychological testing.* Washington, DC: American Educational Research Association.

Americans With Disabilities Act of 1990. (1993). 42 U.S.C. § 12101 et seq.

Berg, W. K., Wacker, D. P., & Steege, M. W. (1995). Best practices in assessment with persons who have severe or profound handicaps. In A. Thomas & J. Grimes (Eds.), *Best practices in school psychology III* (pp. 805–816). Washington, DC: National Association of School Psychologists.

Bracken, B. A., & McCallum, R. S. (1998). *Universal Nonverbal Intelligence Test.* Itasca, IL: Riverside.

Braden, J. P., & Hannah, J. M. (1998). Assessment of hearing impaired and deaf children with the WISC-III. In D. Saklofske & A. Prifitera (Eds.), *Use of the WISC-III in clinical practice* (pp. 175–201). New York: Houghton-Mifflin.

Bradley-Johnson, S. (1994). *Psychoeducational assessment of students who are visually impaired or blind: Infancy through high school* (2nd ed.). Austin, TX: PRO-ED.

Carroll, J. B. (1993). *Human cognitive abilities: A survey of factor-analytic studies.* New York: Cambridge University Press.

Education of All Handicapped Children. (1977). Pub. L. No. 94–142, 20 U.S.C. § 1401 et seq., 42 Fed. Reg. 65082.

Elliott, C. D. (1990). *Differential Ability Scales.* San Antonio, TX: Psychological Corporation.

Hallahan, D. P., & Kauffman, J. M. (1997). *Exceptional learners: Introduction to special education* (7th ed.). Needham Heights, MA: Allyn and Bacon.

Haring, N. G., McCormick, L., & Haring, T. (1994). *Exceptional children and youth* (6th ed.). Columbus, OH: Merrill/Prentice Hall.

Heward, W. L. (1996). *Exceptional children: An introduction to special education* (5th ed.). Columbus, OH: Merrill/Prentice Hall.

Horn, J. L. (1991). Measurement of intellectual capabilities: A review of theory. In K. McGrew, J. K. Werder, & R. W. Woodcock, *WJ-R technical manual* (pp. 197–232). Itasca, IL: Riverside.

Individuals With Disabilities Education Act (IDEA). (1994). 20 U.S.C. § 1400 et seq.

Kaufman, A. S., & Kaufman, N. L. (1983). *Kaufman Assessment Battery for Children*. Circle Pines, MN: American Guidance Service.

Kaufman, A. S., & Kaufman, N. L. (1998). *Kaufman Test of Educational Achievement NU*. Circle Pines, MN: American Guidance Service.

Markwardt, F. (1998). *Peabody Individual Achievement Test-Revised NU*. Circle Pines, MN: American Guidance Service.

Olson, J. F., & Goldstein, A. A. (1997). *The inclusion of students with disabilities and limited English proficient students in large-scale assessment: A summary of recent progress*. Washington, DC: U.S. Department of Education.

Rehabilitation Act of 1973. (1974). 29 U.S.C. § 794.

Reschly, D. J., & Grimes, J. P. (1995). Best practices in intellectual assessment. In A. Thomas & J. Grimes (Eds.), *Best practices in school psychology III* (pp. 763–773). Washington, DC: National Association of School Psychologists.

Thomas, A., & Grimes, J. (Eds.). (1995). *Best practices in school psychology III*. Washington, DC: National Association of School Psychologists.

Thurlow, M. L., Elliott, J. L., & Ysseldyke, J. E. (1998). *Testing students with disabilities: Practical strategies for complying with district and state requirements*. Thousand Oaks, CA: Corwin Press.

Woodcock, R. W. (1998). Extending Gf-Gc theory into practice. In J. J. McArdle & R. W. Woodcock (Eds.), *Human cognitive abilities in theory and practice* (pp. 137–156). Mahwah, NJ: Erlbaum.

APPENDIX A

Worksheet for Developing Testing Accommodations

Developed by Douglas K. Smith

Name of examinee: _____

Date: _____

1. Describe any limitations or disabilities in the examinee's receptive (auditory, visual) skills:

2. Describe any limitations or disabilities in the examinee's expressive (verbal, motor) skills:

3. Indicate the skills to be assessed:

   General level of intelligence _____   Oral expression _____
   Long-term retrieval _____   Reading comprehension _____
   Crystallized intelligence _____   Written expression _____
   Processing speed _____   Spelling _____
   Fluid intelligence _____   General information _____
   Visual intelligence _____   Listening comprehension _____
   Auditory intelligence _____   Mathematics reasoning _____
   Short-term memory _____   Mathematics computation _____
   Word recognition _____
   Other (please specify) _____

   _____

4. Indicate the purpose(s) of assessment:
   Normative comparison _____
   Determine presence/absence of specific skills_____
   Program planning _____
   Develop academic interventions _____
   Other (please specify) _____

   _____

5. Indicate the test(s) you plan to use:

6. List the receptive abilities and expressive abilities required by the test(s) in Step 5:

   Receptive abilities   Expressive abilities

7. Refer to Steps 1 and 2 and indicate:
   A. Examinee has the receptive abilities required by the test
      Yes _____   No _____
   B. Examinee has the expressive abilities required by the test
      Yes _____   No _____

8. A. If 7A and 7B are "Yes," then proceed with testing
   B. If 7A and 7B are "No," describe the type of accommodations that will be needed:

9. Considering the purpose of the assessment, will the accommodations in 8B compromise the test results?

   Yes _____   Explain:

   No _____

10. If the answer to 9 is "Yes," are there are other tests that could be substituted?

    Yes _____   Please list:

11. Describe any cautions or limitations in interpreting the test results:

APPENDIX B

Worksheet for Developing Testing Accommodations—
An Example

Name of examinee: _____Pat_____

Date: ____March 8, 1999_____

1. Describe any limitations or disabilities in the examinee's receptive (auditory, visual) skills:

   None

2. Describe any limitations or disabilities in the examinee's expressive (verbal, motor) skills:

   Pat has a severe expressive language problem. Pat's speech is not understandable to most people.

3. Indicate the skills to be assessed:

General level of intelligence _____	Oral expression _____
Long-term retrieval _____	Reading comprehension __X__
Crystallized intelligence _____	Written expression Spelling _____
Processing speed _____	General information _____
Fluid intelligence _____	Listening comprehension _____
Visual intelligence _____	Mathematics reasoning _____
Auditory intelligence _____	Mathematics computation _____
Short-term memory _____	
Word recognition _____	
Other (please specify) _____	

4. Indicate the purpose(s) of assessment:
   Normative comparison __X__
   Determine presence/absence of specific skills __X__
   Program planning __X__
   Develop academic interventions _____
   Other (please specify) _____

5. Indicate the test(s) you plan to use:

   Reading Comprehension subtest of the Kaufman Test of Educational Achievement

6. List the receptive abilities and expressive abilities required by the test(s) in Step 5:

Receptive abilities	Expressive abilities
Visual and auditory skills	Verbal expressive skills

7. Refer to Steps 1 and 2 and indicate:
   A. Examinee has the receptive abilities required by the test
      Yes __X__   No _____
   B. Examinee has the expressive abilities required by the test
      Yes _____   No __X__

8. A. If 7A and 7B are "Yes," then proceed with testing
   B. If 7A and 7B are "No," describe the type of accommodations that will be needed:
      Since Pat's speech is very, very difficult to understand, a written response will be needed

9. Considering the purpose of the assessment, will the accommodations in 8B compromise the test results?

   Yes __X__   Explain:

   The test was standardized with verbal responses. Writing responses to questions produces greater fatigue and may lead to more condensed responses. This may result in a lower score due to Pat's disability rather than weakness in reading comprehension.

   No _____

10. If the answer to 9 is "Yes," are there are other tests that could be substituted?

    Yes __X__   Please list:

    Reading comprehension subtest of Peabody Individual Achievement Test-Revised

11. Describe any cautions or limitations in interpreting the test results:
    None

6

SCORE REPORTING ISSUES IN THE ASSESSMENT OF PEOPLE WITH DISABILITIES: POLICIES AND PRACTICES

WILLIAM A. MEHRENS AND RUTH B. EKSTROM

This chapter discusses some of the key issues in reporting test scores for individuals with disabilities. Although all types of score reporting are addressed, special attention is given to the problem of reporting scores from nonstandardized administrations of standardized tests, especially in admission testing.

Score reporting varies according to the purpose of the testing. For testing that centers on the needs of the individual, such as clinical, counseling, and rehabilitation testing, score reports typically include a description of the individual's disability and how it may have affected test performance, including a description of any test modifications that were made because of the individual's disability.

Much of this chapter is based on the paper "Flagging Test Scores: Policy, Practice, and Research," prepared by William A. Mehrens as background for the National Academy of Sciences, Board on Testing and Assessment, planning meeting on test score flagging policies, September 19, 1997.

Reporting of scores from tests used to make decisions about admissions or employment, where results for an individual with a disability who has taken a modified test are being compared by a score recipient with a larger population, is handled differently under the law than scores from tests used in clinical, counseling, or rehabilitation testing (see chapter 1, this volume). This has resulted in considerable controversy that centers on the privacy rights of individuals with disabilities and the test interpretation needs of score users.

GENERAL PRINCIPLES OF SCORE REPORTING

For most tests, the score report reflects what has gone before. The testing professional has obtained information about the type and extent of the individual's disability and has used this information to select an appropriate test or to make any needed testing accommodation. For example, when the test taker has a visual impairment, the test administrator may have obtained a copy of the test taker's functional visual assessment to obtain information about things such as lighting needs, preferred type size, and auxiliary aids used. This information and the rationale for test selection or test modification are included in the score report and are described in relation to any accommodation typically used by the individual at school or at work.

The basics of score reporting require identifying test instrument, identifying any normative group to which the given score is being compared, and describing any changes from the standardized testing procedure that may have affected test results. When a test that has not been specifically designed for individuals with a given disability is administered to such individuals, the score report should indicate if the test norms being used are for individuals with disabilities or for the general population. If the norms are for the general population or include both the general population and individuals with disabilities, the score report should provide some indication of whether or not the testing professional believes the results are meaningful and appropriate for the given test taker. If the test has been modified in some way to accommodate the needs of an individual with a disability, the score report should describe the testing accommodation or modification and indicate if the testing professional believes the accommodation may affect test validity. This type of documentation facilitates interpreting test data. Obtaining and using information about the nature and extent of a disability to make a testing accommodation extends to group educational tests, such as those used in state testing programs, but not to admissions tests.

These general principles are reflected in Standard 5.2 of the *Standards for Educational and Psychological Testing* (AERA/APA/NCME, 1999):

"Modifications or disruptions of standardized test administration procedures or scoring should be documented" (p. 63).

THE EXCEPTIONS

Admissions, certification, licensing, and employment testing differs from clinical and counseling testing. The test to be used is specified by the educational institution, employer, or licensing or certification body. Section 504 of the Rehabilitation Act of 1973 and the Americans With Disabilities Act both state that inquiries about a disability are not permitted before making an offer of admission or employment. Thus, the test administrator cannot ask the test taker if she or he has a disability. Test takers can, however, be "invited" to provide information about the existence of a disability so that appropriate testing accommodations can be provided for them. (It is important to remember that some individuals with disabilities will not need testing accommodations and that some will prefer not to request an accommodation.) If accommodations are made, it has been a common practice as an interpretive aid to test score recipients, to mark or "flag" test scores, to indicate that they are from a nonstandard administration. This has typically occurred when it was believed that the accommodation might have an impact on test validity. The legal background for the flagging of test scores and the issues arising from it are discussed next.

TEST-SCORE FLAGGING

Rosenfeld, Tannenbaum, and Wesley (1995) have proposed three key questions about test-score reporting when accommodations have been made for individuals with disabilities:

- Should test scores be flagged?
- If so, under what conditions?
- Who should have access to this information?

Background

In 1977, the U.S. Department of Health, Education and Welfare issued regulations related to implementation of Section 504 of the Rehabilitation Act of 1973. These regulations mandated that admissions tests for individuals with disabilities be validated; they also prohibited, before the admission decision, inquiry into the disability status of the applicant. If test takers were "invited" to reveal a disability, they were to be told that the information was being requested on a voluntary basis and that it would be kept confidential. This confidentiality requirement meant that score recipients could not be told that a testing accommodation had been provided.

Many individuals felt this confidentiality requirement conflicted with good professional practice. As a consequence, when the *Standards for Educational and Psychological Testing* (AERA/APA/NCME, 1999) were prepared, Standard 10.11 was written to describe when test score flagging might and might not be appropriate:

> When there is credible evidence of score comparability across regular and modified administrations, no flag should be attached to a score. When such evidence is lacking, specific information about the nature of the modification should be provided, if permitted by law, to assist test users properly to interpret and act on test scores. (p. 108)

The comment on Standard 10.11 points out that

> the inclusion of a flag on a test score where an accommodation for disability was provided may conflict with legal and social policy goals promoting fairness in treatment of individuals with disabilities. . . . Reporting practices that use asterisks or other nonspecific symbols to indicate that a test's administration has been modified provide little useful information to test users. When permitted by law, if a non-standardized administration is to be reported because evidence does not exist to support score comparability, then this report should avoid referencing the existence of nature of the test taker's disability and should instead report only the nature of the accommodation provided, such as extended time for testing, the use of a reader, or the use of a tape recorder. (1999, p. 108)

The confidentiality requirement also appears to be in conflict with the *Code of Fair Testing Practices in Education* (JCTP, 1988), which states "Test developers should . . . warn test users of potential problems in using standard norms with modified tests or administration procedures that result in noncomparable scores" (p. 3).

The conflict between the Section 504 ban on preadmission inquiry and the desire to alert admissions officers to interpretive problems with nonstandard administrations was addressed by a 1978 interim policy of the Department of Education's Office of Civil Rights (OCR). This policy permitted testing programs (such as the ACT and SAT) to notify score recipients if nonstandard procedures were used in an examinee's test administration. Testing programs could continue to mark or "flag" test results until it could be demonstrated that scores obtained under nonstandard conditions were comparable to those obtained using standard test administrations.

The guidelines for this interim policy were prepared by a joint committee of the American Association of Collegiate Registrars and Admissions Officers (AACRAO) and the American Council on Education (ACE); OCR then endorsed them (see Bennett & Ragosta, 1984, p. 5). As Bennett and Ragosta explained,

> The AACRAO/ACE guidelines were meant to allow time for careful exploration of the issues necessitating flagging, in particular those related to test validity. Recognizing the need to clarify the issues preventing full implementation of the testing provisions of Section 504, the Office of Civil Rights commissioned a study of the problem by the National Research Council (NRC). (p. 5)

The NRC Panel on Testing of Handicapped People issued a report in 1982. As this report stated in its preface,

> Conflicting, apparently reasonable codes, which were created with the best of intentions, had brought to a standstill the implementation of federal regulations regarding the testing of handicapped applicants to schools and for employment. On the one hand, such applicants deserved to be protected from being labeled, that is, from having to reveal possibly prejudicial information about the existence of a handicap; on the other hand, the integrity of standardized testing procedures was also in need of protection so that scores obtained under nonstandard conditions could be "flagged" because of their uncertain validity. (Sherman & Robinson, 1982, p. vii)

The report concluded "current psychometric theory and practice do not allow full compliance with the regulations as currently drafted" (p. 1). The NRC panel called for a research program to include studies of test validity, research on the types of testing accommodations most appropriate for people with various types of disabilities, and investigations into the role of test scores in admissions decisions.

The NRC panel also recommended eliminating the practice of flagging admissions test scores *if it could be demonstrated that the scores were reasonably comparable to those obtained under standard conditions.*

The passage of the Americans With Disabilities Act (ADA) in 1990 has resulted in an increase in the number of tests given under accommodated conditions. But the ADA failed to clarify when a testing accommodation can be made without invalidating the inferences made from the test scores. In fact the ADA probably has complicated the situation by requiring that testing accommodations be made on an individual basis. This makes it extremely difficult to conduct research on test validity, because this would require large numbers of individuals with the same type and degree of disability taking the same test with identical accommodations.

Research on Test Score Comparability

In response to the NRC panel's report, there has been research to determine the comparability of test scores obtained under accommodated or modified conditions and scores obtained under standardized conditions. This has included research on how best to administer tests under accommodated conditions to produce scores that are as comparable as possible to those obtained under standardized conditions.

The Educational Testing Service (ETS), the College Board, and the Graduate Record Examination (GRE) Board undertook a four-year research program with three objectives:

- To develop an improved base of information;
- To evaluate and improve the accuracy of assessment for people with disabilities, and
- To evaluate and enhance the fairness and comparability of tests for individuals with and without disabilities.

This research culminated in the publication of *Testing Handicapped People* (Willingham et al., 1988); it should be noted that the term "handicapped," which is no longer preferred, was the term used in the Rehabilitation Act of 1973 and, thus, in this research. The studies looked at eight dimensions of test score comparability, including reliability, factor structure, prediction of academic performance, admissions decisions, test content, testing accommodations, and test timing. Comparison of the construct and predictive validity of the SAT and the GRE were made when the tests were given in special administrations to individuals with hearing impairment, learning disabilities, physical handicaps, visual impairment, and to individuals with no known disabilities.

Overall, comparability between standard and nonstandard test administrations was quite high, but it varied somewhat according to the type of the disability and the type of accommodation. For example, the factor structure of the tests was similar, although verbal and mathematical factors were less highly related for students with disabilities. For learning disabled students, mathematical ability may be underestimated when an audiocassette version of the test is used. Although little evidence of differential item functioning was found for most groups of students with disabilities, visually impaired students had difficulty with some SAT mathematics items in Braille format.

The prediction of academic performance of individuals with disabilities was less accurate than that of other individuals. The SAT substantially overpredicted performance of individuals with learning disabilities and there was corroborating evidence for this overprediction in the study with the GRE. The two factors believed to contribute most to overprediction for learning disabled students were the imprecise definition of learning disabilities and the time allowed to complete the test.

The executive summary of the *Testing Handicapped People* study stated that the primary source of test score noncomparability was the amount of time provided to test takers. It was suggested that "the problem could be corrected by setting time limits in nonstandard administrations so that handicapped and non-handicapped examinees are equally likely to finish the task. A principle conclusion of this report is that such empirically based timing should be attempted. However, this attempt may prove difficult from a practical standpoint because of problems in differentiating among handicapped examinees as to type and severity of handicap." (Willingham et al., 1988, p. xv)

The American College Testing program (ACT) has conducted two studies related to the validity of scores from special assessments. Laing and Farmer (1984) obtained a correlation between actual and predicted college grade point average (GPA) of 0.39 for special tested students with motor (physical and learning) disabilities and of 0.52 for students with visual impairments. These were compared with previous research indicating a correlation of 0.59 between actual and predicted GPAs for students tested under standardized conditions. Predicted GPAs for special tested students were slightly higher than their actual GPAs.

Ziomek and Andrews (1996) found the correlation between predicted and actual GPAs was 0.47 for students diagnosed with attention deficit disorder and 0.37 for dyslexic students. The results showed a slight overprediction for special-needs tested students with those diagnosed as having attention deficit showing the largest overprediction.

The Law School Admission Test (LSAT) program has also studied data from special administrations. From June 1991 through February 1993, there were accommodated LSAT administrations for 894 individuals with learning disabilities, 258 with visual impairments, 353 with physical impairments, and 11 with hearing impairments, compared to 228,676 individuals with regular administrations. The mean LSAT score for individuals in each disability group except those with hearing impairment exceeded the mean for those who took the test under regular conditions. However, applications with a learning disability had earned the lowest mean undergraduate GPA, significantly lower than the mean GPA for regular administration applicants. Individuals with visual impairments obtained a mean GPA 0.4 of a standard deviation lower than regular administration applicants. There was severe overprediction of GPAs for each group of students who took the LSAT under accommodated conditions.

Based on the results from this study, there is no justification for discontinuing the practice of identifying scores earned under nonstandard conditions. Currently, these scores cannot be relied upon to provide indications of first year performance in law school to the same extent that scores earned by students at regular LSAT administrations can be. (Wightman, 1993, p. 53)

Score Changes for Students With Disabilities Who Retest

There has been special interest in the effect that providing extended testing time has on the test results of students with disabilities because, in many cases, extended time is the only accommodation requested. Two studies have examined the scores for students who tested both under regular conditions and with extended time (Camara & Copeland, 1996; Ziomek, 1996). Students who obtain a testing accommodation that involves additional time, after having first tested without such an accommodation, show substantial score gains. The average gain for this group on the ACT composite was 3.2 points (as compared to an average gain of 0.9 points for students who had extended time for both testings). On the SAT-V, the average gain for such students was 44.6 points (as compared to an average gain of 15.3 points for students who had extended time for both testings); on the SAT-M the average gain was 38.1 points (as compared to 12.4 points for students who had extended time for both testings).

Research on the Use of Flagged Scores in Admission

There has been less research on how flagged test scores are used in the admission process. The NAS panel stated,

> Knowing that an individual is handicapped may, in different situations, have negative, positive, or negligible effects. In short, research does not support the common assumption that knowledge of a person's handicapping condition works to that person's disadvantage. (Sherman & Robinson, 1982, p. 24)

A 1984 study by Oltman and Hartnett (as reported in Willingham, 1987) found the following:

> Very few respondents (2 percent) reported any different weighting of admissions criteria when considering handicapped applicants. When asked whether they interpreted flagged test scores any differently from scores that were not flagged, 6 percent checked "yes" but usually elaborated only to say that other factors were carefully considered. (Willingham, 1987, p. 5)

Willingham looked at data from 1539 individuals with disabilities who had applied for admission to 121 institutions.

> The main finding in this study is that the handicapped applicants were admitted on much the same basis as the nonhandicapped applicants, though there were instances where particular groups of handicapped applicants were somewhat more or less likely to be admitted than would be expected. (Willingham, 1987, p. 16)

Hearing-impaired individuals were more likely to be admitted than would be expected from their high school grades and SAT scores, whereas learning disabled students were slightly less likely to be admitted.

In a study of law school applicants, those who took an accommodated LSAT were compared to applicants to the same schools who took the test under standard conditions.

> The most central finding of this portion of the study is that overall, applicants who present a test score identified as nonstandard are admitted to law school in the same proportions as would be predicted by their LSAT scores and UGPA [Law School Admissions Test and Undergraduate Grade Point Average]. The nonstandard LSAT score does not seem to negatively impact their probability of admissions. (Wightman, 1993, p. 47)

Anecdotal data from the Medical College Admission Test (MCAT) suggest that many college admissions offices simply disregard the flagging and consider the scores standard (Koenig, 1997, personal communication to Mitchell).

Mehrens (1997) concluded that both existing research and anecdotal reports suggest the flagging of test scores has little impact on the admissions process or on admissions decisions. However, the ConsorTium for Equity in Standards and Testing (CTEST) has suggested that

> once a college or university receives a test score with a flag on it, they have a reasonable basis for assuming that the test-taker was disabled and may, as a result, engage in discriminatory conduct against that applicant for admission. Since the accommodations that colleges and universities must provide for students with disabilities can sometimes be expensive, there may be incentives to deny admission to these students. (ConsorTium for Equity in Standards and Testing, 1998)

Deborah May (1994) surveyed 98 colleges about the admission of students with learning disabilities; 10% reported that they did not accept students with such disabilities into all programs offered at their institution and 5% reported having limitations on the number of such students who could be admitted. May commented that postsecondary educational institutions have no legal guidelines for evaluating and educating students with disabilities. However, the American Association of Collegiate Registrars and Admissions Officers provides such guidance in their publication "Recruitment, Admissions, and Students With Disabilities" (AACRAO, 1994).

Score Reporting Practices

Each admission testing program currently sets its own policies and practices regarding score reporting when testing accommodations have been made for individuals with disabilities. Because these policies are regularly reviewed and revised as needed, they are not described in detail. Testing professionals should contact the specific testing program to obtain the most current information.

As indicated in chapter 11, documentation of a disability is often requested by admission testing programs. The test taker and an appropriate professional identifies and verifies the disability, requests a specific accommodation, explains why the disability requires this accommodation, and either verifies that the same accommodation has been given for previous educational tests or explains why it was not given but is currently needed. These requests are evaluated and, if approved, the requested accommodation is provided.

Typically, test scores have been flagged for any nonstandard administration, and neither the specific accommodation nor the reason for the accommodation is reported to the test score user. There appears to be a trend toward reducing the kinds of accommodations that require flagging, especially flagging for minor accommodations that would not be expected to alter test performance (such as large type, marking answers in the test book, or allowing a diabetic to eat a snack during testing). Flagging is most likely to occur when the testing accommodation may have affected test validity or when extra time has been provided to the test taker. Many testing programs have felt they lack sufficient evidence to stop flagging completely without being in violation of the *Standards*.

There is little guidance provided to test score users to assist them in interpreting a flagged test score beyond stating that the flag indicates the test was given under nonstandard conditions. Materials about flagged scores often emphasize the importance of using any test score in conjunction with other information.

The score reporting problem is complicated by the wide variety of policies about when to indicate a testing accommodation has been made. Different testing programs have made different decisions about when a score should or should not be flagged. The rationale for these decisions may be based on test validity research, or it may simply be based on a program administrator's best judgment or even on operational considerations.

Policy and Research Issues Related to Flagging

Flagging appears to violate regulations written after the passage of the ADA. But to report test scores from nonstandard administrations without flagging appears to be contrary to the AERA/APA/NCME *Standards* because there is not yet sufficient evidence to conclude that scores from tests given under accommodated or modified conditions always mean the same thing as scores from a standard administration. In his presentation at the Board on Testing and Assessment (BOTA) planning meeting on test score flagging policies, Mehrens (1997) concluded that the interim policy should not be changed at that time, citing lack of clear evidence that the regression equation for the standardized group applied to the scores obtained under nonstandard administrations, no matter what the type or degree of disability or the type of accommodation.

However, change may be on the horizon. In February 2001 Educational Testing Service announced, as part of a legal settlement, that it would stop flagging the accommodation of extended time on the Graduate Record Examinations, the Graduate Management Admission Test, the Test of English as a Foreign Language, Praxis, and several other admissions tests, effective October 1, 2001. This was not done with any psychometric justification. The College Board, which owns the SAT, is evaluating aspects of the flagging practice and will then make a decision about whether flagging on the College Board tests should be continued, modified, or terminated. Because of the possibility of changes, testing professionals should check to determine the current practices about flagging on any given test.

Mehrens emphasized the need for government funding to increase the quantity of research in this area, something that has been recommended by others (e.g., Orleans, 1982–1983) for more than a decade. Mehrens has also addressed issues for doing high-quality research on this issue when faced with the constraints of small sample sizes, the many different types and degrees of disabilities, and the many different types of testing accommodations and modifications.

W. J. Camara (personal communication, 1997) has provided insightful comments on the problems of doing such research:

> My concern with proposed empirical studies to determine optimum time limits for groups of students with disabilities is with the potential utility of such work. That is, because ADA presently requires individual accommodations I am not sure any research which provides an empirical time limit for establishing comparability would ever be used in an operational program. . . . The difficulty in arriving at agreed upon and valid classifications of learning disabilities in particular is also a concern in conducting research.

Describing the research requirements, Camara stated,

> To help eliminate flagging you would need to: (1) appropriately classify learning disabilities (type and severity), (2) demonstrate the specific accommodations (fixed amount of extended time, etc.) for students, as a group, to perform similarly to students without disabilities testing under standard conditions, and (3) cross validate results with another group of test takers with similar disabilities who receive the same accommodations. Even then differences in the populations of test takers and differences over time may present problems in using the results in an operational program. (personal communication, Camara, 1997)

One of the most useful areas of research would examine the impact of providing extended time as the sole testing accommodation. Although testing without time limits might eliminate the problems associated with this type of accommodation, it is often impractical, especially when large groups of students must take a test in a paper-and-pencil format. Computer-administered tests might offer a better means of examining comparability when extended time is provided. Bennett (1995) has suggested that extended time might not be restricted to examinees with disabilities but be part of a "general design change to enhance comparability for everyone" (p. 2). Other promising research approaches include the use of differential item functioning (DIF) analyses (Geisinger, 1994) or validity generalization techniques (Livingston, 1993).

CONCLUSION

The accommodations and modifications used when testing individuals with disabilities should be clearly documented in any score report except when doing so would violate existing federal legislation (primarily affecting admissions and employment tests). Such documentation facilities the interpretation of the test results. Care should be taken to preserve the confidentiality of information about disabilities and testing accommodations.

We believe the use of test score flagging should be kept to a minimum. We believe testing organizations and admissions score users would benefit from a reduction in the variations in flagging policies and practices and from the development of a clear rationale for such action.

Similar recommendations have been made recently by committees of the National Research Council (Heubert & Hauser, 1999; McDonnell, McLaughlin, & Morison, 1997).

> When testing technology is able to ensure that accommodations do not confound the measurement of underlying constructs, score notations will be unnecessary. Until then, however, flagging should be used only with the understanding that the need to protect the public and policymakers from misleading information must be weighed against the equally important need to protect student confidentiality and prevent discriminatory uses of test information (Heubert & Hauser, 1999, p. 201).

REFERENCES

American Association of Collegiate Registrars and Admissions Officers (AA-CRAO). (1994). *Recruitment, admissions, and students with disabilities: A guide for compliance with Section 504 of the Rehabilitation Act of 1973 and Amendments of 1992 and the Americans with Disabilities Act of 1990* (3rd ed.). Washington, DC: Author.

American Educational Research Association, American Psychological Association, and National Council for Measurement in Education (AERA/APA/NCME). (1999). *Standards for educational and psychological testing*. Washington, DC: American Educational Research Association.

Americans With Disabilities Act. (1990). Pub. Law No. 101–336, 42. USC § 12101 et seq.

Bennett, R. E. (1995). *Computer-based testing for examinees with disabilities: On the road to generalized accommodation* (Research Memorandum 95–1). Princeton, NJ: Educational Testing Service.

Bennett, R. E., & Ragosta, M. (1984). *A research context for studying admissions tests and handicapped populations* (Report No. 1). Princeton, NJ: Educational Testing Service.

Camara, W. J., & Copeland, T. (1996, Oct. 28). *Score changes for students with disabilities testing with extended time on the SAT reasoning tests*. Presentation at the College Board's National Forum, New York.

ConsorTium for Equity in Standards and Testing. (1998, April 21). Testing students with disabilities. *SpotLight Issues* [On-line]. Available at wwwcsteep. bc.edu/ctest.

Geisinger, K. F. (1994). Psychometric issues in testing students with disabilities. *Applied Measurement in Education, 7*(2), 121–140.

Heubert, J. P., & Hauser, R. M. (Eds.). (1999). *High stakes: Testing for tracking, promotion, and graduation*. Washington, DC: National Academy Press.

Joint Committee on Testing Practices (JCTP). (1988). *Code of fair testing practices in education*. Washington, DC: Author.

Laing, J., & Farmer, M. (1984). *Use of the ACT assessment by examinees with disabilities* (Research Report #84). Iowa City: American College Testing Program.

Livingston, S. A. (1993). Small-sample equating with log-linear smoothing. *Journal of Educational Measurement, 30*, 23–39.

McDonnell, L. M., McLaughlin, M. J., & Morison, P. (Eds.). (1997). *Educating one and all: Students with disabilities and standards-based reform*. Washington, DC: National Academy Press.

May, D. D. (1994). Admission of students with learning disabilities into colleges: Policies and requirements. *Journal of College Admission, 145*, 10–19.

Mehrens, W. A. (1997, Sept. 19). *Flagging test scores: Policy, practice, and research*. Background paper for the BOTA Planning Meeting on Test Score Flagging Policies, National Academy of Sciences/National Research Council, Washington, DC.

Orleans, J. H. (1982–1983). Review of *Ability Testing of Handicapped People: Dilemma for Government, Science, and the Public*. *Journal of College and University Law, 9*(3), 347–354.

Rosenfeld, M., Tannenbaum, R. J., & Wesley, S. (1995). Policy issues with psychometric implications. In J. C. Impara (Ed.), *Licensure testing: Purposes, procedures, and practices (pp. 59 87)*. Lincoln: Buros Institute of Mental Measurements, University of Nebraska.

Sherman, S., & Robinson, N. (1982). *Ability testing and handicapped people: Dilemma for government, science, and the public.* Washington, DC: National Academy Press.

Wightman, L. F. (1993). *Test takers with disabilities: A summary of data from special administrations of the LSAT* (Research Report 93–03). Newtown, PA: Law School Admission Council and Law School Admission Services.

Willingham, W. W. (1987). *Handicapped applicants to college: An analysis of admission decisions* (College Board Report No 87–1). New York: College Entrance Examination Board.

Willingham, W. W., Ragosta, M., Bennett, R. E., Braun, H., Rock, D. A., & Powers, D. E. (1988). *Testing handicapped people.* Boston: Allyn and Bacon.

Ziomek, R. L. (1996, Oct.). *Achievement score gains of special-needs tested students who tested at least twice on the ACT assessment.* Paper presented at the annual NACAC convention, Minneapolis, MN.

Ziomek, R. L., & Andrews, K. M. (1996). *Predicting the college grade point averages of special-tested students from their ACT assessment scores and high school grades* (Research Report 96–7). Iowa City: American College Testing.

III

ASSESSMENT IN CLINICAL AND COUNSELING SETTINGS

7

THE CLINICAL ASSESSMENT OF PEOPLE WITH DISABILITIES

WILLIAM E. FOOTE

This chapter provides an overview of situations in which clinicians conduct assessments with disabled people. As such, it will be necessarily superficial in discussing arenas (such as neuropsychology or rehabilitation assessment) that have demanded significant literatures to fully elaborate. Rather, references to these areas are offered as examples of clinical assessment of people with disabilities so that assessment processes may be compared and unique issues may be explored.

I will begin this chapter with some definitions. Then I will assess two broad areas, situations in which the client's–patient's disability is not the focus of the assessment and contexts in which disability assessment is the center of the evaluation process.[1] In this second part of the chapter, I will

The author wishes to thank Polly Stipke for her diligent work in preparing drafts of this chapter. He also expresses his appreciation to Dr. Debra Saslawsky for her review of an early draft of this work.

[1]Throughout this chapter, the term "client" will be used to denote the individual who is the focus of the clinician's interest and professional services. In some settings, notably neuropsychology and rehabilitation assessment, the term "patient" would be more appropriate as the individual is usually encountered in a medical setting. However, the term client will be used for purposes of uniformity.

discuss issues encountered in evaluations related to neuropsychology, rehabilitation, and disability assessment.

DEFINITIONS

It may be helpful to provide some definitions that will be used in this chapter. Pryor (1997) reminded us that a distinction has long been made between *impairment* and *disability*. *Impairment* refers "to organ level abnormalities or restrictions (such as episodes of panic in an anxiety disorder) . . ." (p. 155). *Disability* refers "to restricted ability to perform a social role within the expected range, due to an impairment, the history of an impairment or the perception of an impairment" (Pryor, 1997, p. 155). In other words, one can conceptualize impairments outside of life context. A woman who has lost a leg to amputation may experience some impairment in walking. A child who has experienced a frontal-lobe brain injury may experience impairment in planning, sequencing, or behavioral control. A man diagnosed with severe depression may experience limited energy, optimism, and endurance.

In contrast, disability is impairment within a given context. For example, a woman with an impairment in walking from a lower limb amputation may experience disability in tasks requiring significant ambulation but no disability at all in sedentary work. A child with frontal-lobe impairment may experience considerable disability in situations with little external structure but experience less disability in contexts in which such structure is present. A man experiencing impairment from depression may not be able to do work that requires self-initiation, sustained activity, or long work days, but function much better in tasks in which he is closely supervised and does not have to work a full eight-hour day.

The clinician conducting testing with a client may be interested only in assessing the impairments evidenced in symptoms, interpersonal deficits, or intellectual deficits. However, in most cases, assessments involving impairment are not useful to the consumer of the assessment report unless the impairment is placed in a specific context and discussed in terms of disability. This chapter is largely about different assessment contexts and different ways in which a client's disability is conceptualized.

Clinicians conducting evaluations may encounter clients with disabilities in two general circumstances. In the first, the person's disability is not the main issue. Rather, the clinician is assessing the person with a disability to examine an issue that is not necessarily related to the disability. In the second, the impact of the disability on the person is the main focus of the evaluation. The approach for evaluating the patient may be markedly different, depending on the context.

Disability Not Related to Assessment Focus

Clinicians encounter people with disabilities in a number of assessment contexts. A common context is an evaluation to determine the client's treatment needs (Butcher, 1997; Masling, 1997; Nelson & Adams, 1997; Weiner, 1997). This assessment may occur in an outpatient setting in which a psychotherapist refers the patient for evaluation. The assessment may also occur in an inpatient setting as part of the intake assessment or discharge-planning processes in the hospital, residential treatment facility, or clinic. In either inpatient or outpatient settings the assessment may address a host of issues.

The therapist may have interest in the patient's ability to benefit from specific modes of treatment (Harkness & Lilienfield, 1997). For example, the clinician may want to know if a particular patient would respond better to group rather than individual psychotherapy. Comprehensive personality assessment can determine if the patient has sufficient verbal capacities and social skills to benefit from the group mode. Likewise, determinations about the appropriateness of insight-oriented versus behavioral interventions may rely on the results of psychological assessment (Haynes, Leisen, & Blaine, 1997). The developers of some instruments (Morey, 1991) have isolated specific combinations of scores to assist in modality decisions.

In some cases, the therapist may also require psychological testing to help determine appropriate treatment goals (Ben-Porath, 1997). A patient who has a number of life problems may wish to narrow the range of issues in therapy to generate a higher probability of success within the constraints of managed care, monetary resources, or social support (Finn & Tonsager, 1997). Ascertaining the extent of the patient's resources and the severity of the emotional problem provides not only appropriate targets for intervention but also suggests the tools to be used in implementing the intervention. Psychological testing can identify strengths, such as insight or capacity for bonding with the therapist that make therapy possible (Meyer & Handler, 1997). Testing can also identify barriers, such as guardedness, a tendency to externalize blame, or poor reality testing that would retard the therapy process (Chisolm, Crowther, & Ben-Porath, 1997; Donat, 1997).

The therapist may have interest in narrowing the range of diagnostic alternatives for a client (Morrison, Edwards, & Weissman, 1994). Although many therapists use the interview and therapeutic process to assist in this process, in some cases an independent determination of the patient's diagnosis is an essential predicate for the therapeutic enterprise (Sloan, Arsenault, Hilsenroth, Handler, & Harvill, 1996; Sloan, Arsenault, Hilsenroth, Harvill, & Handler, 1995). For example, a therapist working with a patient to treat a substance abuse problem should have some definitive knowledge of comorbid conditions (Matano, Locke, & Schwartz, 1994).

The presence of an Axis I illness such as major depressive disorder may sufficiently complicate the treatment process to require adjunctive medications and the ability to hospitalize the patient for depressive crises (Shapiro et al., 1995; Wetzler, Khadivi, & Oppenheim, 1995). The presence of an Axis II condition, such as borderline personality disorder, may also complicate treatment because of the patient's affective lability, unstable interpersonal connections, and propensity for self-destructive behavior (Bell-Pringle, Pate, & Brown, 1997; Merritt, Balogh, & Kok, 1998). Anticipating these complications may assist the therapist in a wide range of therapeutic decisions, not the least of which is determining if that particular therapist is the appropriate person for the job.

Related to diagnostic assessments are evaluations to determine if the patient is at risk for suicidal or homicidal behavior (Bongar, 1991). At the same time, interventions to reduce suicide or homicide risk usually involve loss of liberty for the patient or a compromise of the patient's confidentiality (Monahan, 1993). In part because of the criticality of risk assessment, some test instruments (Exner, 1993; Morey, 1991) include one or more measures of suicide risk. Homicide risk assessment is a more complicated process (Quinsey, Harris, Rice, & Cormier, 1998; Webster, Douglas, Eaves, & Hart, 1997) but may include psychological testing to determine clinical as well as historical correlates of violent behavior.

ASSESSING CLINICAL CONDITIONS FOR PEOPLE WITH DISABILITIES

To assess these clinical issues, the assessment process must be both fair and accurate (Nester, 1994). The degree to which accommodation is necessary varies along a continuum of extensiveness and complexity. At the most simple end of that continuum, the patient's disability may pose only a minor challenge to the assessing clinician. For example, a person with compromised lower body function from a spinal cord injury may be able to complete a standard clinical battery with very few modifications. Of course, in accordance with ethical and legal requirements (APA, 1992; Geisenger, 1994), the testing location and the ancillary facilities (e.g., the restroom or cafeteria) should be wheelchair-accessible. Testing procedures may need some modification to accommodate the disability. Modifications might include more frequent breaks for weight shifts to avoid pressure sores (Beggs, 1992).

Following the evaluation, interpretation of the assessment data may require some modification based on unique responses associated with the particular disability (Rodevich & Wanlass, 1995). For example, in the case of a spinal cord disability, because of medical problems associated with the condition, the patient may experience elevations on scales measuring somatic concern (such as the *Hy* scale on the MMPI) or scales reflecting unusual somatic experiences (such as the *Sz* scale on the MMPI; Fow, Yee, Wilson-O'Connor, & Spataro, 1996; Huang, Kim, & Charter, 1990). In interpreting these results, the knowledgeable examiner would view elevations on those scales as artifacts of the disability, rather than reflections of pathologically excessive somatic preoccupation or psychotic symptoms.

At the other end of the continuum, assessment procedures may require significant alteration to accommodate the disability. This would certainly be the case with visual or auditory disabilities. For example, in working with patients with visual disabilities, assessment of cognitive capacities may require significant changes in testing procedures. This demand has arisen from work by some researchers (Tillman, 1973; Vander Kolk, 1977, 1982) who have demonstrated that intellectual assessments based on a group of verbal subtests are effective in generating scores that are equivalent to IQs in visually disabled individuals. Other researchers (Brand, Pieterse, & Frost, 1986; Jordan, 1978) have used haptic (using only the sense of touch) tasks to replace some performance subtests of intellectual test batteries. Although the haptic skills may not map those assessed in performance tasks done by sighted patients, these measures do add a nonverbal component to the assessment and provide a benchmark for comparison to scores from verbal subtests.

For patients with auditory disabilities, the process may be even more complex. First, most prelingually deaf patients require the assessing clinician to be fluent in sign language or to hire an interpreter for the evaluation (Steinberg, 1991). Because very few clinicians possess sign language skills, most use interpreters to conduct assessments. This is not an entirely suitable substitute, as the addition of another person to the evaluative dyad can distort the interpersonal aspects of the evaluation and thus part of the clinician's database. The complications of this triad are further exacerbated if the clinician is not familiar with "deaf culture" (Brown & Gustafson, 1995; Hall, 1991; Reagan, 1995), although it could be expected that the sign language interpreter and deaf patient would interact within the assumptions and conventions of that culture. The patient's confidentiality is compromised by the third party, and the patient may accordingly censor history or symptoms to avoid embarrassment.

Moreover, the literature provides substantial evidence that the skills, intellectual capacities, and habits supporting signing skills in prelingually deaf patients may be quite distinct from those supporting verbal skills in hearing patients (Harry, 1986; Steinberg, 1991). In general, even in those tasks involving reading and writing without an oral component, deaf patients perform more poorly on and may have difficulty communicating in written media (Brauer, 1992).

Because of these significant differences in skill patterns and complications of language, the assessment of deaf patients is difficult, even for the signing clinician. Norms for deaf people do not exist for most cognitive and personality measures (Schwartz, Mebane, & Malony, 1990). Interpreting the responses of deaf people to standard personality measures such as the MMPI or Rorschach without appropriate accommodation and norm-referencing can be extremely misleading (Zieziula, 1982). However, some research using writing of responses on the Rorschach (Schwartz, Mebane, & Malony, 1990) and the presentation of MMPI items by signing via videotape (Brauer, 1992) have yielded more valid measures of the personality functioning of hearing-impaired clients.

In summary, clinical assessment of disabled people focused on issues not related to the person's disability must take into account the impact of the disability on the person's ability to complete the tests themselves. If the assessment context and method is not fair, the assessment may violate ethical standards and laws designed to protect disabled people. More important, if the method and context is not fair, the assessment may not be an accurate measure of the clinical condition it was designed to measure. Depending on the referral question, the interpretation of test instruments may be altered by the patient's disability. In some cases, traditional testing methods are simply invalid for people with specific disabilities. In other cases, interpretation must be altered significantly to accommodate the disability.

Evaluations Focused on Disability

In some cases, the primary purpose of an evaluation is to assess the impact of a disabling condition on the client. These assessments occur in a number of clinical settings. However, because of the limited scope of this chapter, it is not possible to include the broad scope or fine detail inherent in these assessments. Accordingly, this chapter does not include situations that clearly fall into the field of forensic psychology (Committee on Ethical Guidelines for Forensic Psychologists, 1991; Melton, Petrila, Poythress, & Slobogin, 1997). Forensic assessments include those related to the Americans With Disability Act of 1991 (Foote, 2000) and those related to assessments of criminal responsibility and legal capacity (Grisso, 1986; Rogers, 1986). The interested reader may observe that many of the assessment issues addressed in this section find applications in the forensic assessment of plaintiffs in personal injury, products liability, malpractice, and domestic relations cases. However, forensic assessments are both complex and peculiar to the legal context in which the evaluation takes place. For that reason, forensic assessment will not be considered.

However, other arenas of the clinical assessment of disability offer a broad range of issues for consideration. Although some of the following assessment situations may overlap, for purposes of simplicity it is possible to divide disability-related assessments into three separate areas: neuropsychological assessment, rehabilitation assessments, and disability evaluation.

Neuropsychological Assessment

The broad field of neuropsychology focuses in large part on the assessment of impairment and disability related to damage of the tissues of the brain by disease, congenital causes, or trauma. Even a rudimentary summary of the discipline of neuropsychology would be beyond the scope of this chapter. However, it should be noted that many neuropsychologists work as part of an interdisciplinary team including speech therapists, occupational therapists, physical therapists, physiatrists, and neurologists to develop comprehensive treatment programs to remediate the deficits produced by brain injury (Christensen & Uzzell, 1994; Milliren & Gordon, 1994; Prigatano, 1990, 1994). In this context, identifying the quality and extent of cognitive deficits is a necessary foundation for the preparation of a treatment program (Wood & Eames, 1989). Neuropsychological assessment can also delineate appropriate outcome measures to determine the success or failure of the treatment program (Prigatano & Klonoff, 1990). Likewise, the assessment of brain-related learning disabilities forms the foundation for developing a treatment and education program for children or adults with such problems (Gaskill & Brantley, 1996; Trexler, Webb, & Zappala, 1994).

Rehabilitation Assessments

Closely related to the neuropsychological assessment is assessment related to the process of rehabilitation. This is also a broad area of psychology that would require considerable space to explore. However, for the purposes of this chapter, it should be noted that a rehabilitation assessment is usually an integral component of a rehabilitation program for almost any form of disability (Elliot & Gramling, 1990). If other physical or psychological disabilities have a direct impact on cognitive or communicative processes, the psychological testing may help delineate the parameters of the individual's functioning (Barry & O'Leary, 1989; Rosenthal & Kolpan, 1986).

Assessment processes in rehabilitation are focused on specific goals. At early phases in the patient's rehabilitation, the goals may be related to the rehabilitation process itself. For example, increasing the patient's ability to communicate with care givers and family is critical for subsequent adaptation to the hospital environment as well as adaptation to the home or work situation (Wright, 1980). Although most assessments of communicative skills fall within the job description of speech therapists, psychologists may be in an effective position to assess fundamental verbal, abstraction, and memory skills.

Over the longer term, rehabilitation efforts are associated with maximal independence of function both at home by increasing the patient's capacity to engage in activities of daily living (ADLs; Smith-Knapp, Corrigan, & Arnett, 1996). In this regard, psychological testing may join available learning methods with the patient's cognitive strengths and weaknesses to map the rehabilitation process for the patient (Wesolowsky & Zencius, 1994). Of course, the testing clinician is a part of a larger rehabilitation team, as noted previously, and the role may vary depending on the extent of cognitive impairment experienced by the patient (Tun, Tun, & Wingfield, 1997; Wood & Eames, 1989). In other rehabilitation contexts, assessment of emotional functioning can be an important component to the overall rehabilitation process. For example, the existence of a preexisting personality disorder can limit the effectiveness of a physical rehabilitation program (Diller, 1994).

Likewise, the presence of emotional reactions resulting from the injury may interfere with the interventions of rehabilitation professionals from all disciplines (Frank, VanValin, & Elliot, 1987; Hewlett, Young, & Kirwan, 1995; Viney & Westbrook, 1982). Assessment of these reactions is a critical part of the assessment process in rehabilitation (Klonoff & Lamb, 1998; Tun et al., 1997) for several reasons. First, not all patients experience serious emotional reactions (Frank et al., 1987). For example, some research indicates that only about one third of people with spinal cord injuries experience some form of diagnosable depression (Fullerton, Harvey, Klein, & Howell, 1981). For those with serious emotional reactions, personality assessment may assist in identifying the nature of the reaction and in directing psychotherapeutic and psychopharmacologic interventions to relieve the person's distress.

Second, when emotional reactions do occur, they can significantly interfere with the rehabilitation process (Livneh & Antonak, 1990). These reactions are partially a product of the person's predisability psychological make-up (Diller, 1994; Gatchel, Polatin, & Kinney, 1995) but may also correlate with the severity of the patient's injuries and resultant incapacities (Viney & Westbrook, 1982). Depressive and anxiety disorders can impair cognitive functions (Parente & Herrmann, 1996). The low level of energy and social withdrawal associated with depression can reduce the patient's enthusiasm for rehabilitation activities (Frank et al., 1987). Because of this impact of depression, the overall length of the rehabilitation process may be lengthened (Malec & Neimeyer, 1983; Viney & Westbrook, 1982).

Third, as a related issue, emotional reactions play some role in determining the probability that a person who has experienced a disability will reach some degree of adjustment to that disability. Although the long-term adjustment may be considered part of the rehabilitation process, in this case the issue is how the disabled person lives his or her life following maximum medical improvement. For example, in a review of empirical research concerning people with spinal cord injuries, Frank et al. (1987) determined that long-term adjustment may be related to the person's health status, how much control he or she has over day-to-day life, and the quality of their social contacts. In other words, personal and social resources play an important role. Personality assessment can assist by determining the nature of the personal resources the patient has both at the beginning of the rehabilitation process (Diller, 1994) and on repeated testing throughout the life span of the person.

Fourth, emotional reactions can be serious enough to lead to life-threatening conditions. For example, severe depression is associated with increased suicide risk among some groups of people with disabilities (Nyquist & Bors, 1967). Such reactions are also associated with increased morbidity related to inadequate respiratory, bladder and bowel, and skin care (Crewe & Krause, 1990; Tun et al., 1997). As noted previously, personality testing can guide interventions through psychotherapy, counseling, or medication to not only avoid life-threatening emotional deterioration but also to improve the quality of the person's physical health.

DISABILITY STATUS ASSESSMENTS

A number of governmental systems provide financial benefits, health care, and rehabilitation services to people with disabilities. The largest of these is the federal government, with the Social Security Disability Administration and the Veterans' Administration. In addition, some states have welfare programs that offer short-term disability benefits. Worker's compensation systems also provide disability-related benefits for on-the-job injuries both in the public sector (e.g., the federal worker's compensation system, or Office of Worker's Compensation) and the private sector, usually supported by a state insurance pool or a private insurance carrier but operating under legally binding state guidelines.

In addition to governmental systems, disability benefits are also paid by private insurance carriers for individuals who are disabled by injuries that occur off the job or illnesses that are unrelated to the person's work. These benefits are defined by a contract between the employer or worker and the disability insurance carrier and may vary widely in the sorts of disabilities covered, the definitions of disability, and the scope and duration of coverage.

Social Security Disability: An Example

The principles of most disability insurance systems are the same. As Pryor (1997) noted, most systems have goals of preventing disabilities, accommodating disabilities, delivering benefits to disabled people, and supplying those people with rehabilitation services. To accomplish these goals, a clinician must conduct some assessment of the applicant's disability. This assessment is designed to determine the severity of the applicant's disability and the nature of residual skills and capacities. A good example of these systems is the U.S. federal Social Security Disability Insurance program.

In this system, disability is defined as "the inability to engage in any substantial gainful activity by reason of medically determinable physical or mental impairment(s) which can be expected to result in death or which has lasted or can be expected to last for a continuous period of not less than 12 months" (Social Security Administration Office of Disability, 1998, p. 2). This definition contains several elements that are part of most disability definitions. First, it defines the disability in terms of the origin of the disability—in this case, a "medically determinable physical or mental impairment." Second, it defines the duration of the disability necessary to qualify for consideration—at least one year. This is to specifically exclude disabling conditions of short duration, such as those related to recovery from an accident or illness that is only temporarily disabling. Third, the definition delineates the tasks considered in determining the disability —in this case, a broad universe of "any substantial gainful activity." This language focuses on the work that the claimant has done in the past (vocational history); the work the claimant is doing now, if any; and any other work for which the claimant is qualified.

The Social Security Administration uses a "sequential evaluation process" (Pryor, 1997). First, the examiner determines if the claimant is currently engaged in any gainful activity. If the claimant is so engaged, the system yields a finding of "no disability." Second, an assessment is done to determine if the claimant has a severe impairment. If the claimant does not have a severe impairment, the model dictates a finding of "no disability." Third, a determination is necessary to decide if the claimant meets or exceeds listed impairments. Such impairments are found in "the listings" that are published by the Social Security Administration (1998). These cover both medical and mental disabilities and are designed to provide the evaluating professional with specific criteria for determining if the claimant's impairments match with the regulatory standards. If the claimant meets these listings, then the verdict is "disabled." Fourth, an assessment is necessary to determine whether the claimant's impairment prevents him or her from doing relevant work he or she has done in the past. If the claimant can do that work, the system mandates a finding of "no disability." Fifth, the claimant's residual functional capacity (RFC) must be determined, which, along with age, education, and past work experience, determines if the claimant can perform any other work. If the claimant cannot perform any other work, a finding of "disabled" is made.

For mental disabilities, the listings begin with a brief definition of the category of impairment. This is followed by two sections. Section A contains the symptoms that are generally consistent with *DSM-IV* criteria for that or similar disorders (American Psychiatric Association, 1994). For example, for affective disorders, the listings include symptoms of a major depressive episode (e.g., anhedonia, sleep disturbance), a manic episode (e.g., hyperactivity, flight of ideas), and bipolar syndromes (both manic and depressive).

Section B requires the diagnosed condition to result in at least two of the following:

> 1. Marked restriction of activities of daily living; or 2. Marked difficulties in maintaining social functioning; or 3. Deficiencies of concentration, persistence or pace resulting in frequent failure to complete tasks in a timely manner (in work settings or elsewhere); or 4. Repeated episodes of deterioration or decompensation in work or work-like settings which cause the individual to withdraw from that situation or to experience exacerbation of signs and symptoms (which may include deterioration of adaptive behaviors). (Social Security Administration, 1998, pp. 95–96)

Thus, as a disability compensation system, Social Security places impairments in two contexts to define disability. One is the work the claimant has done or can do. The other is a group of activities that are common to a number of work settings and are essential for functioning in most jobs.

Testing can be a critical part of assessing claimants in Social Security cases. First, for some disabilities, notably "Mental Retardation and Autism," the criteria are defined in terms of Full Scale IQ. For example, a person with an IQ from the Wechsler Scales (or similar instruments) of 59 or less qualifies automatically for having a severe disorder. Higher IQs must be coupled with other disorders to meet the listings.

Second, neuropsychological testing may assist in determining specific impairments related to organic mental disorders. For example, one of the criteria for that category is a demonstrated loss of 15 or more IQ points from premorbid levels, or an "impairment index" in the severely impaired range as measured through common neuropsychological batteries.

Third, testing may document the presence of specific symptoms related to other disorders. For example, a personality disorder is defined in terms of "deeply ingrained, maladaptive patterns of behavior," which may be associated with such symptoms as seclusiveness, inappropriate hostility, or pathological dependency. These symptoms may be assessed through actuarial personality measures (e.g., the MMPI-2 or PAI) or through projective measures (e.g., the Rorschach).

Fourth, psychological testing can establish whether the claimant's condition meets the criteria for the listings B3, "concentration, persistence and pace." The guide suggests that "in psychological tests of intelligence or memory, concentration is assessed through tasks requiring short-term memory or through tasks that must be completed within established time limits" (Social Security Administration, Office of Disability, 1998, p. 88).

Disability Evaluation: Summary

The example of the Social Security Disability assessment system illustrates factors common to all disability evaluation systems. All systems have criteria for defining conditions that produce impairments. All systems have criteria for defining contexts in which those impairments are relevant. These include definitions of the range of work situations that qualify (some or all of the jobs that the person has done or can do) and the severity of the impairments necessary to constitute a disability in those situations.

Although the medical standards and guidelines for determining disability as a result of mental conditions have been shown to be a reasonably reliable basis for disability assessment (Pincus et al., 1991), empirical assessment techniques relating to appropriate norms should increase both the reliability and accuracy of such assessments. Likewise, the appropriate use of testing in worker's compensation, Veteran's Administration, and private disability systems should increase the reliability and accuracy of those assessments. For the assessing professional, the key is to appropriately relate the listed criteria to specific test scores or to patterns of test scores. This requires not only a thorough understanding of the criteria but of the range of available test instruments, their base norms, and the range of appropriate applications for those data.

CONCLUSION

Clinicians who conduct assessments using testing work with disabled people in a broad range of situations, with a wide range of goals, and with differing attention to the specific parameters of the client's disability. For clinicians assessing non–disability-related issues, the client's disability must be taken into account to provide a fair and accurate assessment of the issue in question. For those assessing the client's disability, the first task is to determine the nature and severity of impairments caused by the disability. This level of evaluation should include cognitive assessment. Memory, judgment, perceptual, and decision-making processes are the foundation of the client's involvement in most aspects of work and home life. Cognitive processes also undergird interpersonal and personality functions, which are usually assessed through personality assessment measures. These measures allow the clinician to compare the skills, deficits, traits, and symptoms to norms (Finn & Tonsager, 1997; Greene, Gwin, & Staal, 1997; Masling, 1997; Matano, Locke, & Schwartz, 1994; Weiner, 1997).

Likewise, personality assessment measures allow the clinician to compare the client's functioning to diagnostic categories. Both actuarial and projective measures provide comparisons of the client's traits, symptoms, and behavioral patterns to those of established normative groups. Further, personality assessment methods provide an opportunity for the client to list problems, symptoms, and impairments that may directly translate into disability criteria.

However, clinical assessment of disabled people must usually include a broader base of data than testing results. Although testing is an important component of the assessment of people with disabilities, data from other sources are critical for accurate conclusions. Documentary sources including educational, vocational, military, and medical records provide essential background for understanding the test data. Interview data including behavioral observations, mental status assessment, and a client's account of history and the development and current status of symptoms allow for weighting various test data to determine those most germane to the assessment issue. Interviews with collateral sources—the client's family, work supervisors, coworkers, neighbors, or clergy—can provide additional corroborative information about the real-life capabilities and incapacities of the client. It is only through a systematic combination of information from all these sources that the clinician may develop a picture that reflects the full range of the client's skills, talents, and strengths. In this picture, disability is seen not as the central defining characteristic of the client but as an element of the client's life that requires consideration, understanding, and respect.

REFERENCES

American Psychiatric Association. (1994). *The diagnostic and statistical manual of mental disorders* (4th ed.). Washington, DC: American Psychiatric Association.

American Psychological Association. (1992). Ethical principles of psychologists and code of conduct. *American Psychologist, 47*, 1597–1611.

Barry, P., & O'Leary, J. (1989). Roles of the psychologist on a traumatic brain injury rehabilitation team. *Rehabilitation Psychology, 34*(2), 83–90.

Beggs, W. A. (1992). Coping with traveling in the visually impaired. *Psychology and Health, 7*, 15–26.

Bell-Pringle, V. J., Pate, J. L., & Brown, R. C. (1997). Assessment of borderline personality disorder using the MMPI-2 and the Personality Assessment Inventory. *Assessment, 4*(2), 131–139.

Ben-Porath, Y. S. (1997). Use of personality assessment instruments in empirically guided treatment planning. *Psychological Assessment, 9*(4), 361–367.

Bongar, B. (1991). *Suicide risk assessment.* Washington, DC: American Psychological Association.

Brand, H. J., Pieterse, M. J., & Frost, M. (1986). Reliability and validity of the Ohwaki-Kohs tactile block design test for the blind. *Psychological Reports, 58*, 375–380.

Brauer, B. A. (1992). The signer effect on MMPI performance of deaf respondents. *Journal of Personality Assessment, 58*(2), 380–388.

Brown, P. M., & Gustafson, M. S. (1995). Showing sensitivity to deaf culture. *American Speech Hearing Association, 37*(5), 46–47.

Butcher, J. N. (1997). Introduction to the special section on assessment in psychological treatment: A necessary step for effective intervention. *Psychological Assessment, 9*(4), 331–333.

Chisholm, S. M., Crowther, J. H., & Ben-Porath, Y. S. (1997). Selected MMPI-2 scales' ability to predict premature termination and outcome from psychotherapy. *Journal of Personality Assessment, 69*(1), 127–144.

Christensen, A., & Uzzell, B. (1994). *Brain Injury and Neuropsychological Rehabilitation: International Perspectives.* Hillsdale, NJ: Erlbaum.

Committee on Ethical Guidelines for Forensic Psychologists. (1991). Specialty guidelines for forensic psychologists. *Law and Human Behavior, 15*(6), 655–665.

Crewe, N. M., & Krause, J. S. (1990, Winter). An eleven-year follow-up of adjustment to spinal cord injury. *Rehabilitation Psychology, 35*(4), 205–210.

Diller, L. (1994). Finding the right treatment combinations: Changes in rehabilitation over the past five years. In A. Christensen & B. Uzzell (Eds.), *Brain injury and neuropsychological rehabilitation: International perspectives* (pp. 1–16). Hillsdale, NJ: Erlbaum.

Donat, D. C. (1997). Personality traits and psychiatric rehospitalization: A two-year follow up. *Journal of Personality Assessment, 68*(3), 703–711.

Elliot, T., & Gramling, S. (1990). Psychologists and rehabilitation: New roles and old training models. *American Psychologist, 45,* 762–765.

Exner, J. E. (1993). *The Rorschach: A comprehensive system* (3rd. ed.). New York: Wiley.

Finn, S. E., & Tonsager, M. E. (1997). Information-gathering and therapeutic models of assessment: Complementary paradigms. *Psychological Assessment, 9*(4), 374–385.

Foote, W. E. (2000). A model for psychological consultation in Americans With Disability Act cases. *Professional Psychology: Research and Practice, 31*(2), 190–196.

Fow, N. R., Yee, J., Wilson-O'Connor, D., & Spataro, R. (1996). MMPI-2 profiles in traumatic and non-traumatic spinal cord injured patients. *Journal of Clinical Psychology, 52*(5), 573–579.

Frank, R., VanValin, P., & Elliot, T. (1987). Adjustment to spinal cord injury: A review of empirical and non-empirical studies. *Journal of Rehabilitation, 53,* 43–48.

Fullerton, D., Harvey, R., Klein, M., & Howell, T. (1981). Psychiatric disorders in patients with spinal cord injury. *Archives of General Psychiatry, 32,* 1369–1371.

Gaskill, F. W., & Brantley, J. C. (1996). Changes in ability and achievement scores over time: Implications for children classified as learning disabled. *Journal of Psychoeducational Assessment, 14*, 220–228.

Gatchel, R. J., Polatin, P. B., & Kinney, R. K. (1995). Predicting outcome of chronic back pain using clinical predictors of psychopathology: A prospective analysis. *Health Psychology, 14*(5), 415–420.

Geisinger, K. F. (1994, Dec.). Cross-cultural normative assessment: Translation and adaptation issues influencing the normative interpretation of assessment instruments. *Psychological Assessment, 6*(4), 304–312.

Greene, R. L., Gwin, R., & Staal, M. (1997). Current status of MMPA-2 research: A methodologic overview. *Journal of Personality Assessment, 68*(1), 20–36.

Grisso, T. (1986). *Evaluating competencies: Forensic assessment and instruments.* New York: Plenum Press.

Hall, S. A. (1991, Winter). Door into deaf culture: Folklore in an American deaf social club. *Sign Language Studies, 73*, 421–429.

Harkness, A. R., & Lilienfeld, S. O. (1997). Individual differences science for treatment planning: Personality traits. *Psychological Assessment, 9*(4), 349–360.

Harry, B. (1986). Interview, diagnostic, and legal aspects in the forensic psychiatric assessment of deaf persons. *Bulletin of American Academy of Psychiatry Law, 14*(2), 147–162.

Haynes, S. N., Leisen, M. B., & Blaine, D. D. (1997). Design of individualized behavioral treatment programs using functional analytic clinical case models. *Psychological Assessment, 9*(4), 334–348.

Hewlett, S., Young, P., & Kirwan, J. (1995, March). Dissatisfaction, disability, and rheumatoid arthritis. *Arthritis Care and Research, 8*(1), 4–9.

Huang, D. D., Kim, S. W., & Charter, R. A. (1990). Psychological reaction to spinal cord injury and the relationship of personality to the resulting neurological dysfunctions. *Journal of Neurologic Rehabilitation, 4*(3), 157–161.

Jordan, S. (1978). Some clinical interpretations of the Haptic Intelligence Scale for adult blind. *Perceptual and Motor Skills, 47*, 203–222.

Klonoff, P. S., & Lamb, D. G. (1998). Mild head injury, significant impairment on neuropsychological test scores, and psychiatric disability. *Clinical Neuropsychologist, 12*(1), 31–42.

Livneh, H., & Antonak, R. F. (1990, Winter). Reactions to disability: An empirical investigation of their nature and structure. *Journal of Applied Rehabilitation Counseling, 21*(4), 13–21.

Malec, J., & Neimeyer, R. (1983). Psychologic prediction of duration of inpatient spinal cord rehabilitation and performance of self-care. *Archives of Physical Medicine and Rehabilitation, 59*, 359–363.

Masling, J. M. (1997). On the nature and utility of projective tests and objective tests. *Journal of Personality Assessment, 69*(2), 257–270.

Matano, R. A., Locke, K. D., & Schwartz, K. (1994, Oct.). MCMI personality subtypes for male and female alcoholics. *Journal of Personality Assessment, 63*(2), 250–264.

Melton, G. B., Petrila, J., Poythress, N. G., & Slobogin, C. (1997). *Psychological evaluations for the courts* (2nd ed.). New York: Guilford Press.

Merritt, R. D., Balogh, D. W., & Kok, C. J. (1998). *DSM-IV* cluster A personality disorder diagnoses among young adults with a 2–7-8 MMPI profile. *Psychological Assessment, 5*(3), 273–285.

Meyer, G. J., & Handler, L. (1997). The ability of the Rorschach to predict subsequent outcome: A meta-analysis of the Rorschach prognostic rating scale. *Journal of Personality Assessment, 69*(1), 1–38.

Milliren, J. W., & Gordon, W. A. (1994). The development of an integrated rehabilitation system for persons with traumatic brain injury: The evolution of public policy in New York. *Journal of Head Trauma Rehabilitation, 9*(2), 27–34.

Monahan, J. (1993). Limiting therapist exposure to *Tarasoff* liability. *American Psychologist, 48*(3), 242–250

Morey, L. C. (1991). *The Personality Assessment Instrument manual*. Odessa, FL: Psychological Assessment Resources.

Morrison, T. L., Edwards, D. W., & Weissman, H. N. (1994). The MMPI and MMPI-2 as predictors of psychiatric diagnosis in an outpatient sample. *Journal of Personality Assessment, 62*(1), 17–30.

Nelson, L. D., & Adams, K. M. (1997). Challenges for neuropsychology in the treatment and rehabilitation of brain-injured patients. *Psychological Assessment, 9*(4), 368–373.

Nester, M. A. (1994). Psychometric testing and reasonable accommodation for persons with disabilities. In S. M. Bruyere & J. O'Keefe (Eds.), *Implications of the Americans With Disabilities Act for psychology* (pp. 25–36). Washington, DC: American Psychological Association.

Nyquist, R., & Bors, E. (1967). Mortality and survival in traumatic myelopathy during nineteen years from 1946 to 1965. *Paraplegia, 51*, 22–48.

Parente, R., & Herrmann, D. (1996). Emotional issues. In R. Parente & D. Herrmann (Eds.), *Retraining Cognition: Techniques and Applications* (pp. 201–208). Gaithersburg, MD: Aspen.

Pincus, H. A., Kennedy, C., Simmens, S. J., Goldman, H. H., Sirovatka, & Sharfstein, S. S. (1991). Determining disability due to mental impairment: APA's evaluation of Social Security Administration guidelines. *American Journal of Psychiatry, 148*(8), 1037–1043.

Prigatano, G. P. (1990). Effective traumatic brain injury rehabilitation: Team/patient interaction. In E. D. Bigler (Ed.), *Traumatic brain injury: Mechanisms of damage, assessment, intervention, and outcome* (pp. 297–311). Austin, TX: Pro-ed.

Prigatano, G. (1994). *Neuropsychological rehabilitation after brain injury*. Baltimore, MD: Johns Hopkins University Press.

Prigatano, G. P., & Klonoff, P. S. (1990). Psychotherapy and neuropsychological assessment after brain injury. In E. D. Bigler (Ed.), *Traumatic Brain Injury* (pp. 313–329). Austin, TX: PRO-ED.

Pryor, E. S. (1997). Mental disabilities and the disability fabric. In R. J. Bonnie and J. Monahan (Ed.), *Mental disorder, work disability, and the law* (pp. 153–198). Chicago: University of Chicago Press.

Quinsey, V. L., Harris, G. T., Rice, M. E., & Cormier, C. A. (1998). *Violent offenders: Appraising and managing risk.* Washington, DC: American Psychological Association.

Reagan, T. (1995). A sociocultural understanding of deafness: American sign language and the culture of deaf people. *International Journal of Intercultural Relationships, 19*(2), 239–251.

Rodevich, M. A., & Wanlass, R. L. (1995). The moderating effect of spinal cord injury on MMPI-2 profiles: A clinically derived Tscore correction procedure. *Rehabilitation Psychology, 40*(3), 181–190.

Rogers, R. (1986). *Conducting insanity evaluations.* New York: Van Nostrand Reinhold.

Rosenthal, M., & Kolpan, K. (1986). Head injury rehabilitation: Psychology issues and roles for the rehabilitation psychologist. *Rehabilitation Psychology, 31,* 37–46.

Schwartz, N. S., Mebane, D. L., & Malony, H. N. (1990). Effects of alternate modes of administration on Rorschach performance of deaf adults. *Journal of Personality Assessment, 54*(3&4), 671–683.

Shapiro, D., Rees, A., Barkham, M., Hardy, G., Reynolds, S. & Startup, M. (1995). The effects of treatment duration and severity of depression on the maintenance of gains after cognitive-behavioral and psychodynamic-interpersonal psychotherapy. *Journal of Consulting and Clinical Psychology, 63*(3), 378–387.

Sloan, P., Arsenault, L., Hilsenroth, M., Handler, L., & Harvill, L. (1996). Rorschach measures of posttraumatic stress in Persian Gulf War veterans: A three-year follow up study. *Journal of Personality Assessment, 66*(1), 54–64.

Sloan, P., Arsenault, Hilsenroth, M., Harvill, L., & Handler, L. (1995). Rorschach measures of posttraumatic stress in Persian Gulf War veterans. *Journal of Personality Assessment, 64*(3), 397–414.

Smith-Knapp, K., Corrigan, J. D., & Arnett, J. A. (1996). Predicting functional independence from neuropsychological tests following traumatic brain injury. *Brain Injury, 10*(9), 651–661.

Social Security Administration Office of Disability. (1998). *Disability evaluation under social security.* Washington, DC: Social Security Administration.

Steinberg, A. (1991). Issues in providing mental health services to hearing-impaired persons. *Hospital and Community Psychiatry, 42*(4), 380–389.

Tillman, M. H. (1973). Intelligence scales for the blind: A review with implications for research. *Journal of School Psychology, 11*(1), 80–87.

Trexler, L. E., Webb, P. M., & Zappala, G. (1994). Strategic aspects of neuropsychological rehabilitation. In A-L. Christensen & B. P. Uzzell (Eds.), *Brain injury and neuropsychological rehabilitation: International perspectives* (pp. 99–123). Hillsdale, NJ: Erlbaum.

Tun, C. G., Tun, P. A., & Wingfield, A. (1997). Cognitive function following long-term spinal cord injury. *Rehabilitation Psychology, 42*(3), 163–182.

Vander Kolk, C. J. (1977, April). Intelligence testing for visually impaired persons. *Visual Impairment and Blindness, 71*(4), 158–163.

Vander Kolk, C. J. (1982). A comparison of intelligence test score patterns between visually impaired subgroups and the sighted. *Rehabilitation Psychology, 27*(2), 115–120.

Viney, L., & Westbrook, M. (1982). Patients' psychological reactions to chronic illness: Are they associated with rehabilitation? *Journal of Applied Rehabilitation Counseling, 13,* 38–44.

Webster, C. D., Douglas, K. S., Eaves, D., & Hart, S. D. (1997). Assessing risk of violence to others. In C. D. Webster & M. A. Jackson (Eds.), *Impulsivity: Theory, assessment, and treatment* (pp. 251–277). New York: Guildford Press.

Weiner, I. B. (1997). Current status of the Rorschach inkblot method. *Journal of Personality Assessment, 68*(1), 5–19.

Wesolowski, M. D., & Zencius, A.H. (1994). *A practical guide to head injury rehabilitation: A focus on postacute residential treatment.* New York: Plenum Press.

Wetzler, S., Khadivi, A., & Oppenheim, S. (1995). The psychological assessment of depression: Unipolars versus bipolars. *Journal of Personality Assessment, 65*(3), 557–566.

Wood, R. L., & Eames, P. (1989). The structure and content of a head injury rehabilitation service. In L. L. Rodger, R. L. Wood, & P. Eames (Eds.), *Models of brain injury rehabilitation* (pp. 31–47). London: Chapman and Hall.

Wright, G. N. (1980). *Total rehabilitation.* Boston: Little, Brown.

Zieziula, F. (1982). *Assessment of hearing impaired people.* Washington, DC: Gallaudet College Press.

8

COUNSELING ASSESSMENT

JANET E. HELMS AND RUTH B. EKSTROM

Counselors are concerned with preventing and treating mental health problems associated with normal life transitions and the fulfillment of developmental tasks and goals. As a result, assessment and counseling are closely linked. For children and adults with life-long disabilities, assessment and counseling are the first steps in developing individualized plans for education and training. For adults who have developed disabilities through accidents, illness, or aging, assessment and counseling are the first steps in rehabilitation and development of an individualized life plan that might address issues of employment, education, family relationships, lifestyle, or some combination of these factors.

In this chapter, we discuss some of the topics that are important for counselors who carry out the assessment of individuals with disabilities. We use the term *counselor* generically to refer to counseling professionals providing services to children or adults with disabilities regardless of the discipline in which the counselors were trained. Counselors are trained in a variety of disciplines whose knowledge bases, professional standards, and domains of practice may vary. In this chapter, we focus on those aspects of counseling and assessment that are common to the various disciplines as they pertain to effective assessment of individuals with disabilities.

As Hood and Johnson (1997) pointed out, using assessment to assist individuals in fulfilling personal needs and goals has always been important in counseling.

> During the early days, counseling and assessment were virtually synonymous. Many of the counseling centers established during the 1930s and 1940s were called Counseling and Testing Centers. At that time, counseling typically involved helping students make educational or vocational plans on the basis of test results. (p. 3)

In recent years counseling has expanded to include a wider array of personal concerns in addition to vocational and educational planning, but assessment continues to be one of the eight core areas of knowledge and skill for all counselors. According to the standards of the Council for the Accreditation of Counseling and Related Educational Programs (CACREP, 1994), the assessment component of counselor education minimally should include the following:

- Theoretical and historical bases for assessment techniques;
- Validity, including evidence supporting content, construct, and empirical validity;
- Reliability, including methods of establishing stability, internal consistency, and cultural equivalence;
- Appraisal methods, including environmental assessment, performance assessment, individual and group test and inventory methods, behavioral observations, and computer-managed and computer-assisted methods;
- Psychometric statistics, including types of assessment scores, measures of central tendency, indexes of variability, standard errors, and correlations;
- Age, gender, ethnicity, language, disability, and cultural factors related to the assessment and evaluation of individuals and groups;
- Strategies for selecting, administering, interpreting, and using assessment and evaluation instruments and techniques in counseling; and
- Ethical and legal considerations in appraisal.

Thus, every counselor who has completed a CACREP-accredited program should have acquired the assessment and appraisal skills and knowledge specified by CACREP. (However, some educators would argue that the completion of courses does not guarantee that the person has acquired such knowledge.) Counselors trained in other disciplines should have comparable expertise as specified by their professional associations. Given the focus of this book, it is important to note that all counselors should be aware of disability factors at the individual and systemic levels that may affect assessments and evaluations.

THE COUNSELOR ROLE

The main purpose of assessment in counseling persons with disabilities is to provide information that counselors and their clients can use in evaluating strengths and weaknesses, needs, goals, competencies, and potential impediments. Counselors may conduct the assessments themselves. However, because "clients" may include a variety of constituencies in addition to the person being assessed, counselors are often involved in multiple roles including empathic listener, advisor, educator, advocate, and intermediary, as well as practitioner–scientist.

In addition to basic counseling and communication skills, these roles require special expertise when working with persons with disabilities and their families, employment and educational institutions, mental health and social services agencies, and society in general. The counselor has to integrate knowledge of existing laws and principles of assessment with an understanding of the client's needs and concerns, regardless of how "client" is defined, and communicate that information in a useful manner to the relevant parties. When serving as an assessor or interpreter of assessment information, counselors should be able to anticipate or use existing assessment procedures to estimate the likely effects of the person's particular disability on the assessment process and outcome(s) and to make or recommend appropriate compensatory procedures, if necessary. In the role of practitioner–scientist, counselors must be attuned to criteria for evaluating the scientific quality of the assessment, as implied in the CACREP standards and specified in the *Standards for Educational and Psychological Testing* (AERA/APA/NCME, 1999), before, during, and after the assessment takes place. Such multifaceted foresight and pragmatism can sometimes prevent problems and misunderstandings in using assessment procedures.

Even when counselors are not engaged in extensive amounts of assessment themselves, they may serve as a resource for assessment information for those with whom they work. Impara and Plake (1995) found that secondary school counselors were more knowledgeable about assessment than were either secondary school teachers or administrators. It is not surprising, then, that counselors are seen as a resource for assessment information (see, for example, Ginter, Scalise, & Presse, 1990). Given these expectations, all counselors need to know about assessing individuals with disabilities, whether they carry out such assessments, interpret and use the information from them, or advise colleagues and clients.

Lombana (1982) outlined some basic areas of knowledge for counselors of clients with disabilities that can be augmented and generalized to assessment roles:

> (a) Counselors need a general understanding of various types of disabilities and the effects of a person's particular disability on her or his needs and personal concerns and behaviors;

(b) Counselors need to be aware of the ways in which assessing clients with disabilities is both similar to and different from assessing individuals without disabilities;

(c) Counselors should know how to investigate the effects of a person's disability on the assessment process as well as on relevant parties (e.g., family, employers) who might have access to or use the results of the assessment process;

(d) Counselors should be aware of the extent to which a client with a disability has internalized negative expectations, labels, and stereotypes that might adversely affect his or her performance during the assessment process.

TYPES OF ASSESSMENT

There is some variety in the types of assessment tools most frequently used in different counseling settings. Mental health counselors most often use personality inventories, interest inventories, intelligence tests, projective tests, and achievement tests (Bubenzer, Zimpfer, & Mahrle, 1990). Vocational counselors most often use interest inventories and aptitude tests (Watkins, Campbell, & Nieberding, 1994). School counselors most frequently use academic aptitude and achievement tests, intelligence tests, and interest inventories (Elmore, Ekstrom, Diamond, & Whittaker, 1993). In rehabilitation settings, counselors may use psychological tests and evaluations of work activities, work samples, on-the-job activities, or a combination of these approaches (Berven, 1980).

These measures and procedures vary along several dimensions, which include test format (e.g., relatively structured or nonstructured), type of behavior assessed (e.g., primarily verbal or performance), method of administration (e.g., oral, paper-and-pencil, or computer), type of response format (e.g., written rather than verbal or other motor responses), scoring procedures (i.e., items with correct answers versus descriptive statements), and the assessment process (e.g., individual or group administration). Effective performance on each aspect of assessment may assume some test-taker characteristics that are not present for persons with certain disabilities. Thus, the counselor has to be aware of the extent to which the assessment methodology may interact with the client's particular disability. Perhaps it is stating the obvious to suggest that not every type of disability will interact with every type of assessment tool in the same way.

It is especially important for counselors to know that the regulations that apply to an assessment depend on the purpose(s) for which the assessment is being conducted and the setting in which it occurs. The regulations for employment testing and testing for admissions, licensing, or certification differ in a number of ways from the regulations for testing conducted for other purposes. Also, counselors need to be aware of variations in state level regulations regarding the assessment of individuals with disabilities.

LEGISLATION

Major topics about which counselors should be informed are the federal and state requirements pertaining to delivering assessment services to individuals with disabilities. As discussed by Pullin in chapter 1, the three major pieces of federal legislation about which counselors should be aware are

1. Section 504 of the Rehabilitation Act of 1973;
2. The Education for All Handicapped Children Act of 1975 (now called the Individuals With Disabilities Education Act of 1991, which was reauthorized and expanded in 1997); and
3. The Americans With Disabilities Act of 1990.

Counselors need to be aware of the scope of this legislation. It defines who qualifies as having a disability deserving of compensatory action during the assessment process. It specifies the rights of persons with disabilities during the assessment and counseling process. Often the legislation recommends the types of services and conditions of accommodation that must be provided in the domains of education, employment, health care, welfare, or social services.

These laws have an impact not only on assessment but also on counseling, education, and employment. Counselors must know the implications of these laws and regulations so that they can advise clients about various types of assessments, laws that protect them from having to reveal possibly prejudicial information about the existence of a disability before receiving a job or admission offer, as well as how to seek redress in situations in which they feel that they have been discriminated against because of their disability.

In chapter 1 Pullin's focus is on the administration of tests of maximal performance. Counselors should familiarize themselves with the information that she presents. These three acts also collectively mandate less formal psychoeducational interventions and environmental assessments.

As they work to assess individuals with disabilities, school counselors may become aware of disability harassment. Recently the U.S. Department of Education issued *Guidelines on Disability Harassment* (Cantu & Heumann, 2000), which include the following:

1. Counseling the individual(s) who has been harmed by disability harassment and the individual(s) responsible for such harassment;

2. Implementing monitoring programs to follow up on resolved issues of disability harassment; and
3. Regularly assessing and, as appropriate, modifying existing disability harassment policies and procedures for addressing the issues to ensure effectiveness.

Counselors will often share the responsibilities for assessing "harm" and the effectiveness of counseling, as well as conducting program evaluations and follow-up studies. Often structured tests and measures will be used for these purposes and, if so, counselors also must attend to issues pertaining to the interactions between disabilities and performance on these types of measures.

The regulations implementing Section 504 of the Rehabilitation Act (1973) addressed admission to college or graduate–professional school. These institutions may not use "any test or criterion for admission that has a disproportionate, adverse effect on handicapped persons" unless it has been validated as a predictor of academic success, and other tests or criteria with fewer adverse effects are not available. Title III of the Americans With Disabilities Act (ADA) has somewhat expanded these requirements. As a consequence, unless special tests for individuals with specific disabilities are available and appropriate, existing tests must be modified or testing accommodations must be made.

With respect to the Individuals With Disabilities Education Act (IDEA), school counselors need to be aware of the policies in their state regarding access to special education and services. In most states school psychologists carry out these assessments, but Missouri and Kentucky require school counselors to be trained in such assessments. Frequently, school counselors join parents, school psychologists, and teachers in Individual Educational Plan conferences. This is a good example of a situation in which counselors use their knowledge of assessment of individuals with disabilities even though they have not themselves conducted the actual assessment.

The IDEA also calls for activities to promote the transition of individuals with disabilities from education to employment. School counselors may be called on to work with special education programs to assist students with disabilities in making the transition from school to adulthood. One possible approach to such counseling is described in Fox, Wandry, Pruitt, and Anderson (1998). Their Transition Intervention Model describes four domains of practices (i.e., working with the student individually, implementation of preventative and remedial environmental interventions intended to overcome existing problems, and community outreach) in which counselors may serve as invaluable resources.

Thus, counselors can integrate their knowledge of the legislation and skills in individual and systemic interventions to assist people with disabilities in obtaining appropriate assessments, including testing accommodations if they are needed. Counselors may also use knowledge of the legislation to assist individuals with disabilities who are seeking admission to college or graduate or professional school or who are seeking employment. Knowledge of this legislation is also helpful to counselors when determining conditions under which mental health or social services may be provided.

ACCESS TO SERVICES

Access to state and national testing programs has been a particular concern for students with disabilities. Excluding students with disabilities from state and national testing programs limits counselors' ability to obtain policy-relevant information on educational outcomes for this population (McGrew, Thurlow, Shriner, & Spiegel, 1992).

The IDEA requires that most students with disabilities be included in district, state, and national assessments. Despite this requirement, until recently many students with disabilities have been excluded from such testing. For example, in 1994, the National Assessment of Educational Progress (NAEP) included only 50% of fourth-grade students, 38% of eighth-grade students, and 36% of 12th-grade students who were identified as having an IEP. Under new procedures, students with IEPs will be included in NAEP assessments unless the IEP team determines that the student cannot participate or if the student's cognitive functioning is so severely impaired that she or he cannot participate, even with accommodations (Olson & Goldstein, 1996). Counselors participating in IEP teams can work to see that inclusion procedures are implemented.

Assessment results may be used in making promotion or graduation decisions. This is sometimes known as "high stakes" testing, as has been discussed in previous chapters. The National Research Council's Committee on Appropriate Test Use has made several recommendations regarding the testing of students with disabilities in these situations (Heubert & Hauser, 1999):

- Having the IEP team ensure that the curriculum and instruction is aligned with the test content and that the student has an adequate opportunity to learn the material covered by the test; and
- Ensuring that high-stakes decisions about students with disabilities consider other sources of evidence (such as grades, teacher recommendations, and work samples) as well as the assessment results.

School counselors should work to see that these recommendations are implemented. Counselors will find helpful information about this type of testing in the chapter on students with disabilities in *High Stakes: Testing for Tracking, Promotion, and Graduation* (Heubert & Hauser, 1999). They will also find much helpful information in *Educating One and All: Students With Disabilities and Standards-Based Reform* (McDonnell, McLaughlin, & Morison, 1997).

School counselors need to know the policies for including students with disabilities in state- and district-mandated testing. Counselors in educational settings generally also need to be able to assist educators to make sure that students receive appropriate and allowed accommodations in high-stakes testing situations, especially because teachers and professors are often unaware of or are misinformed about which testing accommodations are permitted in state-mandated programs or formal testing programs (DeSteffano, 1998; Siskind, 1993).

There are other disability-related policies about which counselors should be knowledgeable. The law requires different policies for admissions and employment tests, where individuals with disabilities are being compared to other test takers, than are required for tests intended to help diagnose a disability, or to aid in the rehabilitation of individuals with disabilities, or for tests used in educational and career planning. Counselors need to be aware of these differences, especially as they affect what test takers can and cannot be asked before being assessed in each situation.

PSYCHOMETRIC ISSUES

When testing accommodations are provided for individuals with disabilities, the question of test validity arises. Does the test still measure the same construct? Does the testing accommodation affect the meaning of the test results? In chapter 2 Geisinger, Noble, and Boodoo discuss these and other validity issues.

Validation of tests for individuals with disabilities has always presented problems because of the relatively small numbers of individuals with the same type and degree of any given disability. This has become even more complex with the passage of the ADA, which requires individualization of test accommodations. As a consequence, there are relatively small numbers of test takers with the same type and degree of disability using identical test accommodations. Nevertheless, the numbers of studies of the validity of educational tests as used with individuals under similar conditions of accommodation are increasing. Counselors ought to keep abreast of this literature as it accrues (Pomplun & Omar, 2000).

Counselors need to be able to use their knowledge of test validity and psychometric concepts when interpreting the results of assessments given to individuals with disabilities to determine if the test results for a given individual with a specific accommodation can be considered equivalent to the test results for other individuals. This is a special concern when individuals both with and without disabilities are being compared, such as in college admissions or in employment decision making.

TESTING ACCOMMODATIONS

According to a survey of 2,224 members of the "general public" described by Bowe (1980), people in general support accommodations for people with disabilities to a greater extent than they support special efforts for women or ethnic minorities. He reported that when asked "whether they supported special efforts [e.g., accessibility modifications, affirmative action in employment] on behalf of disabled people," 79% of the survey respondents endorsed such compensatory efforts in the abstract for persons with disabilities compared with 47% who supported such efforts on behalf of women and 44% on behalf of ethnic minorities (p. 13). Nevertheless, when faced with the actuality of such accommodations in testing situations, people without legally defined disabilities may not understand the rationale for such accommodations, what types of accommodations are legally mandated, who is entitled to such accommodations under existing law, and the assessed person's rights under current law and professional standards.

As a consequence, they may view testing accommodations as "unfair" or use them as support for their preexisting negative stereotypes and harassment of individuals with disabilities regardless of whether the individual's disability is "visible" (e.g., mobility impairments) or "invisible" (e.g., learning disabilities; Cantu & Heumann, 2000). In their work counselors may have responsibilities pertaining to counseling and assessment in each of these areas of potential confusion, including clarification and implementation of regulations.

Rationale

Testing accommodations are intended to "level the playing field" for individuals with disabilities. Counselors or other test users must first determine whether a testing accommodation will be needed and, if so, what kinds of accommodations have been used with the specific test or are allowed by the state or by a testing organization. Next they must review IEPs and medical data, as well as the kinds of accommodations used by the test taker in performing similar tasks. Will providing similar accommodations alter the construct being measured and affect test validity? Are there any normative data, or is other information available about test results when individuals with disabilities have used the testing accommodation under consideration? Carrying out an analysis of the skills needed to complete the test can aid in developing a rationale for a testing accommodation. If an appropriate accommodation is not possible for a given test, the counselor or test user must decide if alternative measures or types of information will be useful.

Types

There are many different types of testing accommodations or modifications. They may involve changes in the test setting or administrative environment (such as individual rather than group testing), changes in the way that the test directions or the items are presented (such as directions given in sign language or items presented in Braille), changes in the amount of time allowed for responding or in the response mechanism (such as responding orally rather than in writing), or using assistive devices. In chapter 3, Behuniak presents more detailed information on the types of accommodations and modifications most often provided to individuals with disabilities. Counselors should remember that, because the ADA mandates that accommodations be individualized, some clients may require types of accommodations not discussed in this book. Also, accommodations may be required for effective use of types of tests often used by counselors that are not discussed in this book (e.g., diagnostic, lifestyle).

Documentation Requirements

When individuals with disabilities request a testing accommodation for admissions or employment tests, they may be asked to provide documentation of the need for this accommodation. Counselors who are experienced in working with individuals with disabilities may be asked to serve as documenters. In these cases, counselors need to review the relevant documentation guidelines, evaluate their own qualifications, and either assist the person in the documentation activity or refer the person to someone who is more qualified in this area.

SCORE REPORTING

For most tests used by counselors to help a person with a disability formulate an individualized plan for rehabilitation, education, or employment, any testing accommodations used should be fully described to all parties for whom the test results are relevant. When admissions or employment test scores are being provided to test users, a current "interim" policy allows scores to be marked or "flagged" to indicate that the test was given under nonstandard conditions. Counselors need to be aware that test-score flagging is a controversial topic (see chapter 6, this volume) and is an area in which there may be changes in government policy.

Because there are different standards for test score reporting for different types of tests, counselors should make certain that they know the intended purpose of an assessment before endorsing changes in standard assessment procedures or making a decision about how scores will be reported. As is always the case, counselors need to ensure that all relevant parties understand the counselor's role and legal and ethical responsibilities in any given situation.

CONCLUSION

When working with clients with disabilities, counseling and assessment knowledge and skills (historical allies) become intricately linked with several other knowledge domains. In this chapter we have discussed federal legislation, multiple counselor roles, types of tests, and legal requirements for accommodations as critical knowledge bases for counselors whose work includes assessing clients with disabilities or using assessment information to help such clients develop individualized life plans. We suggest that counselors develop the capacity to anticipate how specific disabilities may interact with standard assessment procedures, using whatever empirical evidence is available to support such inferences. Finally, we advise that counselors will need to make use of their interpretive and communication skills in explaining the accommodations and outcomes of assessment to interested parties using language that is meaningful to them, legally sound, and scientifically and ethically based.

REFERENCES

American Educational Research Association, American Psychological Association, and National Council on Measurement in Education (AERA/APA/NCME). (1999). *Standards for educational and psychological testing*. Washington, DC: American Educational Research Association.

Americans With Disabilities Act. (1990). 42 U.S.C. § 12111–12213, Pub. L. No. 101–336.

Berven, N. L. (1980). Psychometric assessment in rehabilitation. In B. Bolton & D. W. Cook (Eds.), *Rehabilitation client assessment* (pp. 46–64). Baltimore: University Park.

Bowe, F. (1980). *Rehabilitating America*. New York: Harper and Row.

Bubenzer, D. L., Zimpfer, D. G., & Mahrle, C. L. (1990). Standardized individual appraisal in agency and private practice: A survey. *Journal of Mental Health Counseling, 12*, 51–66.

Cantu, N. V., & Heumann, J. E. (2000, July 26). *Dear College Letter on U.S. Department of Education Guidelines on Disability Harassment*. Washington, DC:

Office for Civil Rights Education and Office of Special Rehabilitative Services.

Council for the Accreditation of Counseling and Related Educational Programs (CACREP). (1994). *Accreditation procedures manual and application.* Alexandria, VA: Author.

DeStefano, L. (1998, April). *Translating classroom accommodations to accommodations in large-scale assessment.* Paper presented at the annual meeting of the American Educational Research Association, San Diego, CA.

Elmore, P. B., Ekstrom, R. B., Diamond, E. E., & Whittaker, S. (1993). School counselors' test use patterns and practices. *The School Counselor, 41,* 73–80.

Fox, R. W., Wandry, D., Pruitt, P. & Anderson, G. (1998). School to life transitions for students with disabilities: Forming a new alliance. *Professional School Counseling, 1*(4), 48–52.

Ginter, E. J., Scalise, J. J., & Presse, N. (1990). The elementary school counselor's role: Perceptions of teachers. *The School Counselor, 38*(1), 19–23.

Heubert, J. P., & Hauser, R. M. (Eds.). (1999). *High stakes: Testing for tracking, promotion, and graduation.* Washington, DC: National Academy Press.

Hood, A. B., & Johnson, R. W. (1997). *Assessment in counseling: A guide to the use of psychological assessment procedures.* Alexandria, VA: American Counseling Association.

Impara, J. C., & Plake, B. S. (1995). Comparing counselors', school administrators', and teachers' knowledge in student assessment. *Measurement and Evaluation in Counseling and Development, 28*(2), 78–87.

Lombana, J. H. (1982). Counseling handicapped children and youth. *Counseling and Human Development, 15,* 1–12.

McDonnell, L. M., McLaughlin, M. J., & Morison, P. (Eds.). (1997). *Educating one and all: Students with disabilities and standards-based reform.* Washington, DC: National Academy Press.

McGrew, K. S., Thurlow, M. L., Shriner, J. G., & Spiegel, A. N. (1992). *Inclusion of students with disabilities in national and state data collection programs* (Tech. Rep. No. 2). Minneapolis: University of Minnesota, National Center on Educational Outcomes.

Olson, J. F., & Goldstein, A. A. (1996, July). Increasing the inclusion of students with disabilities and limited English proficiency students in NAEP (NCES 96–894). *Focus on NAEP, 2*(1).

Pomplun, M., & Omar, M. H. (2000). Score comparability of a state mathematics assessment across students with and without reading accommodations. *Journal of Applied Psychology, 85,* 21–29.

Siskind, T. G. (1993). Teachers' knowledge about test modifications for students with disabilities. *Diagnostique, 18*(2), 145–157.

Watkins, C. E., Jr., Campbell, V. L., & Nieberding, R. (1994). The practice of vocational assessment by counseling psychologists. *The Counseling Psychologist, 22,* 115–128.

IV

ASSESSMENT IN EDUCATION SETTINGS

9

LARGE-SCALE EDUCATIONAL ASSESSMENT

PETER BEHUNIAK, CAROLE PERLMAN, AND AUDREY QUALLS

This chapter focuses on the participation of students with disabilities in large-scale educational assessments. Decisions concerning the extent to which students with disabilities should participate and the form and scope of appropriate accommodations for those students are discussed in light of the considerations and issues that affect local, state, and national assessments. A general principle that forms a basis for the points made in this chapter is the need to provide students with access to the assessments and any benefits these students might derive from them. This is consistent with the intent of the 1997 amendments to the Individuals With Disabilities Education Act (see chapters 1 and 9, this volume)—that is, to improve educational outcomes for students with disabilities by having them participate more fully in the general curriculum, assessments, and accountability systems. The presumption is that most students are capable of taking part in large-scale assessments, given appropriate accommodations or modifications.

We begin with a discussion of the nature and purpose of many large-scale assessments. One dimension of large-scale assessment that is dealt with at length is the purposes for which the test results are used. The stakes of large-scale assessments are important because accommodations that may be possible for low- or moderate-stakes assessments may not be reasonable for high-stakes tests. Throughout the chapter, we discuss the accommodations and related issues in the contexts that typically prevail in educational settings.

FEATURES OF LARGE-SCALE ASSESSMENTS

It is useful to begin by identifying some of the features common to typical large-scale assessments, as well as to highlight a few of the ways in which they differ from each other.

Large-scale assessments are frequently developed or operated by large district or state educational agencies. Such assessments may be built entirely to custom specifications or they may be adopted or adapted from commercially available measures. These assessments are often legislatively mandated and, as a result, report individual or group results for accountability purposes, often by establishing standards or performance levels against which student achievement may be judged. In recent years there has been an increased tendency for these assessments to include performance tasks and multiple-step problems, which can pose special difficulties for students with disabilities.

One dimension relevant to a discussion of large-scale assessment is whether the assessment is a criterion-referenced test (CRT) or norm-referenced test (NRT). A CRT is based on specific objectives with test results interpreted in relation to established criteria or standards. The results of an NRT are interpreted in relation to the performance of specified groups of students; the content of a CRT tends to cover a broader spectrum. However, many large-scale assessments have some characteristics of both a CRT and an NRT. For example, a statewide assessment may be designed as a CRT, based on specific objectives and established standards. However, this same test may report an individual student's results in relation to other students in the district, region, and state. These features of large-scale assessments affect the manner in which test scores are properly interpreted and therefore represent important considerations when making accommodations decisions.

Other features of large-scale assessments are also relevant to decisions regarding accommodations. One example is that large-scale assessments may be administered only once per year or only in selected grades (e.g., grades 4, 8, and 11). These infrequent administrations can limit the ability of test administrators to use certain options such as out-of-level or functional-level testing. For instance, a Grade 8 student with disabilities might be well-served by being administered a Grade 6 or Grade 7 test, but this option would not be available in a system with tests at only the Grade

4 and Grade 8 levels. Another example is that test administration procedures are often set by the test developer to achieve standardization and
can further constrain available accommodations. These and other examples
will be discussed later in this chapter. It is first necessary to examine the
way in which the purposes of large-scale assessments differ from one setting
to another. This crucial dimension of large-scale assessment affects many
practical and philosophical elements of accommodating students' needs.

STAKES OF LARGE-SCALE ASSESSMENTS

The decisions made on the basis of test score information for students
with disabilities represent a continuum ranging from minor adjustments in
classroom instructional strategies to high-stakes decisions regarding promotion and high school graduation. The type of accommodation offered
or the use of alternative assessments for individual students should be
guided by the importance of the intended educational decisions. As previously indicated, the primary purposes in providing accommodations or
alternative assessments to students with disabilities is to provide access to
the assessments offered to all other students and to improve the validity
of the test results for students with disabilities. Granting students with
disabilities access to large-scale assessments promotes the extension of the
full range of educational opportunities and resources to all students.

The use and consequences associated with a student's performance on
a large-scale assessment have come to be associated with particular stakes.
Madaus (1988) defined these stakes on a relative scale whereby the level
of the stakes is related directly to the extent to which administrators, teachers, students, and parents perceive test performance to be used to make
important decisions that immediately and directly affect them. For example, an informal classroom reading test administered by a student's teacher
to monitor weekly progress and guide the selection of reading material
would not generate as much concern regarding available accommodations
as would a district-mandated test used to determine grade promotion. Accordingly, the level of stakes associated with a given educational decision
should be taken into account when accommodation decisions are made.

Low-stakes assessments are not as common in large-scale applications
as are moderate- or high-stakes assessments. This is because the typical
purposes of large-scale assessment include far-reaching issues of accountability, instructional improvement, and curriculum redesign. In contrast,
low-stakes assessments often yield information used in the classroom by
teachers primarily for diagnostic purposes or to monitor student progress
within and across programs of study. Some educators feel that as soon as
test results are used to inform individuals outside the direct learning environment (i.e., reporting to parents, school administrators, or the com-

munity at large), the stakes rise to at least a moderate level (Canner, 1991). Lower stakes applications offer more flexibility to the test administrator, usually the student's teacher, because the interpretation of the test score can more readily take into account any accommodations afforded to a particular student.

The stakes of an assessment can be elevated in a variety of ways. As indicated previously, sharing test results with a larger audience tends to raise the stakes. Designating test results for multiple purposes can have the same effect. For example, a test intended for use in the classroom as a diagnostic measure may be low-stakes whereas the same test used as both a diagnostic tool and a vehicle to award grades may be moderate-stakes. Clearly, the relative stakes of any assessment occur across a continuum, and the determination of these stakes must consider all of the purposes and uses of the measure.

The stakes of large-scale assessment sometimes vary for different individuals or groups. A test that determines a student's opportunity to be promoted or to graduate may be moderate-stakes for teachers but high-stakes for students. It is also possible that assessments may have high-stakes for teachers or administrators but not students, as may be the case when test results are used to award merit pay or to serve as evidence that an administrator's contract should be renewed. In addition, not all students would necessarily be affected equally by the assessment. Students with high grades and an excellent achievement record may view the assessment as little more than a formality. For a student with borderline grades and achievement, however, the assessment may have life-changing consequences and may become the highest of stakes.

The consequences associated with individual student level performance at a low or moderate level of stakes are not usually associated with the denial of benefits or resources. Decisions can be modified if additional evidence (e.g., classroom performance, teacher's judgment) warrants change. What is perhaps most salient about assessments with low- or moderate-level stakes is that the assessment is almost always correctly viewed as being only one source of information regarding student learning that is used along with other appropriate sources to make sound educational decisions.

MAKING PARTICIPATION AND ACCOMMODATIONS DECISIONS

The extent to which a student with disabilities participates in large-scale assessments, and the type of accommodations or alternative assessments provided for a student with a disability, must be carefully considered in light of the student's needs, the instruction the student receives, and the stakes associated with the assessment. In general, lower stakes assessments will allow more flexibility, whereas higher stakes assessments demand greater standardization. In all cases, however, determining appropriate assessments and accommodations depends in large measure on maintaining a successful balance between assessment validity and individual student needs.

One principle that should govern these decisions is that they need to be made at the individual student level. Sometimes an explicit set of criteria is used to delimit the range of accommodations depending on the goals of the test. For example, states often create guidelines that govern accommodations decisions on a statewide large-scale assessment (Connecticut State Department of Education, 1998; North Carolina Department of Public Instruction, 1996). These criteria, however, should not be rigidly used to dictate appropriateness for all students who may be loosely grouped together by disability type. The variation of student need within a particular disability grouping is quite large and the successful participation of these students in large-scale assessments will vary. As noted by McDonnell, McLaughlin, and Morison (1997),

> Some students with disabilities already participate fully in the general education curriculum, participation in common standards and assessments for them will be compatible with their individualized programs, with or without appropriate accommodation or supports. (pp. 4–5)

Nonetheless, as Phillips (1994) observed, although participation and accommodation decisions must be made on an individual basis, students with similar circumstances should be afforded similar opportunities to participate in assessments. Districts and states should provide school personnel with guidelines for making decisions regarding assessment participation and accommodations.

A small percentage of students have instructional goals that have little in common with the predominantly academic general education curriculum. These students, many with significant cognitive disabilities, may receive little instruction in the general curriculum. However, alternatives need to be carefully crafted that still represent challenging expectations for these students. Other students, affected with somewhat less severe disabilities, may require some modifications to the common standards and assessments to ensure compatibility of their individualized programs with the general curriculum. Decisions for these students must be made on an individual basis and must focus on whether alternative assessments and accommodations are necessary and, if so, what kinds of assessments are appropriate. Decisions about participation or accommodations may vary across subjects and may change for any given student as he or she progresses through school; it also must take into consideration the relevance of prevailing standards, curricula, and instruction.

A second principle to consider is the extent to which the student has had an opportunity to learn the content and skills that the test measures. This is an especially salient concern when the assessment has high stakes for the student. Many large-scale assessments are based on state or local content standards. For example, 40 states report that statewide assessments are based in whole or in part on state content standards (Olson, Bond, & Andrews, 1999). If the assessment has significant consequences for the student, it is necessary to consider the extent to which the student is receiving instruction on the knowledge and skills being assessed. To what instructional materials does the student and his or her teacher have access? If the student has not been mainstreamed into a classroom of peers without disabilities, has the student's teacher had the same opportunities for standards-related inservice training?

Opportunity to learn is not always a critical issue when the assessments have low stakes. Some large-scale assessments can appropriately be administered to students who have received little or even no instruction in a portion of the content. For example, a district with high mobility might find it useful to administer a criterion-referenced mathematics test to all incoming students to inform diagnostic and placement decisions. Students who never received instruction on some of the skills would be more likely to be properly identified and served. However, it would be inappropriate for both legal and ethical reasons to subject the same students to this mathematics test if the resulting scores were to be used to deny the students scoring below a certain level the right to graduate.

A third principle relevant to making accommodations decisions concerns the importance of reviewing the instructional practices used with a particular student in the classroom. For example, a student who only writes using a keyboard in class could be accommodated by allowing him or her to use a keyboard on a large-scale assessment in writing that he or she might otherwise not be able to participate in. However, a student who writes with a pencil but simply prefers a keyboard may not be afforded the same accommodation. It is also necessary to recognize that not all instructional practices can be translated into assessment accommodations. A student whose disability renders him or her unable to read may regularly receive oral classroom instruction. This does not justify presenting the material on a reading assessment orally to the student, because such an accommodation would alter the construct being assessed and impair the validity of the measure.

As defined earlier, low-stakes assessments are typically given to provide additional information to be used directly in the learning environment. In this setting, almost any accommodation would be permissible as long as it is provided to offset a student disability that is unrelated to the ability or skill being measured. However, caution needs to be exercised when accommodations are being made to norm-referenced tests. Normative score information such as percentile ranks or stanines should generally be ignored unless the accommodation is judged to be acceptable based on the procedures used with the norming sample. Even if the normative information is compromised, criterion-referenced interpretations of the test results may allow a teacher to identify a student's areas of strengths and needs. Such information might help the teacher to adapt instruction to the student's specific needs. (See Pitonick & Royer, 2001, for more on accommodations.)

PRESERVING ASSESSMENT VALIDITY

It should be the goal of all individuals involved in making assessment and accommodation decisions that each test score produced by every assessment be valid for all students. Unfortunately, the issues under consideration sometimes cause the discussion to take on an adversarial tone, with some arguing for flexibility to meet perceived student needs and others defending the importance of objectivity and standardization to support test validity. Both of these perspectives are important. Attending to standards of test validity is crucial to providing a meaningful test score for a student; to do any less means the student's effort was wasted. On the other hand, test developers and administrators should recognize that the valid measurement of any given construct for some students may require accommodations to allow the student appropriate access to the assessment. The best way to do justice to these considerations is to weigh the merits of the unique circumstances that apply for each student and each test.

Many times it will be possible for the needs of the student to be met through alternative assessments or accommodations of one type or another. This will be possible most often in low-stakes assessments but can occur to some degree on higher stakes measures as well. (Examples of accommodations were provided in chapter 3.) The rationale for providing these accommodations is to ensure that the resulting scores will reflect the student's ability on the same construct as those students not receiving an accommodation. If, for example, the assessment was designed to measure a child's listening comprehension and the child was hearing-impaired, a printed reading comprehension test could not be interpreted as yielding the same type of information.

There are times when accommodations that maintain the validity of the original assessment are not possible for a given student, as was discussed in chapter 2. The most desirable choice in these situations is an alternative assessment that looks at the same construct measured by the regular assessment. Determining the effect of substituting an alternate assessment is difficult and may require separate validation efforts. If using an alternative assessment that measures the same construct is impossible, it may still be feasible to identify one that measures a construct that is sufficiently related to provide valuable information. This will depend largely on the purpose of the large-scale assessment.

In the United States, decisions about the education of a student with disabilities, including the student's participation in large-scale assessments, are made by the team that developed the student's individualized education program (IEP). The team typically consists of the student's parents and various educational and medical professionals; all members of the team, including parents, should be informed about district and state policies governing assessment of students with disabilities. They should also be aware of the implications of participating or not participating in each assessment; at least some members of the team should be familiar with the general curriculum in the various content areas. The IEP not only identifies the nature of a student's disability, it outlines the ways in which the general educational program is modified to fit the student's unique needs. The 1997 IDEA amendments require the IEP to directly address large-scale assessment participation issues. As reported by Heubert and Hauser (1999), the IEP must include a statement that specifies whether the student will or will not participate in large-scale assessments. If participation is deemed appropriate, needed accommodations must be delineated. If participation is not recommended, alternative methods of assessment must be specified.

Even when large-scale assessment administration procedures are specified, there can be widespread differences in how those procedures are implemented from one school or district to another (DeStefano, 1998). Validity of test scores depends in part on the success achieved in maintaining consistent applications of the assessments to all students. Through the IEP process, accommodations can be given careful consideration and decided well in advance of administering the assessment. This can help to improve the consistency of the decisions. In general, accommodations for assessment purposes should mirror the types of accommodations that are normally provided during the course of instruction. The IEP can help to ensure that accommodations are noted and considered when interpreting score information (see chapter 6, this volume). Thus, the IEP can be a useful vehicle for helping to achieve a reasonable balance between student needs and measurement validity

POLICY AND ACCOUNTABILITY ISSUES

System-level accountability is becoming more widely associated with high-stakes large-scale assessments. Assessments of this nature generally inform a broader public of the current status of student achievement on a widely accepted domain of knowledge. These systems typically operate at a district or statewide level. Although the highest stakes may be primarily focused on the district or state, teachers and students often experience significant consequences on the basis of student performance on these assessments.

There are often additional constraints to consider when accountability is a primary purpose of a large-scale assessment. Not only do the stakes increase, but security and standardization requirements are frequently more stringent. The standards and even the definition of the content being assessed may be rigidly established by policy or legislation. Under these conditions, the provision of accommodations may be restricted. In some cases this has led to students with disabilities being excluded from accountability-driven assessments. Although the reasons for exclusion are numerous, this practice has created a source of concern regarding the possibility that excluded students may be experiencing a commensurate exclusion from full participation in the general education curriculum. This concern increases the importance of establishing procedures that ensure that appropriate accommodations are offered to students with disabilities.

This concern was an important factor in the 1997 IDEA amendments as described earlier. This legislation now requires all states to develop policies and implement procedures that will include all students in statewide assessments. States currently vary widely in their procedures regarding accommodations (Roeber, Bond, & Braskamp, 1997) and have begun the process of determining the adjustments that must be made to include even students with the most severe disabilities in statewide large-scale assessment. In fact, a consortium of states has been meeting regularly since 1997, coordinated by Council of Chief State School Officers (CCSSO), for the purpose of sharing information and pooling resources to meet these requirements. Although these changes will take considerable time to fully implement, it is clear that all states will be examining and revising the manner in which accommodations are provided to students with disabilities.

Large-scale assessment in accountability systems poses many issues regarding validity and fairness that are critical and must frame accommodation discussions. The desired inferences from score information are the same for students with and without disabilities. Any accommodation to be provided must leave essentially unchanged the construct being assessed. Accommodations must be administered in settings that preserve test security. Presentation options, such as using a large-print edition as opposed to standard paper copy, would generally be acceptable. Reading the test to the student in domains where reading is not the attribute being measured could also be a reasonable accommodation. Extended time, rest periods, and abbreviated testing sessions would be other acceptable accommodations.

Policy changes also have implications for reporting test results (see chapter 6, this volume). As the federal legislation described earlier shapes state and district practices, test score reports will continue to change. New reporting practices will not only reflect changes in state policies on accommodations but will also need to attend to the variation that exists from district to district with regard to how these policies are implemented. Assessment reports in the future are likely to be closely scrutinized to determine their adequacy with regard to descriptions of the population of students with disabilities included in the assessment, the nature of all accommodations provided, the relative frequency of use of each accommodation, and descriptions of alternate assessments. The nature of alternate assessments offered will be changing (Ysseldyke & Olsen, 1999). As they do, it will be necessary to ensure that results from alternate assessments are appropriately included in the overall summaries of system achievement whenever large-scale assessment results are presented.

CONCLUSION

The following factors should also be taken into consideration in making accommodations in a large-scale educational assessment. Some issues associated with making accommodations decisions are specific to the content area being assessed. Some disabilities will result in student needs that can be reasonably accommodated for assessments in some content areas but not in others. For example, a student with a reading disability may have a mathematics or science test read to him or her; that particular accommodation would not result in a valid score on a reading comprehension test, however. Accordingly, each accommodations decision must be identified for each content area based on student need and the desired inferences. Within a large-scale assessment that measures several content areas, it would not be surprising to find accommodations for certain content areas (e.g., having a math problem-solving test question read to the student), alternative assessments for another content area (e.g., obtaining a measure of listening comprehension instead of reading comprehension), and no assessment of a third content area (e.g., map reading). It should be recognized that in this example the math problem-solving results are the only domain from which inferences for the student accommodated may be reasonably similar to students assessed via the standard form.

Out-of-level testing is the practice of using a test level different from (usually lower than) the typical level used by students in a given grade. It is an option that can be useful with students with or without disabilities. Out-of-level testing is a method of aligning the level of instruction and testing. For some assessment purposes (e.g., diagnostic), out-of-level testing can provide more relevant information than could the original measure. Hoover, Hieronymus, Frisbie, and Dunbar (1993) indicated that the most important consideration in selecting the appropriate test level for a student is the particular set of objectives to be measured. The selected test should match as closely as possible the student's classroom instructional focus as well as his or her current level of academic development. The student's disability may have influenced the choice of instructional strategies and will as a result indirectly influence selection decisions regarding testing levels.

However, it is necessary to be aware that an out-of-level option is not always available, particularly when the assessment is part of a standards-based instructional system. Most commercial large-scale achievement batteries do provide this alternative, but many state and district assessments do not. Nevertheless, when available, selective use of the out-of-level option combined with sound teacher judgment can be an effective accommodation.

Communication among school personnel, including all of a student's teachers and the local school testing coordinator, can promote appropriate assessment of students with disabilities. It is critical that the teachers and other school staff know early in the school year which assessments are scheduled for each student and the circumstances and stakes under which these assessments will be taken. In addition to providing teachers with the necessary information to coordinate instruction and assessment, early notification should make the actual administration of assessments easier. The testing coordinator can plan how and where testing will take place, reserve special physical facilities as needed, order appropriate assessment materials (e.g., large-print tests), and request additional staff that may be needed (e.g., scribes, proctors for individually administered assessments). School staff should accurately enter onto the student's answer document any needed information regarding testing accommodations.

For those students with disabilities who have IEPs, the IEP should be used to facilitate early planning for accommodations or alternative measures for regularly scheduled assessments. For those students who do not have IEPs but may potentially require accommodations, a testing checklist should be prepared. Using either the IEP or the testing checklist, all regularly scheduled assessments should be listed. For each, it should be noted whether the student can take the regular assessment under normal conditions, the regular assessment under accommodated conditions, an alternative measure, or receive no assessment. If an accommodation is deemed feasible, the specific accommodation should be indicated. Alternative measures should also be identified. The subtests or subjects to be tested on each assessment must also be indicated as well, because it may be the case that a student may take some parts of an assessment but not others or that the student might need accommodations in one subject but not in others.

REFERENCES

Canner, J. (1991). *Regaining trust: Enhancing the credibility of school testing programs.* NCME Task Force Report (Chair). New York: Test Committee of the Association of American Publishers.

Connecticut State Department of Education. (1998). *Assessment guidelines* (5th ed.). Hartford, CT: Bureau of Research, Evaluation and Student Assessment.

DeStefano, L. (1998, April). *Translating classroom accommodations to accommodations in large-scale assessment.* Paper presented at the annual meeting of the American Educational Research Association, San Diego.

Hoover, H. D., Hieronymus, A. N., Frisbie, D. A., & Dunbar, S. D. (1993). *Iowa tests of basic skills: Interpretive guide for teachers and counselors, Forms K and L.* Chicago: Riverside.

Heubert, J. P., & Hauser, R. M. (Eds.). (1999). *High stakes testing for tracking, promotion and graduation.* Washington, DC: National Academy Press.

Madaus, G. (1988). The influence of testing on the curriculum. In L. Tanner (Ed.), *Critical issues in curriculum: 87th yearbook of the NSSE, Part 1.* Chicago: University of Chicago Press.

McDonnell, L. M., McLaughlin, M. J., & Morison, P. (Eds.). (1997). *Educating one and all.* Washington, DC: National Academy Press.

North Carolina Department of Public Instruction. (1996). *Testing modifications and accommodations for students with disabilities.* Raleigh, NC: Office of Instructional and Accountability Services.

Olson, J. E., Bond, L., & Andrews, L. (1999). *Data from the annual survey of state student assessment programs. Volumes I & II.* Washington, DC: Council of Chief State School Officers.

Phillips, S. E. (1994). High-stakes testing accommodations: Validity versus disabled rights. *Applied Measurement in Education, 7*(2), 93–120.

Pitonick, M., & Royer, J. (2001). Testing accommodations for examinees with disabilities: A review of psychometric, legal and social policy issues. *Review of Educational Research, 71,* 53–104.

Roeber, E., Bond, L., & Braskamp, D. (1997). *Annual survey of state student assessment programs.* Washington, DC: Council of Chief State School Officers.

Ysseldyke, J., & Olsen, K. (1999). Putting alternate assessments into practice: What to measure and possible sources of data. *Exceptional Children, 65,* 175–185.

10

INDIVIDUAL NORM-REFERENCED ABILITY TESTING

DOUGLAS K. SMITH AND DONALD L. STOVALL

The focus of this chapter is the educational assessment of individuals with disabilities using individually administered, norm-referenced ability tests. The purposes of such assessments include determination of special education eligibility, program planning, and evaluation of educational progress. The chapter provides practitioners with information to make informed decisions regarding the utility and appropriateness of specific ability tests with individuals with disabilities. In addition, information is provided regarding acceptable accommodations and modifications.

There is a plethora of ability tests designed for use with the schoolage population. To provide in-depth coverage of each instrument is, therefore, not possible. As a result, the focus of this chapter is the most frequently used normative measures of ability or cognitive processes.

To determine the tests to be included in this chapter a review of recent studies of test usage was conducted. This included studies that were national in scope (e.g., Archer, Maruish, Imhof, & Piotrowski, 1991; Hammill, Fowler, Bryant, & Dunn, 1992; Hutton, Dubes, & Muir, 1992; Laurent & Swerdlik, 1992; Piotrowski & Keller, 1989; Stinnett, Havey, & Oehler-Stinnett, 1994; Watkins, Campbell, Nieberding, & Hallmark, 1995,

1996; Wilson & Reschly, 1996), international in scope (e.g., Chan & Lee, 1995; Oakland & Hu, 1992) and regional in scope (e.g., Zaske, Hegstrom, & Smith, 1999). From these a list of the most frequently used ability tests was developed. This includes the Kaufman Assessment Battery for Children (K-ABC; Kaufman & Kaufman, 1983), Stanford Binet Intelligence Scale: Fourth Edition (SB: FE; Thorndike, Hagen, & Sattler, 1986), Wechsler Intelligence Scale for Children-Third Edition (WISC-III; Wechsler, 1991), Wechsler Adult Intelligence Scale-Revised (WAIS-R)/Wechsler Adult Intelligence Scale-Third Edition (WAIS-III; Wechsler, 1997), and Wechsler Preschool and Primary Scale of Intelligence-Revised (WPPSI-R; Wechsler, 1989).

During the past few years several new ability tests have been developed. We decided to include several of these in this chapter, including the Differential Ability Scales (DAS; Elliott, 1990), Kaufman Adolescent and Adult Intelligence Test (KAIT; Kaufman & Kaufman, 1993), and the Das-Naglieri Cognitive Assessment System (CAS; Naglieri & Das, 1997).

For individually administered tests, accommodations as cited in the respective test manuals are largely confined to changes in timing (e.g., allowing additional time to respond to test items, eliminating bonus points for rapid performance, allowing additional exposure time for test stimuli, or allowing unlimited time for responding to items); changes in presentation format (e.g., use of sign language, Braille, large print, or repeating directions); and changes in response format (e.g., pointing to a response rather than circling the response, writing responses instead of verbally responding, or using a word processor instead of writing). Because all of the tests discussed in this chapter are norm-based measures, the use of accommodations or modifications to the standardized testing format must be carefully considered. Such changes may affect the appropriateness of the test norms when interpreting the student's test performance. The reader may find it helpful to use the Worksheet for Developing Testing Accommodations presented in chapter 5.

SPECIAL CONSIDERATIONS IN ABILITY ASSESSMENT

The practitioner assessing an individual's cognitive abilities must work from a perspective that is sensitive to a variety of issues, including the individual's age, culture, language skills, developmental stage, and the impact of the disability (Janda, 1998; Sattler, 1988). Special attention should be given to the individual's attention span, ability to concentrate for extended periods of time, and potential to become distracted through the course of assessment. Some disabilities may accentuate difficulties in these areas. It should be remembered that children are in a dynamic and rapidly changing period of growth (Papilia & Olds, 1990; Vasta, Haith, & Miller,

1999). During the preschool years, in particular, significant changes can occur within a period of months.

During the course of assessment, the practitioner might find it necessary to adapt traditional standardized methods to gain supplemental information about an individual's performance. These adaptations could be crucial in developing appropriate interventions for the individual or in making placement recommendations. They could assist in understanding the reasons an individual responded to a situation in a specific way.

For ability assessment, especially, the purpose of assessment is crucial. Is the purpose of testing designed to produce a standard score that will be used with other information to make a placement decision about the individual? If so, assessment is oriented toward program eligibility or documentation of special learning needs (McLoughlin & Lewis, 1990; Salvia & Ysseldyke, 2000). Testing accommodations, therefore, must be made cautiously to allow use of the test norms. If the focus is not a normative comparison, testing accommodations have less impact on interpretation of performance. Testing to produce observations of performance and behavior or to explain or expand on the individual's way of responding is consistent with an orientation related to programming needs and decisions.

Adaptations for children, adolescents, and adults fall into several categories (McLoughlin & Lewis, 1990). One involves changes to subtests that are timed. On tests in which an individual's performance is assessed based on completion within a specific time period, the examiner may seek to determine if the individual could perform the skill if given more time. This may be necessary if the examiner has reason to believe that the individual possesses the skill but may be penalized by the time factor. Some individuals may process information more slowly than others. In other cases, the individual may require more time because of difficulties in manipulating objects. The individual may perceive the correct solution of a puzzle, yet have difficulty with the motor skills needed to place the pieces correctly. Such accommodations, of course, prevent the use of normative comparisons.

A second type of accommodation involves modification of verbal instructions to the individual. After the test is administered in the standardized format, the examiner may test the limits by rewording or attempting to simplify instructions using words that are different from those in the standardized instructions (Sattler, 1988). Such practices have been incorporated into several cognitive ability measures, including the K-ABC, DAS, and CAS through the use of sample items and teaching items and to a limited degree in the Wechsler scales through sample items on selected subtests. If the individual's disability involves comprehension of verbal instructions, the examiner should consider the use of tests with sample items and teaching items.

The importance of rapport in working with individuals with a disability and preschool children cannot be overemphasized. Examiners should remember that there are stages in which it is appropriate for children to be wary of strangers or unfamiliar adults. This may be exaggerated in preschool children with disabilities. In some situations it may be necessary to have the parent or caregiver present during the test administration. Another alternative is to have the parent or caregiver present the test directions after training from the examiner about the administration of a particular subtest. This procedure may invalidate the scores if the deviation in administration from the standardized format is considerable. However, examiners may learn that the student possesses the skill in question.

AN ANALYSIS OF FREQUENTLY USED COGNITIVE ABILITY TESTS

This section provides information on the selected cognitive ability tests. The reader should consult the test manuals for more detailed information. For each test we present an overview; suggestions from the test author regarding accommodations–modifications; a description of the subtests the test comprises; an analysis of the presentation–response format of each subtest; and our recommended use of the test with students with disabilities based on our analysis of the subtests. Reviews of each test can be found in *Buros Mental Measurements Yearbooks* (2001) and such textbooks as Salvia and Ysseldyke (2000). Readers should refer to the test manuals for additional information about the measures discussed in this chapter and for descriptions of the subtests.

Wechsler Intelligence Scale for Children-Third Edition

The WISC-III is an individually administered test for assessing the intellectual ability of students 6 years and 0 months through 16 years and 11 months. It is based on David Wechsler's conception of intelligence as the "capacity of the individual to act purposefully, to think rationally, and to deal effectively with his or her environment" (Wechsler, 1991, p. 1). Three composite scores are provided: verbal IQ, performance IQ, and full-scale IQ. Students with learning disabilities, speech–language impairments, emotional disturbance, physical impairments, and reading problems made up 7% of the sample.

Accommodations–Modifications

The test author provides some guidance on the use of the WISC-III with individuals with disabilities:

> For a child who is at a disadvantage on tasks requiring manual manipulation because of motor or visual impairments, one should consider

administering only the Verbal subtests and using the Verbal scores as estimates of the child's cognitive abilities. Similarly, for a child with a hearing impairment, one may find it preferable to place greater weight on the Performance subtests as estimates of the child's abilities. (1991, p. 38)

The test author emphasizes that the test was not standardized with modifications of test procedures. If modifications are needed, they should be noted on the record form. Accommodations such as sign language and visual aids for the student with hearing impairments may have an impact on test scores, and the examiner "will need to rely on clinical judgment to evaluate the impact of such modified procedures on the test scores" (Wechsler, 1991, p. 38). For students with physical impairments, the test author wrote that "other tests designed for such populations should be used to supplement the WISC-III" (Wechsler, 1991, p. 38). Although the use of test accommodations may invalidate the use of norms, they may provide valuable qualitative information about the student's cognitive strengths and weaknesses.

Recommended Use of the WISC-III With Students With Disabilities

The presentation–response formats and recommendations for use of each subtest with individuals with hearing disabilities, speech disabilities, vision disabilities, and physical disabilities are presented in Table 10–1.

All verbal subtests are presented verbally and require verbal responses. This causes much difficulty for students with hearing impairments. Use of sign language in presenting items is fraught with difficulty, as is the performance scale with its extensive reliance on verbal instructions. These issues are explored in depth by Braden and Hannah (1998). Substituting written responses for verbal responses is problematic because one-word responses are not sufficient on many subtests, and several subtests are scored 0, 1, or 2 and demand query in response to certain answers.

For individuals with visual impairments, the verbal subtests are appropriate as presented. If the verbal scale alone is used, however, the examiner should keep in mind that the IQ score is the verbal IQ and not a composite score.

Performance subtests use visual stimuli and verbal directions. As a consequence, use with individuals with hearing impairments is compromised even if directions are presented in sign language or by gesture.

For individuals with motor impairments, the requirements and time limits–bonuses on coding, picture arrangement, block design, and symbol search are problematic. There is no provision for administering these subtests without the time limits. Only picture completion does not have a motor component in the response. The verbal scale can be used, however, without modification. If this is done, the examiner should keep in mind that the IQ score is the verbal IQ and not a composite score.

TABLE 10-1

WISC-III Subtests: Presentation/Response Format and Appropriateness for Individuals With Disabilities

Subtest	Presentation Format	Response Format	Hearing	Speech	Vision	Physical
					Use With Individuals With Disabilities	
Information	Verbal	Verbal	No	No	Yes	Yes
Similarities	Verbal	Verbal	No	No	Yes	Yes
Arithmetic	Verbal[a]	Verbal	No	No	Items 6–18 only	Yes
Vocabulary	Verbal[b]	Verbal	Yes[c]	No	Yes	Yes
Comprehension	Verbal	Verbal	No	No	Yes	Yes
Digit span	Verbal	Verbal	No	No	Yes	Yes
Picture completion	Visual (verbal directions)	Verbal	No	Yes	No	Yes
Coding	Visual (verbal directions)	Copies symbols	No	Yes	No	No[d]
Picture arrangement	Visual (verbal directions)	Arranges picture cards	No	Yes	No	No[d]
Block design	Visual (verbal directions)	Assembles blocks	No	Yes	No	No[d]
Object assembly	Visual (verbal directions)	Assembles puzzles	No	Yes	No	No[d]
Symbol search	Visual (verbal directions)	Draws lines through	No	Yes	No	No[d]

[a]Picture cards for items 1–5; problem cards for items 19–24.
[b]Examinee can be shown the word.
[c]If examinee is shown the word.
[d]Subtests are timed with bonus points for rapid, correct performance so any physical disability can affect score.

152   SMITH AND STOVALL

Wechsler Preschool and Primary Scale of Intelligence-Revised

The WPPSI-R is an individually administered test for assessing the intellectual ability of children 3 years and 0 months through 7 years and 3 months. It is based on Wechsler's conception of intelligence as a global aggregate of skills. Three composite scores are provided: verbal IQ, performance IQ, and full-scale IQ.

Accommodations–Modifications

The test author provides some guidance in the use of the WPPSI-R with children with disabilities. Examiners are advised not to use the test with children with severe visual or auditory impairments or with children with significant physical impairments. Furthermore, the test author indicates that there "is no empirical support for altering the WPPSI-R to accommodate a child's handicapping condition and then comparing that child's performance to the normative sample" (Wechsler, 1989, p. 9). If standard administration of the test to a child with a disability "places the child at a disadvantage, then the WPPSI-R should not be used to assess the child's intellectual potential" (Wechsler, 1989, p. 9). Examiners are advised to "adhere strictly to the directions . . . for administering and scoring the WPPSI-R" (Wechsler, 1989, p. 13).

Recommended Use of the WPPSI-R With Students With Disabilities

The presentation–response formats and recommendations for use of each subtest with individuals with hearing disabilities, speech disabilities, vision disabilities, and physical disabilities are presented in Table 10–2.

Initial items on four of the verbal subtests use visual stimuli and verbal directions. Otherwise, all verbal subtests and items are presented verbally and require verbal responses, causing difficulty for children with hearing impairments. As with the WISC-III, use of sign language in presenting items presents difficulties, as does the performance scale with its extensive verbal instruction.

For children with visual impairments, the verbal subtests with the exception of the initial items on information, arithmetic, vocabulary, and similarities are appropriate as presented. Again, if the verbal scale alone is used, the examiner should keep in mind that the IQ score is the verbal IQ and not a composite score.

Performance subtests use visual stimuli and verbal directions. As a consequence, use with individuals with hearing impairments is compromised even if directions are presented in sign language or by gesture.

For children with motor impairments, the motor requirements and time limits–bonuses on object assembly, block design, mazes, and animal pegs are problematic. There is no provision for administering these subtests

TABLE 10-2
WPPSI-R Subtests Presentation/Response Format and Appropriateness for Individuals With Disabilities

Subtest	Presentation Format	Response Format	Use With Individuals With Disabilities			
			Hearing	Speech	Vision	Physical
Information	Visual (verbal directions)	Pointing (items 1–7)	No	No	No	Yes
	Verbal	Verbal (items 8–27)	No	No	Yes	Yes
Comprehension	Verbal	Verbal	No	No	Yes	Yes
Arithmetic	Visual (verbal directions)	Pointing (items 1–7)	No	No	No	No
	Verbal	Verbal (items 8–10)	No	No	No	Yes
	Verbal	Verbal (items 11–23)	No	No	Yes	Yes
Vocabulary	Visual (verbal directions)	Verbal (items 1–3)	No	No	No	Yes
	Verbal	Verbal (items 4–25)	No	No	Yes	Yes
Similarities	Visual (verbal directions)	Pointing (items 1–6)	No	No	No	Yes
	Verbal	Verbal (items 7–20)	No	No	Yes	Yes
Sentences	Verbal	Verbal	No	No	Yes	Yes
Object assembly	Visual (verbal directions)	Assembles puzzles	No	Yes	No	No
Geometric design	Visual (verbal directions)	Pointing (items 1–7)	No	Yes	No	No
	Visual (verbal directions)	Copying designs (items 8–16)	No	Yes	No	No
Block design	Visual (verbal directions)	Assembles blocks	No	Yes	No	No
Mazes	Visual (verbal directions)	Draws lines in mazes	Yes	Yes	No	No
Picture completion	Visual (verbal directions)	Verbal or pointing	No	Yes	No	Yes
Animal pegs	Visual (verbal directions)	Places pegs in holes	No	Yes	No	No

without the time limits. Only picture completion does not have a motor component in the response. The verbal scale can be used, however, without modification, again keeping in mind that the IQ score is the verbal IQ and not a composite score.

Except for arithmetic, all WPPSI-R subtests begin with items on which the correct response is demonstrated or taught if the child does not respond correctly. This procedure may be especially useful for some students with disabilities.

Kaufman Assessment Battery for Children (K-ABC)

The K-ABC is an individually administered test for assessing the intelligence and achievement of children 2 years and 6 months through 12 years and 6 months. Intelligence is defined as the problem-solving style of the child. The mental processing scales measure the child's ability to solve problems in a sequential manner or a simultaneous manner. The achievement scale measures the child's acquired knowledge and reading skills (word recognition and reading comprehension). Teaching items and sample items are used on the mental processing subtests and verbal instructions are minimized. Four scores are provided: simultaneous processing; sequential processing; mental processing composite; and achievement. A special nonverbal scale, composed of subtests that may be administered in pantomime and responded to motorically, is provided. Children with disabilities were included in the standardization sample. (Note that a revision of the K-ABC is currently in progress.)

Accommodations – Modifications

There is some flexibility allowed for verbal responses.

Whenever a verbal response is required, it makes no difference whether the child responds in English, sign language, a subcultural slang, or another language such as Spanish or Japanese. Give the child credit for any response that can clearly be defended as correct. It is therefore always desirable that examiners be familiar with the child's subcultural and linguistic background and know sign language if the child is hearing-impaired. (Kaufman & Kaufman, 1983, p. 38)

A special nonverbal scale is provided. It allows for administration of selected subtests in pantomime with motor responses. At age 4, the scale consists of face recognition, hand movements, and triangles. At age 5, the scale consists of hand movements, triangles, matrix analogies, and spatial memory. At ages 6 through 12, the scale consists of hand movements, triangles, matrix analogies, spatial memory, and photo series. Separate nonverbal norms are available for these scales. The test authors recommend that the nonverbal scale be reserved for "deaf, hearing-impaired, speech-impaired, and language-disordered children with moderate to severe handicaps, and for children who are virtually non–English-speaking" (Kaufman & Kaufman, 1983, p. 41). These nonverbal norms were derived by administering the scale nonverbally rather than to a separate sample of students with hearing impairments.

The test authors indicate that one achievement subtest, reading/understanding, can be administered in pantomime and responded to motorically. This subtest is not part of the nonverbal scale but "offers some insight into the child's school achievement" (Kaufman & Kaufman, 1983, p. 42).

The test authors recommend that prorating be used in certain situations to evaluate students with disabilities. Students with visual impairments may not be able to complete the "magic window" portion of the assessment. Students with physical disabilities may have difficulties with hand movements (sequential processing), triangles (simultaneous processing), and reading/understanding (achievement). In these cases, the problematic subtests can be eliminated and prorating, as described in the test manual, can be used to obtain the sequential, simultaneous, and achievement scores.

The test authors indicate that having the child point to the pictures in the photo series with the examiner placing them in his or her own hand is an acceptable accommodation for students with disabilities.

Recommended Use of the K-ABC With Students With Disabilities

The presentation–response formats and recommendations for each subtest with individuals with hearing disabilities, speech disabilities, vision disabilities, and physical disabilities are presented in Table 10–3.

For students with hearing impairments or auditory receptive disabilities, hand movements, Gestalt closure, triangles, word order, matrix analogies, spatial memory, and photo series may be administered by gesture or pantomime. The nonverbal norms may then be used. This scale may also be used for students with speech disabilities and expressive language disabilities. For students with visual disabilities, only number recall and riddles can be administered. For students with verbal expressive disabilities, number recall and Gestalt closure are not appropriate. The remaining mental processing subtests, however, can be administered and prorating can be used to calculate the sequential processing, simultaneous processing and mental processing composite scores.

For students with motor impairments, hand movements and triangles may be problematic. They can be omitted and prorating can be used to calculate the sequential processing, simultaneous processing, and mental processing composite scores. Photo series can be administered using the procedure described previously.

TABLE 10-3
K-ABC Subtest Presentation/Response Format and Appropriateness With Individuals With Disabilities

Subtest	Presentation Format	Response Format	Use With Individuals With Disabilities			
			Hearing	Speech	Vision	Physical
Magic window	Visual (verbal directions)	Verbal	No	No	No	Yes
Face recognition	Visual (verbal directions)[a]	Points to response	Yes[b]	Yes	No	No
Hand movements	Visual (verbal directions)[a]	Copies hand movements	Yes[b]	Yes	No	No
Gestalt closure	Visual (verbal directions)[a]	Verbal	Yes[b]	No	No	Yes
Number recall	Verbal	Verbal	No	No	Yes	Yes
Triangles	Visual (verbal directions)[a]	Assembles triangles	Yes[b]	Yes	No	No
Word order	Visual (verbal directions)[a]	Points to response	No	No	No	Yes[d]
Matrix analogies	Visual (verbal directions)[a]	Places sticker on easel grid	No	Yes	No	No
Spatial memory	Visual (verbal directions)[a]	Points to response	No	Yes	No	Yes[d]
Photo series	Visual (verbal directions)[a]	Picks up cards or points	No	Yes	No	Yes[d]
Achievement Subtests						
Expressive vocabulary	Visual (verbal directions)	Verbal	No	No	No	Yes
Faces and places	Visual (verbal directions)	Verbal	No	No	No	Yes
Riddles	Verbal	Verbal	No	No	Yes	Yes
Arithmetic	Visual (verbal directions)	Verbal	No	No	No	Yes
Reading decoding	Visual	Verbal	No	No	No	Yes
Reading understanding	Visual (verbal directions)	Acts out word or phrase	Yes[c]	Yes	No	No

[a] Can be presented in pantomime/gesture.
[b] Directions presented by gesture/pantomime and scores produce a nonverbal score.
[c] Directions presented by gesture/pantomime.
[d] If student has the skills to point to the response.

Stanford-Binet Intelligence Scale: Fourth Edition

The SB: FE is an individually administered test of intelligence for students 2 years and 0 months through 23 years. A hierarchical model of intelligence is used with general intelligence reflected by the test composite score. Area scores (verbal reasoning, abstract/visual reasoning, quantitative reasoning, and short-term memory) represent the next level of intelligence, and subtest scores represent the third level. Students with disabilities were included in the standardization sample. (Note that revision of the SB: FE is currently in progress.)

Accommodations—Modifications

The test authors provide no guidelines or suggestions for developing accommodations for individuals with disabilities. Examiners are advised to adhere to standard procedures in administering the instrument. Subtests should be administered in the prescribed order, although changes that are "necessary for the practical requirements of testing" can be made (Thorndike, Hagen, & Sattler, 1986, p. 13). Because area scores can be calculated from combinations of one to four subtests, the examiner has considerable flexibility in which subtests in an area to administer. Thus, individualization to meet the needs of students with disabilities is possible.

Recommended Use of the SB: FE With Students With Disabilities

The presentation—response formats and recommendations for use of each subtest with individuals with hearing disabilities, speech disabilities, vision disabilities, and physical disabilities are presented in Table 10–4.

As noted previously, the SB: FE was designed for flexibility in administration; various combinations of subtests can be administered and used to develop area and composite scores. This is an advantage for students with disabilities, because all subtests in an area do not have to be administered to obtain a score.

All subtests in the verbal reasoning, quantitative reasoning, and short-term memory areas use verbal stimuli or a combination of visual stimuli and verbal directions. There are no provisions for use of gestures or pantomime in place of the verbal directions. Responses to the verbal reasoning subtests are exclusively verbal at schoolage levels. The memory subtests require verbal responses on two subtests (memory for sentences and memory for digits) and pointing or motoric responses for two subtests (bead memory and memory for objects). Written responses in place of verbal responses are allowed on two quantitative reasoning subtests (number series and equation building), and the quantitative subtest uses both motoric and verbal responses.

All subtests in the abstract/visual reasoning area use visual stimuli

TABLE 10-4
SB: FE Subtests Presentation/Response Format and Appropriateness for Individuals With Disabilities

Subtest	Presentation Format	Response Format	Use With Individuals With Disabilities			
			Hearing	Speech	Vision	Physical
Vocabulary	Visual (items 1–14)	Verbal	No	No	No	Yes
	Verbal (items 15–46)	Verbal	No	No	No	Yes
Comprehension	Visual (verbal directions)	Pointing to response	No	Yes	No	Yes
	Verbal (items 7–42)	Verbal	No	No	No	Yes
Absurdities	Visual (verbal directions)	Pointing to response (1–4)	No	Yes	No	Yes
	Visual (verbal directions)	Verbal (items 5–32)	No	No	No	Yes
Verbal relations	Verbal	Verbal	No	No	Yes	Yes
Pattern analysis	Visual (verbal directions)	Assembles blocks	No	Yes	No	No
	Visual (verbal directions)	Assembles blocks (1–12)	No	Yes	No	No
Copying	Visual (verbal directions)	Draws designs (13–28)	No	Yes	No	No
Matrices	Visual (verbal directions)	Verbal/pointing to response	No	Yes	No	Yes[a]
Paper folding and cutting	Visual (verbal directions)	Verbal/pointing to response	No	Yes	No	Yes[a]
Quantitative	Visual and verbal	Manipulating cubes/verbal	No	No	No	No
Number series	Visual and verbal	Verbal or writing numbers	No	Yes	No	Yes
Equation building	Visual and verbal	Verbal or writing numbers	No	Yes	No	Yes
Bead memory	Visual (verbal directions)	Pointing to response (1–10)	No	Yes	No	No
	Visual (verbal directions)	Placing beads on stick (11–42)	No	Yes	No	No
Memory for sentences	Verbal	Verbal	No	No	Yes	Yes
Memory for digits	Verbal	Verbal	No	No	Yes	Yes
Memory for objects	Visual (verbal directions)	Pointing to response	No	Yes	No	Yes[a]

[a] If student can point to response.

with verbal directions. There are no provisions for use of gestures or pan-tomime in place of the verbal directions. Responses are motoric on pattern analysis and motoric and paper–pencil on copying. Verbal or pointing responses are acceptable for matrices and paper folding and cutting.

For students with hearing impairments use of the verbal reasoning subtests is problematic because there is no provision for modifying the verbal stimuli and verbal directions. The abstract/visual reasoning subtests use visual stimuli and verbal directions. Although no provisions are made for use of gestures or pantomime to present these subtests, in some cases such accommodations may have minimal impact on score interpretation. Nonverbal responses are allowed on all four subtests. Likewise, administration of two memory subtests (bead memory and memory for objects) in this way may be acceptable.

For students with visual impairments use of the verbal reasoning subtests at the schoolage level, with the exception of absurdities, is appropriate. This combination of subtests will yield an area score. The abstract/visual reasoning subtests are not appropriate for students with visual impairments. Likewise, the quantitative reasoning subtests and two memory subtests (bead memory and memory for objects) are not appropriate because of the visual stimuli used. A memory score, however, can be calculated from the memory for sentences and memory for digits subtests. In such cases the score represents auditory short-term memory.

For students with motoric impairments the verbal reasoning subtests at the school-age level, the matrices and paper folding and cutting subtests from the abstract/visual reasoning area, the number series and equation building subtests from the quantitative reasoning area, and the memory for sentences and memory for digits subtests from the memory area are appropriate. This makes it possible to calculate all area scores as well as the test composite. If the motor impairments are not severe, it may be possible to administer memory of objects as it only requires a pointing response.

Differential Ability Scales (DAS)

The DAS is an individually administered cognitive abilities battery for students 2 years and 6 months through 17 years and 11 months. It is designed to provide an overall cognitive ability score and achievement scores as well as to measure specific abilities. The composite score (general conceptual ability) is a measure of conceptual and reasoning ability. Three cluster scores are also produced at the schoolage level: verbal ability, nonverbal reasoning, and spatial ability. At the earliest preschool level (ages 2.5 to 3.6) only the general conceptual ability score is provided. At the upper preschool level (ages 3 years and 6 months through 5 years and 11 months) there are verbal ability and nonverbal ability scores as well as the general conceptual ability score. Students with disabilities (learning disabilities, speech impairments, emotional disturbance, physical impairments, mental retardation, gifted–talented) were included in the standardization sample in approximate proportions that occur in the U.S. schoolage population.

Accommodations–Modifications

A special nonverbal composite is provided. The directions for the subtests in the composite can be conveyed through gestures; responses are by pointing, drawing, or manipulating objects. The nonverbal scale consists of recall of designs, pattern construction, matrices, and sequential and quantitative reasoning at the schoolage level. At the early preschool level block building and picture similarities compose the nonverbal scale. At the upper preschool level the scale is composed of picture similarities, pattern construction, and copying. The nonverbal scale is appropriate for children suspected of severe hearing loss, children with verbal expressive difficulties, or other disabilities affecting verbal receptive and verbal expressive skills. It should be noted that these nonverbal scores were derived by administering the scale nonverbally rather than to a separate sample of students with hearing impairments.

The test author warns that subtests "with verbal content should not be administered in translation" (Elliott, 1990, p. 36). These subtests include naming vocabulary, recall of digits, recall of objects, similarities, spelling, verbal comprehension, word definitions, and word reading.

Recommended Use of the DAS With Students With Disabilities

The presentation–response formats and recommendations for use of each subtest with individuals with hearing disabilities, speech disabilities, vision disabilities, and physical disabilities are presented in Table 10–5.

For schoolaged students with hearing impairments, there is a nonverbal scale consisting of recall of designs, pattern construction, matrices, and sequential and quantitative reasoning. This scale can be administered without verbal directions and uses visual input. Motoric responses (pointing, assembling blocks, using a pencil) are required. The special nonverbal composite norms can then be used to interpret the student's performance. Similar scales are available at the lower and upper preschool levels.

For students with motoric impairments or difficulties with time limits, pattern construction can be administered in a nontimed format. Scores are then interpreted with a special set of norms established for this purpose.

It should be noted that only core subtests are used to produce the general composite ability score. At the lower preschool level, those subtests include block building, picture similarities, naming vocabulary and verbal comprehension. Block building and picture similarities compose the nonverbal scale and are suitable for students with hearing disabilities and

TABLE 10-5

DAS Subtests Presentation/Response Format and Appropriateness for Individuals With Disabilities

Subtest	Presentation Format	Response Format	Use With Individuals With Disabilities			
			Hearing	Speech	Vision	Physical
Block building	Visual (verbal directions)[a]	Assembles blocks	Yes[b]	Yes[b]	No	No
Verbal comprehension	Visual and verbal	Manipulates small objects	No	Yes	No	No
Picture similarities	Visual (verbal directions)	Manipulates a card	Yes[b]	Yes[b]	No	No
Naming vocabulary	Visual (verbal directions)	Verbal	No	No	Yes	Yes
Early number concepts	Verbal	Manipulates chips/pictures	No	Yes	Yes	No
Copying	Visual (verbal directions)[a]	Draws designs	Yes[b]	Yes[b]	No	No
Matching letter-like forms	Visual (verbal directions)	Pointing to response	No	Yes	No	Yes[d]
Recall of designs	Visual (verbal directions)[a]	Draws designs	Yes[b]	Yes[b]	No	No
Word definitions	Verbal	Verbal	No	No	Yes	Yes
Recall of objects-immediate	Visual/verbal	Verbal	No	No	Yes	Yes
Pattern construction	Visual (verbal directions)[a]	Assembles blocks	Yes[b]	Yes[b]	No	Yes[c]
Matrices	Visual (verbal directions)[a]	Pointing to response	Yes[b]	Yes[b]	No	Yes[c]
Recall of objects-delayed	Not readministered	Verbal	No	No	No	Yes
Similarities	Verbal	Verbal	No	No	Yes	Yes
Sequential and quantitative reasoning	Visual (verbal directions)[a]	Writing numbers	Yes[b]	Yes[b]	No	No
Recall of digits	Verbal	Verbal	No	No	Yes	Yes
Speed of information pro-cessing	Visual (verbal directions)	Marks a circle with pencil	No	Yes	No	No
Basic number skills	Visual (verbal directions)	Points/writes numbers/verbal[e]	No	Yes	No	No
Spelling	Verbal	Writing words	No	Yes	No	No
Word reading	Visual (verbal directions)	Verbal	No	No	No	Yes

[a] Can be eliminated and administered in pantomime or by gesture.
[b] Scores generate a nonverbal composite.
[c] Can be administered in a nontimed format.
[d] If child can point to a response.
[e] Pointing on item 1; writing numbers on items 6–44; verbal responses on items 2–5 and 45–48.

speech disabilities. At the upper preschool level the core subtests include naming vocabulary, verbal comprehension, early number concepts, copying, pattern construction, and picture similarities. Copying, pattern construction, and picture similarities compose the nonverbal scale and are suitable for students with hearing disabilities and speech disabilities. At the school-age level the core subtests include similarities, word definitions, matrices, sequential and quantitative reasoning, pattern construction, and recall of designs. Of these subtests only similarities and word definitions are not part of the nonverbal scale. The other four core subtests are suitable for students with hearing disabilities and speech disabilities.

Das-Naglieri Cognitive Assessment System

Its authors describe the CAS as a nontraditional approach to intelligence testing based on a theory of cognitive processing. The test "was developed to evaluate Planning, Attention, Simultaneous, and Successive (PASS) cognitive processes of individuals between the ages of 5 and 17 years" (Naglieri & Das, 1997, p. 1). A full-scale score is provided as well as scores on the four cognitive processing scales. Students with disabilities (learning disabilities, speech–language impairments, serious emotional disturbance, mental retardation, gifted) were included in the standardization sample in approximate proportions that occur in the U.S. population.

Accommodations–Modifications

The authors provide some guidance on use of the test with students with disabilities. Examiners are advised that the "CAS needs to be administered and scored exactly as prescribed" and that it "is absolutely necessary that all standardized instructions be followed precisely" (Naglieri & Das, 1997, p. 3). At the same time examiners are informed that

> it is possible to augment the English instructions through other means. The opportunities to "provide additional help when needed" during introductory portions of the subtests can be utilized by examiners who have the knowledge to interact with the child in another language or through another means such as sign language. (Naglieri & Das, 1997, p. 3)

Recommended Use of the CAS With Students With Disabilities

The presentation–response formats and recommendations for use of each subtest with individuals with hearing disabilities, speech disabilities, vision disabilities, and physical disabilities are presented in Table 10–6.

Nine of the twelve subtests have visual input and verbal directions, and three are presented with verbal stimuli only.

For students with hearing impairments, examiners are permitted to

TABLE 10-6
CAS Subtests Presentation/Response Format and Appropriateness for Individuals With Disabilities

Subtest	Presentation Format	Response Format	Use With Individuals With Disabilities			
			Hearing	Speech	Vision	Physical
Matching numbers	Visual (verbal directions)	Underlines response/verbal[a]	Yes[b]	Yes	No	No[c]
Planned codes	Visual (verbal directions)	Draws symbols/verbal[a]	Yes[b]	Yes	No	No[c]
Planned connections	Visual (verbal directions)	Draws lines/verbal[a]	Yes[b]	Yes	No	No[c]
Nonverbal matrices	Visual (verbal directions)	Pointing to response	Yes[b]	Yes	No	Yes[d]
Verbal–spatial relations	Visual (verbal directions)	Pointing to response	Yes[b]	Yes	No	No[c]
Figure memory	Visual (verbal directions)	Draws geometric figures	Yes[b]	Yes	No	No
Expressive attention	Visual (verbal directions)	Verbal	Yes[b]	No	No	Yes
Number detection	Visual (verbal directions)	Underlines response	Yes[b]	Yes	No	No
Receptive attention	Visual (verbal directions)	Underlines response	Yes[b]	Yes	No	No
Word series	Verbal	Verbal	No	No	Yes	Yes
Sentence repetition	Verbal	Verbal	No	No	Yes	Yes
Sentence questions	Verbal	Verbal	No	No	Yes	Yes

[a] Verbal responses for reports on strategies used to solve the items.
[b] Directions can be presented in pantomime or by gesture.
[c] Time limits make the subtest unsuitable for individuals with physical disabilities.
[d] If individual can point to answer.

use sign language or gestures during introductory portions of the subtests and on the teaching items.

For students with visual impairments, word series, sentence repetition, and sentence questions can be administered and used to calculate the sequential score. All other subtests use visual stimuli and are not appropriate.

Six of the subtests require use of a pencil to respond, four require verbal responses, and two use a pointing response. Thus, administration of many of the subtests to students with motor impairments may not be possible. The sequential subtests (word series, sentence repetition, and sentence questions) can be appropriately administered. If the student is able to point to responses, nonverbal matrices and verbal–spatial relations from the simultaneous scale can be administered and the scores prorated for that cognitive processing scale.

Students with expressive language deficits may be less penalized on this battery than on other cognitive ability tests. The planning subtests require a paper and pencil response with a verbal response to report the strategies used to solve the items. This verbal response is not needed for the normative scoring of the subtests, so the planning score can be calculated with the nonverbal response. In addition, all three of the simultaneous subtests can be administered along with two of the attention subtests (number detection and receptive attention). A prorated score can be calculated from these two subtests. The sequential subtests may not be appropriate (depending on the severity of the language disability) because verbal responses are required.

The inclusion of sample and demonstration items in which the examiner in essence teaches the item facilitates use of the test with students with disabilities. These teaching opportunities allow the examiner to use gestures or verbal instruction in any language.

Wechsler Adult Intelligence Scale-Third Edition

The WAIS-III is an individually administered test for assessing the intellectual ability of individuals from 16 years and 0 months through 89 years. It is based on Wechsler's original conception of intelligence but new subtests including letter-number sequencing, matrix reasoning, and symbol search were added in the third edition. Three composite scores are provided: verbal IQ, performance IQ, and full-scale IQ. Individuals with disabilities were not included in the standardization sample.

Accommodations–Modifications

The test author provides some guidance on the use of the WAIS-III with individuals with disabilities. It is recommended that the examiner "consider administering only the Verbal subtests and using the Verbal scores as estimates of the examinee's cognitive abilities" (Wechsler, 1997, p. 33) when evaluating examinees with motor or visual impairments. Likewise, examinees with hearing impairments or speech disabilities should be administered the performance subtests and estimates of the examinee's cognitive abilities made from the performance score.

The test author emphasizes that the test was not standardized with modifications of test procedures. If modifications are needed, they should be noted on the record form. Accommodations such as sign language and visual aids for individuals with hearing impairments or visual impairments may have an impact on test scores, and the examiner "will need to rely on clinical judgment to evaluate the impact of such modified procedures on test scores" (Wechsler, 1997, p. 34).

Recommended Use of the WAIS-III With Individuals With Disabilities

The presentation–response formats and recommendations for use of each subtest with individuals with hearing disabilities, speech disabilities, vision disabilities, and physical disabilities are presented in Table 10–7.

All verbal subtests are presented verbally and require verbal responses severely limiting their use with students with hearing impairments. Use of sign language in presenting items presents many difficulties, as does the use of the performance scale with its extensive reliance on verbal instructions.

For individuals with visual impairments, the verbal subtests are appropriate as presented. If the verbal scale alone is used, the examiner should keep in mind that the IQ score is the verbal IQ and not a composite score.

Performance subtests use visual stimuli and verbal directions. As a consequence, use with individuals with hearing impairments is compromised even if directions are presented in sign language or by gesture.

For individuals with motor impairments, the motor requirements on the performance subtests may make these subtests inappropriate, depending on the severity of the motor impairment. Only picture completion does not have a motor component in the response. The verbal scale can be used without modification. If this is done, the examiner should keep in mind that the IQ score is the Verbal IQ and not a composite score.

Kaufman Adolescent and Adult Intelligence Test

The KAIT is an individually administered test of general intelligence "composed of separate Crystallized and Fluid Scales. The Crystallized Scale measures acquired concepts and depends on schooling and acculturation for success, while the Fluid Scale measures the ability to solve new problems" (Kaufman & Kaufman, p. 1). The theoretical base of the test integrates Horn and Cattell's theory of fluid and crystallized intelligence, the

TABLE 10-7
WAIS-III Subtests: Presentation/Response Format and Appropriateness for Individuals With Disabilities

Subtest	Presentation Format	Response Format	Use With Individuals With Disabilities			
			Hearing	Speech	Vision	Physical
Vocabulary	Verbal[a]	Verbal	Yes[b]	No	Yes	Yes
Similarities	Verbal	Verbal	No	No	Yes	Yes
Arithmetic	Verbal	Verbal	No	No	No	Yes
Digit span	Verbal	Verbal	No	No	Yes	Yes
Information	Verbal	Verbal	No	No	Yes	Yes
Comprehension	Verbal	Verbal	No	No	Yes	Yes
Letter-number sequencing	Verbal	Verbal	No	No	Yes	Yes
Picture completion	Visual (verbal directions)	Verbal	No	Yes	No	Yes
Digit symbol coding	Visual (verbal directions)	Copies symbols	No	Yes	No	No[c]
Picture arrangement	Visual (verbal directions)	Arranges picture cards	No	Yes	No	No[c]
Block design	Visual (verbal directions)	Assembles blocks	No	Yes	No	No[c]
Object assembly	Visual (verbal directions)	Assembles puzzles	No	Yes	No	No[d]
Symbol search	Visual (verbal directions)	Draws lines through	No	Yes	No	No[c]
Matrix reasoning	Visual (verbal directions)	Points to response or says number of the response	No	Yes	No	Yes

[a] Examinee can be shown the word.
[b] If the examinee is shown the word.
[c] Subtests are timed with bonus points for rapid, correct performance so any physical disability can affect score.

Luria-Golden definition of planning ability, and Piaget's stage of formal operations. Three composite scores are provided: crystallized IQ, fluid IQ, and composite IQ. The authors do not indicate whether individuals with disabilities were included in the standardization sample.

Accommodations–Modifications

The test authors emphasize that the KAIT must be administered in accordance with set procedures. "Any deviation from the prescribed procedures represents a violation of the ground rules, thereby making the norms of limited (and sometimes no) value" (Kaufman & Kaufman, 1993, p. 22). Some guidance on use of the instrument with individuals with disabilities is provided. For most subtests that require a verbal response it makes no difference whether the examinee responds in English, sign language, or a foreign language. (The only exception is the definitions subtest.) It is recommended that the examiner have a knowledge of sign language when testing individuals with hearing impairments.

Alternate subtests, one fluid and one crystallized, are provided and can be substituted for a core subtest under certain conditions. Individuals with receptive language difficulties can be given memory for block designs (alternate fluid subtest) for logical steps. Individuals with expressive language difficulties can be given memory for block designs instead of rebus learning. A third-grade reading level is needed for some crystallized subtests. Famous faces (alternate crystallized subtest) can be substituted for definitions or double meanings.

Recommended Use of the KAIT With Individuals With Disabilities

The presentation–response formats and recommendations for use of each subtest with individuals with hearing disabilities, speech disabilities, vision disabilities, and physical disabilities are presented in Table 10–8.

For individuals with visual disabilities, only auditory comprehension and auditory delayed recall can be administered. All other subtests use visual and verbal stimuli.

Definitions, rebus learning, logical steps, and famous faces use both visual and verbal input. For individuals with hearing impairments, the verbal stimuli could be presented in sign language. Standardization procedures used both types of stimuli, so scores for individuals with limitations in either verbal or visual receptive skills should be interpreted cautiously and may be conservative estimates of the skills measured by the subtests.

Mystery codes, double meanings, memory for block designs, and rebus delayed recall use visual stimuli and verbal directions. For individuals with hearing impairments, the directions could be presented in sign language.

Although verbal responses are indicated for definitions, rebus learning, logical steps, auditory comprehension, mystery codes (easel items),

TABLE 10-8
KAIT Subtests: Presentation/Response Format and Appropriateness for Individuals With Disabilities

Subtest	Presentation Format	Response Format	Use With Individuals With Disabilities			
			Hearing	Speech	Vision	Physical
Definitions	Visual/verbal	Verbal	No[a]	No[b]	No	Yes
Rebus learning	Visual/verbal	Verbal	No[a]	No[b]	No	Yes
Logical steps	Visual/verbal	Verbal	No[a]	No[b]	No	Yes
Auditory comprehension	Verbal	Verbal	No[a]	No[b]	Yes	Yes
Mystery codes	Visual (verbal directions)	Verbal[c]/circles response[d]	No[a]	No[b]	No	Yes
Double meanings	Visual (verbal directions)	Verbal	No[a]	No[b]	No	Yes
Memory for block designs	Visual (verbal directions)	Assembles blocks	No[a]	Yes	No	No
Famous faces	Visual/verbal	Verbal	No[a]	No[b]	No	Yes
Rebus delayed recall	Not readministered	Verbal	No[a]	No[b]	No	Yes
Auditory delayed recall	Not readministered	Verbal	No[a]	No[c]	Yes	No

[a]Sign language presentation permitted.
[b]Written or typed responses could be substituted.
[c]Easel items.
[d]Booklet items.

double meanings, famous faces, rebus delayed recall, and auditory delayed recall, a written or typed response could be substituted provided the individual has the necessary skills in this area.

CONCLUSION

This chapter presents an approach to modifying individually administered, norm-referenced ability tests for individuals with disabilities. Some of the important factors related to test modifications and accommodations were discussed. Analyses of the most frequently used ability tests were presented along with suggestions on their use with individuals with disabilities. By using the Tables 10–1 through 10–8 and the Worksheet for Developing Testing Accommodations, it is hoped that testing professionals will be able to make more informed decisions in selecting appropriate ability measures for individuals with disabilities.

REFERENCES

Archer, R. P., Maruish, M., Imhof, E. A., & Piotrowski, C. (1991). Psychological test usage with adolescent clients: 1990 survey findings. *Professional Psychology: Research and Practice, 22,* 247–252.

Braden, J. P., & Hannah, J. M. (1998). Assessment of hearing-impaired and deaf children with the WISC-III. In A. Prifitera & D. Saklofske (Eds.), *WISC-III clinical use and interpretation* (pp. 175–201). San Diego, CA: Academic Press.

Chan, D. W., & Lee, H. (1995). Patterns of psychological test usage in Hong Kong in 1993. *Professional Psychology: Research and Practice, 26,* 292–297.

Elliott, C. D. (1990). *Differential Ability Scales administration and scoring manual.* San Antonio, TX: Psychological Corporation.

Hammill, D. D., Fowler, L., Bryant, B., & Dunn, C. (1992). *A survey of test usage among speech/language pathologists.* Unpublished manuscript.

Hutton, J. B., Dubes, R., & Muir, S. (1992). Assessment practices of school psychologists: Ten years later. *School Psychology Review, 21,* 271–284.

Janda, L. H. (1998). *Psychological testing: Theory and applications.* Needham Heights, MA: Allyn and Bacon.

Kaufman, A. S., & Kaufman, N. L. (1983). *Kaufman Assessment Battery for Children administration and scoring manual.* Circle Pines, MN: American Guidance Service.

Kaufman, A. S., & Kaufman, N. L. (1993). *Kaufman Adolescent and Adult Intelligence Test manual.* Circle Pines, MN: American Guidance Service.

Laurent, J., & Swerdlik, M. (1992, March). *Psychological test usage: A survey of internship supervisors.* Paper presented at the annual meeting of National Association of School Psychologists, Nashville, TN.

McLoughlin, J. A., & Lewis, R. B. (1990). *Assessing special students* (3rd ed.). New York: Maxwell Macmillan International.

Naglieri, J. A., & Das, J. P. (1997). *Das-Naglieri Cognitive Assessment System administration and scoring manual.* Itasca, IL: Riverside.

Oakland, T., & Hu, S. (1992). The top 10 tests used with children and youth worldwide. *Bulletin of the International Test Commission, 19,* 99–120.

Papalia, D. E., & Olds, S. W. (1990). *A child's world: Infancy through adolescence* (5th ed.). New York: McGraw-Hill.

Piotrowski, C., & Keller, J. W. (1989). Psychological testing in outpatient mental health facilities: A national study. *Professional Psychology: Research and Practice, 20,* 423–425.

Salvia, J., & Ysseldyke, J. E. (2000). *Assessment* (8th ed.). Boston: Houghton Mifflin.

Sattler, J. M. (1988). *Assessment of children.* San Diego, CA: Author.

Stinnett, T. A., Havey, J. M., & Oehler-Stinnett, J. (1994). Current test usage by practicing school psychologists: A national survey. *Journal of Psychoeducational Assessment, 12,* 331–350.

Thorndike, R. L., Hagen, E. P., & Sattler, J. M. (1986). *The Stanford-Binet Intelligence Scale: Fourth Edition guide for administering and scoring.* Chicago: Riverside.

Vasta, R., Haith, M. M., & Miller, S. A. (1999). *Child psychology: The modern science* (3rd ed.). New York: John Wiley and Sons.

Watkins, C. E., Campbell, V. I., Nieberding, R., & Hallmark, R. (1995). *Contemporary practice of psychological assessment by clinical psychologists. Professional Psychology: Research and Practice, 26,* 54–60.

Watkins, C. E., Campbell, V. I., Nieberding, R., & Hallmark, R. (1996). On Hunsley, harangue, and hoopla: Contemporary practice of psychological assessment by clinical psychologists. *Professional Psychology: Research and Practice, 27,* 316–318.

Wechsler, D. (1989). *Wechsler Preschool and Primary Scale of Intelligence-Revised manual.* San Antonio, TX: Psychological Corporation.

Wechsler, D. (1991). *Wechsler Intelligence Scale for Children-Third edition manual.* San Antonio, TX: Psychological Corporation.

Wechsler, D. (1997). *Wechsler Adult Intelligence Scale-Third Edition administration and scoring manual.* San Antonio, TX: Psychological Corporation.

Wilson, M. S., & Reschly, D. J. (1996). Assessment in school psychology training and practice. *School Psychology Review, 21,* 9–23.

Zaske, K. K., Hegstrom, K. J., & Smith, D. K. (1999, Aug.). *Survey of test usage among clinical psychologists and school psychologists.* Paper presented at annual meeting of American Psychological Association, Boston.

11

POSTSECONDARY ADMISSIONS TESTING

JULIE P. NOBLE, WAYNE CAMARA, AND JOHN FREMER

Today increasing numbers of individuals with disabilities are taking part in postsecondary education. This chapter addresses issues related to testing students with disabilities for admission to college or to graduate or professional education. A recent National Center for Education Statistics (NCES) report, *An Institutional Perspective on Students With Disabilities in Postsecondary Education*, provides national data about the enrollment of such students and the accommodations they receive (Lewis & Farris, 1999).

PURPOSES OF ADMISSIONS TESTING

Institutions of higher education face a continuing challenge to ensure that admitted students are qualified to meet their academic requirements. Those students who appear to have the requisite abilities, skills, and knowledge are eligible for admissions. The admissions criteria used to admit students vary widely across institutions, however.

As noted by Whitney (1989), resource limitations and restrictive institutional policies can lead to higher selectivity in college admissions policies. Highly selective institutions and programs seek to admit students with the greatest potential for success, whereas less selective institutions or programs admit all students with a reasonable chance of success.

The admissions criteria therefore differ across institutions and programs. These criteria usually include nontest information such as prior coursework and grades, educational needs, and background characteristics. For the majority of postsecondary institutions admissions criteria also include results from standardized admissions tests such as the ACT, SAT, or TOEFL (Test of English as a Foreign Language) for undergraduate admissions, and the Graduate Record Examination (GRE), the Graduate Management Admissions Test (GMAT), the Law School Admissions Test (LSAT), or the Medical College Admissions Test (MCAT) for admission to graduate or professional schools or programs. In 1992, for example, 93% of four-year public and 86% of four-year private institutions required either the ACT or SAT for undergraduate admissions (AACRAO, 1995). The companies that develop such tests (e.g., the American Association of Medical Colleges; Educational Testing Service; ACT, Inc.; and the Law School Admissions Council) are subject to the provisions of the Americans With Disabilities Act, as are all public and private postsecondary institutions. This chapter focuses exclusively on issues concerning the use of standardized admissions tests with students with disabilities.

FORMAT AND DELIVERY OF ADMISSIONS TESTS

Admissions tests are developed, administered, scored, and supported either by the testing companies that own them or by companies that are under contract to test-sponsoring organizations. Most college admissions tests are currently administered in paper-and-pencil format: The GRE, GMAT, and TOEFL are available in a computer-administered format. In the near future, other admissions testing programs will be moving to a computer-administered format. It remains to be seen whether both paper-and-pencil and computer formats will be available for any given test.

Admissions testing programs may include several components. The basic testing program includes one or more tests of varying item and time length. Some testing programs include additional tests that are administered separately (e.g., SAT-II and GRE) or with the basic test administration (the Test of Written English). A nontest section, in which students provide information about their backgrounds, career plans, and educational preferences, may also be included as part of the testing program.

The majority of paper-and-pencil admissions testing is done on national test dates scheduled several times a year. Other standard administrations of admissions tests are conducted as residual testing on college campuses, as Defense Activity for Non-Traditional Educational Support

(DANTES) testing for armed forces members or dependent testing on a military base, or as a component of international testing or state-mandated in-school testing. In addition, individual administrations are arranged for students in areas not served by established test centers. For those tests administered by computer, students can complete the tests at local test centers. In general, students are required to preregister for all admissions tests; students with disabilities who are requesting test accommodations must do so at the time of registration.

Paper-and Pencil Tests

Paper-and-pencil admissions tests are administered to groups of students under fixed time limits and prescribed testing conditions. Each content test has its own specified time limit; the content tests are administered in a particular sequence with a limited number of breaks between tests. For example, students complete the ACT, SAT-I, or TOEFL over a three- to four-hour period, typically in the morning.

The test booklets are printed in standard black type and bound in booklets, with separate scannable answer sheets for the students' responses. The item format for most standardized admissions tests is multiple-choice, though the SAT-I and SAT-II also include short-answer items. The SAT-II writing test includes a 20-minute essay. The MCAT, GMAT, and GRE also include a writing test. The Test of Written English, a 30-minute writing test, can be taken with the TOEFL. For a given test, students are allowed to review their responses to items, skip items and return to them later, or change their answers, as long as it occurs within the specified time limit.

Computer Adaptive Tests

The General Test of the GRE and the TOEFL both include three tests, each with a maximum specified time limit. All items are multiple-choice (except the writing tests). Because of their computer-adaptive format, individual students can arrange to take the tests at a local test center. However, on computer-administered tests students typically cannot review or change their responses to test items or skip items and return to them later.

STANDARDS AND LEGISLATION

Section 504 of the Rehabilitation Act of 1973 states that, in appropriate circumstances, institutions involved in admissions testing must make reasonable accommodations for students with documented disabilities.

However, institutions are not required to lower their admissions standards to accommodate applicants with disabilities. These applicants must meet the same academic standards for admission as students without disabilities (Heaney & Pullin, 1998).

Section 504 also requires that colleges not conduct preadmissions inquiries about students' disabilities that might result in a student not being admitted because of the disability. Once a student has been admitted, such inquiries can be made to assist in accommodating matriculating students' needs. For a more detailed discussion of the laws related to testing individuals with disabilities, see chapter 1.

Companies that develop and administer standardized college admissions tests are subject to the Americans With Disabilities Act. Under the ADA, testing companies must provide reasonable accommodations for students with qualifying disabilities, unless the accommodation will alter the intended purposes of the test or result in an undue burden. Moreover, the accommodation must be a reasonable one, but might not always be the preferred accommodation.

A major consideration in testing, as mentioned in chapter 2, is that testing modifications might affect the validity of the interpretations made from the test scores. At the time this chapter was written, admissions-testing companies typically indicated with a mark or "flag" the test scores of students who took a test under nonstandardized conditions. The reader is referred to the final section of this chapter and to chapter 6 for a detailed discussion of this issue.

PROCEDURES FOR REQUESTING ACCOMMODATIONS

The sponsors and developers of admissions testing programs strive to provide the same access to testing for individuals with disabilities as is available to others who are being tested. As has been noted, this is not only a matter of simple fairness, it is also required by law. A critical first step in providing accommodations is determining whether there is a need for an accommodation. If such a need exists, it is then necessary to determine if the requested accommodation is both reasonable and appropriate for the test. It is important to recognize that some accommodations, such as using a reader for some types of reading skills examinations, may invalidate the results as a measure of a test taker's competence.

Organizations administering admissions testing programs provide procedures for individuals with disabilities to follow to obtain accommodations. The typical steps include

- Identifying the specific disability;
- Providing the basis for determining the disability—for

example, testing, medical history, as determined by an appropriate professional qualified to make a diagnosis;

- Describing the functional limitations of the individual as a result of the disability; and
- Requesting a specific accommodation, providing a rationale for this accommodation.

For information about specific admissions testing programs, refer to chapter 16.

TYPES OF ACCOMMODATIONS

One important step in serving the needs of individuals with disabilities is including easily understandable and appropriate information in admissions testing programs, publications, Websites, and other sources about the procedures to follow to learn about and receive appropriate accommodations. In this section, five types of accommodation are reviewed:

1. Facilities;
2. Test formats;
3. Delivery (such as the use of a signer/response recorder);
4. Extended time; and
5. Technological possibilities.

For a detailed discussion on types of accommodation, see chapter 3.

Facilities

The same considerations that govern access for individuals with disabilities to all facilities apply to the testing setting. Accommodations may be readily arranged at an existing "regular" test site; however, it may be more appropriate to use another facility to meet the needs of the test taker. For example, if the test taker must have wheelchair access, this may require arrangements for elevator access to the testing site, the use of escorts to assist the examinee in reaching the testing site, as well as assignment to a testing room so that facilities such as rest rooms and water fountains are readily accessible.

Test Formats

The adaptation of the test used in admissions testing involves modifications to formats and directions and, in some instances, the content and presentation of particular test questions or sets of test questions, because of their features (e.g., pictures, graphics, etc.). Among the most common format modifications are the following:

- Large-type test booklet and answer documents;
- Overlays for tests (and answer sheets) that change the color of the print;
- Braille; and
- Cassette presentation.

For many test questions, adaptation to one of these formats is straightforward, but adaptations present considerable challenges. For example, when mathematical questions contain complex figures, preparing a cassette description may require decisions about what characteristics of the figure need to be described. The typical guideline is first to give a general statement about a figure in precise, nontechnical language, followed by the description of essential details. Occasionally, raised figures are used instead of or in addition to descriptions of the diagram.

Delivery

Among the accommodations available for admissions tests are the use of a reader and/or a response recorder. Such assistance may be needed both for recording background and identifying information and for responding to the test questions. Communication concerning the interpretation of test content is not permitted, because this type of interaction with another person is not available to other test takers. In addition, for some testing programs it is recommended that a personal reader not record answers for a test taker.

When a qualified test taker requires assistance in recording answers to multiple-choice questions on admissions tests, it may be sufficient for the test taker to mark the answers in the test book for later transcription to an answer sheet or for direct scoring from the booklet. Alternatively, the test taker may dictate the answers to a test supervisor or other individual designated by the testing company but not the test taker's personal reader. Similarly, a test taker who needs assistance responding to free response questions of the short-answer or essay type could dictate her or his responses to a designated representative of the testing company.

Extended Time

As part of the process for requesting accommodations, individuals with disabilities can request additional testing time. Additional time is frequently required when Braille or cassette versions of the test are provided. For test takers with learning disabilities, extended time is the most frequently requested accommodation. The amount of additional time required must be determined on an individual basis, using information provided about the test taker. Some programs provide test takers with a recommended amount of extended time (e.g., time and a half), and individuals requesting additional amounts of extended time must submit appropriate documentation of the need.

In many instances, accommodations, including extended-time arrangements, are stipulated in a confirmation letter from the testing agency to the test taker. The test taker is not only given specific timing instructions regarding each test section but also guidelines concerning rest periods, breaks, and so forth, as needed. To help students pace themselves through testing, they are reminded of the timing for each test section as the test proceeds.

Technological Possibilities

New assistive technologies offer the promise of empowering people with disabilities to achieve their academic and professional objectives in ways that were not possible even a few years ago. Assistive technologies represent a broad range of access strategies, including simple solutions such as magnifying devices, adjustable lighting, or providing alternative foreground and background colors. Some of these devices are so widely used within testing, as in other areas, that many do not even think of them as specialized or adaptive equipment. Technologies such as the conventional computer keyboard, mouse, trackball, or monitor can be modified or replaced to provide equal access to computer-based tests.

Among the technological advances that are being explored are such access strategies as large, adjustable keyboards and touch screens with raised-line images, speech and Braille output, zoom capabilities, and color options.

MAKING DECISIONS ABOUT ACCOMMODATIONS

Individuals with disabilities are entitled to similar access to admissions testing as other test takers, and are also entitled to be tested in such a way that the tests results reflect what the tests are intended to measure rather than an individual's disability. How does one evaluate the adequacy of accommodations that are provided?

In academic situations, where students are receiving accommodations in the classroom, it seems relatively straightforward to evaluate whether a student should be tested under conditions as similar as is feasible to the instructional setting. The use of readers, large-type booklets, extended time, and so forth can then all be examined for the degree of comparability between the educational and testing settings.

When a prospective test taker requests accommodations that are not consistent with his or her educational circumstances, such as a request for extended time on an admissions test or when such accommodations have not been provided for any school or classroom tests, reasonableness is more difficult to evaluate. The choice of accommodations must always be an individual one, taking into account the nature of the disability and the nature of the test involved. The process for arriving at a determination of what is reasonable can be evaluated. Were the individuals making the decisions regarding the need for accommodation appropriately trained to evaluate need? Was the information used relevant and current? Was a rationale provided for the accommodation that was requested? When well-qualified professionals are requesting accommodations that are supported by appropriate documentation, the task of judging reasonableness is greatly simplified. For a detailed discussion about requesting accommodations, see chapters 3 and 4.

REPORTING SCORES FROM ACCOMMODATED TESTS AND FLAGGING

In most instances score reports for accommodated testing of individuals with disabilities are identical to those reports issued for tests administered under standardized conditions. Scores are reported on the same scales and the same interpretive information is provided on the score reports. The major exception has been the policy of "flagging" admissions test scores of students testing with extended time. When test scores from accommodated administrations are reported by the major admissions testing organizations, the test score is marked with an asterisk or an "X." Most testing programs provide a short explanation of the flag, such as "nonstandard administration" provided on the ACT or SAT score report. This "flag" does not specify the test taker as being disabled, nor does it specify the nature of the accommodations or modifications provided.

There are a variety of types of score reports associated with admissions testing programs. First, in all cases, students receive their score reports indicating their level of performance and how to interpret their overall scores. In most instances score reports are mailed to the students; most testing programs (e.g., ACT, GRE, SAT) offer telephone transmission of scores, and accessing one's score via the Web appears to be on the horizon. In undergraduate admissions testing, paper copies of score reports are also mailed to the students' high schools, if authorized by the student. Finally, once students select which institutions should receive their test scores, score reports are transmitted to the designated colleges, universities, or professional schools.

Flagging of scores to designate nonstandard administration of tests in score reports is still a controversial practice and is confined primarily to admissions testing,[1] as explained earlier in chapters 1, 2, and 6 of this volume. Most admissions testing programs will only designate a flagged score if (a) extended time is provided, or (b) the modification results in a change in the construct measured. Research has consistently demonstrated that extended time is a primary source of the noncomparability of accommodated testing and results in differential validity for many groups of students with disabilities (see Mehrens, 1997; Wightman, 1993; Willingham et al., 1988; Ziomek & Andrews, 1996, 1998). Extended time is the cause of flagging in the overwhelming majority of instances.[2] It is the most requested accommodation for the largest proportion of students with disabilities taking admissions tests (i.e., students with learning disabilities) and for students testing under modalities such as cassette or Braille that require extended time.

Occasionally, changes in the testing modality or the items administered differ markedly from the test administered under standardized conditions (even if completed within current time limits), thereby altering the underlying construct measured by the test. For example, some forms of the SAT-II foreign language tests include a listening component. If a student with an auditory disability requests a script to read the section or has a signer, the task no longer involves listening comprehension and the construct is changed. Similarly, if a language test includes both a reading and a writing section, but a student with a visual disability can only complete the writing section, the language construct is much narrower than that on tests administered without such modifications. Another instance when a construct may change would be when a sizeable number of items cannot be translated to an alternative modality (e.g., Braille, cassette), such as when pictures or graphics that represent an important component of the test content cannot be appropriately presented.

As part of a recent legal settlement with the International Dyslexia Association, Californians for Disability Rights, and Mark Breimhorst, the Educational Testing Service (ETS) has agreed to stop flagging for the accommodation of extended time on the GRE, GMAT, TOEFL, and other standardized tests it administers as of October 1, 2001 (ETS, 2001). The settlement does not apply to the SAT and other tests that are owned by the College Board and administered by the ETS. Flagging will continue for students receiving extended time on College Board-owned tests while an external panel reviews evidence and submits recommendations concerning this practice. As of the date of this publication no other postsecondary admissions testing program had announced any changes to their current flagging practices.

---

[1]Some licensure and certification tests also "flag" nonstandard administrations. See chapter 15, this volume.
[2]This applies to all admissions tests examined in this chapter (SATI, SAT II, ACT, GRE, GMAT, LSAT, and MCAT).

ASSUMPTIONS ABOUT ACCOMMODATIONS AND FLAGGING

There appear to be a number of assumptions concerning the nature and number of students with disabilities, the types of accommodations provided and their impact on test scores, the use of flagging in admissions and the impact of flagging on admissions processes and decisions. We will briefly discuss some of the most frequently mentioned myths about testing students with disabilities.

First, since passage of the ADA the number of students requesting and testing with accommodations has increased dramatically in most admissions testing programs. For example, the number of requests for accommodations on both the ACT and SAT has more than doubled in a five-year span (Camara, Copeland, & Rothchild, 1998). Similarly, requests for accommodations on graduate admissions tests such as the GRE, GMAT, LSAT, and the MCAT have increased. By far the greatest amount of growth has been among students with learning disabilities (Camara et al., 1998; HEATH, 1995).

In 1994, 13% of eighth graders and 12% of fourth graders had an Individual Educational Plan (IEP); however, the majority of these students might not have needed any accommodation on standardized tests (Mazzeo, Carlson, Voelkl, & Lutkus, 1999). Similarly, in 1998 to 1999 approximately 50,000 accommodations were granted for the SAT (Mandinach, Cahalan, & Camara, in press), but this represented less than half of all students reporting that they have a disability when registering for the test and about 2% of all SATs administered. Nearly 90% of accommodations were requested by students with a learning or attention deficit disorder (ADD). Among other major testing programs at ETS, accommodations for learning disabilities or ADD made up less than 1% of test takers for each program in 1998 to 1999: (a) the PSAT/NMSQT: 16,800 (.79%); (b) Graduate Management Admissions Test: 832 (.41%), (c) Advanced Placement Program: 2,600 (.23%), (d) The Praxis Series: 4,321 (.53%), (e) Graduate Record Examination General Test: 3,316 (.70%), and (f) Test of English as a Foreign Language: 318 (.05%; Mandinach et al., in press). In the 1997 to 1998 testing year more than 30,000 accommodations were granted for the ACT (J. Noble, personal communication, October 2000), representing 50% of all students reporting they have a disability when registering for the test, and about 2% of all ACTs administered in that time period. There is some concern among admissions professionals that a small number of students requesting accommodations for extended-time testing may not have a bona fide disability.

These concerns appear to be related primarily to students who report that they have a learning disability but who do not have an IEP. Students with diagnosed learning disabilities are more likely to be Caucasian American and to come from higher income and better educated families than students with other types of disabilities (Henderson, 1995). In 1997, an ad hoc committee established by the Association of Higher Education and Disability (AHEAD) developed standard criteria for documenting learning disabilities and attention-deficit/hyperactivity disorders in adolescents and adults. The primary intent of these guidelines was to provide standard criteria for documenting these disabilities. Such documentation could be used by postsecondary personnel and consumers requiring documentation to determine appropriate accommodations required by individuals, resulting in greater uniformity in the provisions of accommodations of students with such disabilities (AHEAD, 1997). The AHEAD guidelines[3] described the documentation needed to substantiate learning disabilities and attention-deficit hyperactivity disorder (ADHD), including diagnostic interviews and assessments, documentation of a specific diagnosis, the currency of documentation, recommended accommodations with a rationale, the interpretative summary, and confidentiality provisions. However, given the relatively large percentage of students who state that they have a disability when registering for the test but who never request an accommodation, it may be more likely that a higher proportion of students who might benefit from accommodations are uninformed about or are reluctant to request them.

Second, admissions officers may assume that a student has a learning disability when they see a score with a flag (Pullin & Heaney, 1997), and may view accommodations such as extended time as providing an advantage to these students (see Ziomek & Andrews, 1998). Research (Braun, Ragosta, & Kaplan, 1988; Wightman, 1993; Willingham et al., 1988; Ziomek & Andrews, 1998) shows a moderate overprediction of college performance and lack of comparability for students with learning disabilities who test with extended time. Admissions officers and others may overestimate the potential impact of extended time, as well as other testing modifications, on student performance. Camara et al. (1998) reported that the effects of extended time for students with learning disabilities who retest on the SAT are, on average score increases of 32 and 26 points more than the corresponding score increases for retesting students without disabilities, on the verbal and mathematics tests, respectively. Ziomek and Andrews (1998) showed that students with disabilities who first tested under standard conditions and retested under extended-time conditions increased their ACT composite scores by an average of 3.2 scale score points. Students testing and retesting under standard conditions showed average score gains of .7 scale score points. Pullin and Heaney (1997) explained, "modifications on an admission test must merely be a means of more accurately measuring the disabled student's abilities, not as a basis for a competitive advantage over nondisabled students" (p. 825).

---

[3] AHEAD is no longer distributing these guidelines.

A third myth associated with admissions testing of students with disabilities is that any variation to standard test administration will result in a flagged score. Each year several hundred students receive accommodations that do not result in a flagged test score. A number of accommodations are provided by one or more admissions testing program to eligible students with disabilities that will not (in and of themselves) result in flagged scores.[4]

In addition, an increasing number of additional accommodations for computer-based admissions tests are afforded to qualifying students without flagging, such as

- Alternative input devices (e.g., trackball, head-mounted mouse emulator);
- Zoom text;
- Alternative screen foreground and background colors;
- Individual or off-site administration of the CBT, as well as accommodations to eliminate distractions from other test takers;
- Enlarged keyboards; and
- Adjustable testing surfaces and seating to accommodate physical disabilities.

Similarly, some students with a temporary disability (e.g., broken arm, temporary visual difficulty) may also require extended time to complete admissions tests in other modalities (e.g., reader, recorder) and will receive a flagged test score, even when the temporary disability will not be present when they enroll in college.

Finally, many advocates for individuals with disabilities fear that flags may be used to discriminate against students either in how applications are processed or in the ultimate admissions decision. One fear is that, once aware of a potential disability, admissions staff may process applications differently, constituting an illegal preadmission inquiry. In a survey of colleges, May (1984) reported that more than half of these institutions required some additional materials from students with disabilities before admission, and a small portion of these had different procedures for determining a student's eligibility (e.g., separate committees).

In addition, these concerns raise a number of interesting questions about admissions processes for students with disabilities. Pullin and Heaney

---

[4]Large-block answer sheets, distraction-free environments (e.g., individual or small group test administration, headphones to eliminate distracting noise), overlays for tests and answer sheets that change the color of the print, special paper to prevent allergic reactions, longer breaks between test sections (as long as time on the test itself does not increase) to reduce fatigue, cardboard or paper to track text, snacks for students with diabetes or other disabilities, individual (e.g., Tourette's syndrome) or off-site administration (e.g., hospital administration, at-home administration), and alternative furniture and seating to accommodate physical disabilities.

(1997) argued that there is seemingly no justification for viewing flagged test results differently from test results for students without disabilities. However, students with disabilities typically score about one half of a standard deviation lower on undergraduate admissions tests than the average test taker, and their scores appear less valid for predicting college performance for some groups. The test taker with a disability therefore may be at a distinct disadvantage if admissions officials consider his or her admissions test score as comparable to those of students without disabilities and do not look for other factors that may indicate their ability to succeed in college (e.g., courses taken, high school grades). A student with a learning disability who is applying to college or graduate school needs "to decide whether or not to 'disclose' the fact that he or she has a disability . . . by disclosing the disability the student may explain possible discrepancies within various pieces of information" (HEATH, 1995, p. 9). For example, some students with learning disabilities may have discrepant scores within an admissions test (e.g., much higher scores on SAT verbal than SAT math) or have lower grades in foreign language courses than other academic coursework taken in high school. When students disclose their disability in their written statements, admissions officers may better understand these discrepancies and be able to consider them in admissions and placement decisions.

A National Research Council (NRC, 1982) panel noted that research does not support the common assumption that knowledge of a person's disability works to their disadvantage (Sherman & Robinson, 1982). In chapter 6 of this volume, Mehrens and Ekstrom summarize research that illustrates that students with flagged test scores were generally admitted at the same or greater rates than students with comparable scores without disabilities at undergraduate and professional schools.

Mandinach et al. (in press) completed interviews, focus groups, and surveys with college admissions counselors, secondary school guidance counselors, and college disability service providers to determine current policies and practices concerning flagging, as well as implications for test takers with disabilities. Eighty percent of admissions officers felt that test scores resulting from a nonstandard test administration should retain a flag. Nearly 90% of admissions officers stated the flag had no impact on admissions decisions, whereas 6.5% felt it occasionally could increase a student's chances of admissions. When admissions officers see a student has taken both standard and nonstandard administrations of an admissions test, 69% percent say they place the greatest weight on whichever test yielded the higher score. Nearly half of the admissions officers reported attending more to other factors such as grades, courses taken, and personal statements or references when a student only submits one admission test completed under nonstandardized administrations. It is interesting to note that only 20% of admissions officers reported seeing the flag when scores were electronically transmitted by ETS, and 75% reported that the flag appeared when the applicant's folder was reviewed personally. Guidance counselors were also supportive of retaining the flag, with 64% recommending that it be retained and 18% having no opinion. Again, nearly 20% of guidance counselors expressed no opinion on the extent to which a flag might impact admissions decisions, with 34% and 31% stating that the flag had no impact or might decrease a student's chances for admissions, respectively. Disability service providers in higher education strongly agreed that the flag had no impact on admissions (81%), yet 54% of them felt the flag should be removed. On average, they reported that about 73% of students with flagged scores would seek assistance or accommodations at college once they matriculated, compared to about 82% of students who had an IEP during high school.

INTERPRETING AND USING SCORES FROM ACCOMMODATED TEST ADMINISTRATIONS

Admissions testing programs generally do not provide any additional information to test users on how to appropriately interpret and use scores from accommodated test administrations. As noted earlier, score reports that are flagged include a simple statement cautioning the test user that the score is based on a nonstandard administration. Yet the four-year study of the SAT and GRE (Willingham, 1988), as well as additional research cited in chapters 2 and 6 of this volume, do offer several conclusions about scores from accommodated admissions testing:

1. Scores from accommodated and standard administrations are comparable in terms of reliability.
2. Scores generally represent the same or comparable cognitive abilities and are not distorted by the disability or the accommodation in most instances, although cognitive constructs (e.g., math and verbal reasoning) appear less related for these students.
3. There is little to no evidence that items are differentially more difficult or less difficult for most modifications.
4. Students with disabilities generally score well below other students completing admissions tests, and their predicted grades are slightly lower than are those of students without disabilities.
5. The relationship between admissions test scores and high school grades with college grades is typically weaker for students with disabilities (especially for students with learning disabilities) than it is for students without disabilities, and

other factors beyond test scores and grades may play a larger part in the ultimate success of students with disabilities attending institutions of higher education.

6. When test scores are used alone with students with disabilities, there is a substantial risk of error. For example, hearing-impaired students are likely to do much better than predicted (called "under-prediction"), whereas students with learning disabilities are likely to perform much more poorly than predicted (called "overprediction"). However, when previous grades and test scores are used together, performance will be as accurately predicted for students with disabilities as it is for students without disabilities.

7. Extended time is the primary reason for overprediction of college performance for students with learning disabilities (Braun et al., 1988; Camara et al., 1998; Wightman, 1993; Willingham et al., 1988; Ziomek & Andrews, 1998).

Test users could benefit by paying special attention to the use of test scores and other admissions materials from students with disabilities. If excessive weight, in the form of minimum scores or cut scores, is applied to admissions tests completed by students with disabilities, there is increased risk of decision errors because of the weaker relationship between test scores and high school grades with college performance for these students. Students with disabilities are more likely to have more pronounced and distinctive academic or cognitive strengths and weaknesses, and these should be carefully considered in admissions. It is especially important to look beyond admissions test scores to previous grades, grade-point average, quality of courses completed, and other academic indicators when evaluating the probability of academic success for students with disabilities.

CONCLUSION

Many persons with disabilities go to college, graduate, and professional schools, and increased numbers of such persons are identifying themselves as in need of accommodations on admissions tests. Three areas that are likely to have significant implications for students requiring testing accommodations in the future include (a) accommodations available through technology, (b) test design and development issues related to access and interface for persons with disabling conditions, and (c) access.

Bennett (1995) noted that computer-based testing (CBT) offers substantial promise in providing task comparability for students with various types of disabilities. CBT offers more than an additional mode of testing for students unable to hold a pencil. "Those who can't read text can have it directed to a speech synthesizer, Braille printer, or Braille display (as well as speech-readable forms and sign-language); and those with limited mobility can work, play, learn or communicate through electronic networks" (p. 8). Standardized presentation of tests through such a wide variation of modalities and features can reduce the uneven quality of human readers and interpreters. In addition, speech recognition and oral responses received by a computer are not permitted in any admissions testing program as of the time this chapter was written, yet commercial software has made these options more viable for admissions testing programs.

Although timing constraints remain in the current generation of CBT, primarily for economic reasons, as new delivery mediums arrive (e.g., Web-based delivery, school-based testing) time constraints may be relaxed for all students, removing extended time as the primary source of noncomparability—all students can have a generous amount of extended time to complete the test.

Automated item generation or item cloning may permit near simultaneous generation of similar items across multiple modalities. Research is exploring alternative methods of generating several test items based on a single item and on measurement models that permit us to estimate item-level data. Test makers may ultimately be able to produce equivalent forms of tests with little or no pretesting of items. In much the same ways, technology may help identify items that may and may not translate easily to Braille, speech synthesizer, or other modalities, thereby eliminating some of the existing inefficiencies in developing alternative forms of current tests retrospectively. Currently four major admissions testing programs are operating or plan to operate CBT (i.e., GRE, GMAT, LSAT, TOEFL). Additional research on the impact of seemingly minor accommodations available through CBT on test performance may also change our assumptions about task comparability (e.g., verbally describing certain geometric figures may change the construct measured and difficulty of an item) and how we modify testing to accommodate students with disabilities.

Finally, the Web may offer greater access to persons with physical disabilities who either experience difficulty in getting to test centers or test at home at great expense to testing programs. Even if Web-based delivery remains impractical for most students because of security concerns, exceptions may be made for students with disabilities providing that a proctor is onsite. Soon score reports will be available on the Web, and all students will have more immediate access to their scores, even within existing paper-based testing.

REFERENCES

American Association of Collegiate Registrars and Admissions Officers (AACRAO) and the American Council on Education (ACE). (1978). *Re-*

cruitment, admissions, and handicapped students: A guide for compliance with Section 504 of the Rehabilitation Act of 1973. Washington, DC: Author.

American Association of Collegiate Registrars and Admissions Officers (AACRAO); ACT, Inc.; the College Board; Educational Testing Service; and National Association of College Admissions Counselors. (1995). Challenges in college admissions: A report of a survey of undergraduate admissions policies, practices, and procedures. Washington, DC: Author.

Association on Higher Education and Disability (AHEAD). (July, 1997). Guidelines for documentation of a learning disability in adolescents and adults. Columbus, OH: AHEAD.

Bennett, R. (1995). Computer-based testing for examinees with disabilities: On the road to generalized accommodations. Unpublished manuscript.

Braun, H., Ragosta, M., & Kaplan, B. (1988). Predictive validity. In W. Willingham, M. Ragosta, R. E. Bennett, H. Braun, D. A. Rock, & D. E. Powers (Eds.), Testing handicapped persons (pp. 109–132). Boston: Allyn and Bacon.

Camara, W. J., Copeland, T., & Rothchild, B. (1998). Effects of extended time on the SAT I: Reasoning test score growth for students with learning disabilities (College Board Research Report (98–7)). New York: College Board.

Educational Testing Service (ETS). (2001, Jan. 24). ETS agrees with disability groups to stop "flagging" on graduate admissions tests [On-line]. Available at www.ets.org/aboutets/news/01020701.html.

Heaney, K. J., & Pullin, D. C. (1998). Accommodations and flags: Admission testing and the rights of individuals with disabilities. Educational Assessment, 5(2), 71–93.

HEATH. (1995). Getting ready for college: Advising high school students with learning disabilities. Washington, DC: American Council on Education.

Henderson, C. (1995). College freshmen with disabilities: A triennial statistical profile. Washington, DC: American Council on Education.

Lewis, L., & Farris, E. (1999). An institutional perspective on students with disabilities in postsecondary education (NCES 1999–046). Washington, DC: U.S. Department of Education, Office of Educational Research and Improvement.

Mandinach, E. B., Cahalan, C., & Camara, W. J. (in press). The impact of flagging on the admissions process: Policies, practices and implications. College Board Research Report Series. New York: College Board.

May, D. C. (1984) Admission of students with learning disabilities into college. Policies and Requirements. Journal of College Admissions, 17, 11–19.

Mazzeo, J., Carlson, J. E., Voelkl, K. E., & Lutkus, A. D. (1999). Increasing participation of special needs students in NAEP: A report on 1996 research activities (NCES 2000-473). Washington, DC: National Center for Educational Statistics.

Mehrens, W. A. (1997, July 24). Flagging test scores: Policy, practice and research. Paper presented at the National Research Council Workshop on Flagging Admissions Tests, Washington, DC.

Pullin, D. C., & Heaney, K. J. (1997). The use of "flagged" test scores in college and university admissions: Issues and implications under Section 504 of the

Rehabilitation Act and the Americans With Disabilities Act. *Journal of College and University Law, 23*(4), 797–828.

Sherman, S., & Robinson, N. (1982). *Ability testing and handicapped people: Dilemma for government, science and the public.* Washington, DC: National Academy Press.

Whitney, D. (1989). Educational admissions and placement. In R. L. Linn (Ed.), *Educational Measurement* (pp. 515–526). New York: American Council on Education/Macmillan.

Wightman, L. (1993). *Test takers with disabilities: A summary of data from special administrations of the LSAT* (Research Report 93–03). Newtown, PA: Law School Admissions Council and Law School Admission Services.

Willingham, W. W., Ragosta, M., Bennett, R. E., Braun, H., Rock, D. A., & Powers, D. E. (1988). *Testing handicapped people.* Boston: Allyn and Bacon.

Ziomek, R. L., & Andrews, K. M. (1996). *Predicting the college grade point average of special-tested students from their ACT assessment scores and high school grades* (ACT Research Report No. 96-7). Iowa City: ACT.

Ziomek, R. L., & Andrews, K. M. (1998). *ACT assessment score gains of special-tested students who tested at least twice* (ACT Research Report No. 98-8). Iowa City: ACT.

V

EMPLOYMENT, CERTIFICATION, AND LICENSING

12

TESTING INDIVIDUALS WITH DISABILITIES IN THE EMPLOYMENT CONTEXT: AN OVERVIEW OF ISSUES AND PRACTICES

WANDA J. CAMPBELL AND HEATHER ROBERTS FOX

Title I of the Americans With Disabilities Act (ADA) prohibits employment discrimination against qualified individuals with disabilities. The act extends its protections not only to employment opportunities but also to the processes used to select candidates. Organizations subject to the ADA include private and public employers as well as employment agencies and labor organizations. To benefit from the protections afforded by the act, a candidate must have, be perceived to have, or have a record of a disability that substantially limits a major life activity and be able to perform the essential functions of the job with or without accommodation.

This chapter addresses four key aspects of the ADA as it applies to employment tests: (a) definition of a "qualified individual with a disability"; (b) "essential functions of the job"; (c) employment tests that can withstand scrutiny under the act and those that are prohibited; and (d) types of accommodations and considerations when granting them. We begin with the definition of a qualified individual with a disability, because this is central to the act, and no other consideration is relevant to the act in the absence of such a person. The identification of essential job functions parallels in many ways the job analysis procedure, which is a critical component in the development of valid employment tests. A number of different types of employment tests are discussed relative to the provisions of the ADA and the interpretive guidance issued by the Equal Employment Opportunity Commission (EEOC). Once the essential job functions have been identified and a valid employment test has been developed and implemented, the issue of reasonable accommodations presents itself. There are a number of types of accommodations available. Each of the accommodations are described in turn, along with considerations in choosing those that reduce the effects of the disability while yielding useful information in making the selection decision.

QUALIFIED INDIVIDUAL WITH A DISABILITY

Although many physical and mental impairments can be classified as disabilities under the ADA, only a qualified individual with a disability is protected by the act. "Qualified individual with a disability" refers to an employee or job applicant who meets the applicable qualification standards *and* is able to perform the essential functions of the job, with or without the employer making a reasonable accommodation for that disability.

Qualification standards may include requisite skill, experience, education, licenses, credentials, or other job-related requirements of an employment position that the individual seeks. An employer is not required to hire an individual who does not have the necessary qualifications to perform the job. However, qualification standards or selection criteria that screen out an individual with a disability or a class of such individuals on the basis of disability must be job-related and consistent with business necessity. Further, the ADA requires that even if a qualification standard *is* job-related and consistent with business necessity, it may not be used to exclude an individual with a disability if this individual could satisfy the legitimate standard with a reasonable accommodation. Given this standard, an employer should first establish that the applicant's qualifications satisfy the minimum job prerequisites before evaluating whether or not the applicant can perform the essential job functions with or without reasonable accommodation. This step is often referred to as determining if an individual with a disability is "otherwise qualified." Of course, such standards must be applied uniformly to all candidates—those with disabilities and those without.

Requiring the ability to perform "essential functions" of the job ensures that an individual with a disability will not be considered unqualified simply because of inability to perform marginal or incidental job functions.

If the individual is qualified to perform essential job functions except for limitations caused by a disability, the employer must consider whether the individual could perform these functions with a "reasonable accommodation." Relative qualifications of candidates must be compared assuming that the candidate will be provided a reasonable accommodation.

"Essential functions of the job" and "reasonable accommodations" are the two key aspects of nondiscrimination under the act. These concepts are more complex in nature, involving a large degree of subjectivity, and thus are considered in more detail next.

ESSENTIAL FUNCTIONS OF THE JOB

The ADA legislation does not define the term "essential job functions"; however, the EEOC regulations state that they are "fundamental job duties of the employment position the individual with a disability holds or desires" (29 C.F.R. Pt. 1630). In the employment context, a qualified individual with a disability must be able to perform the essential functions of the job with or without reasonable accommodation. Essential functions do not include marginal functions or those that the employer would *like* to have the employee perform. An employer may prefer to have a secretary who has a driver's license, so that he or she may occasionally deliver documents to clients, but if it is not considered an essential function of that job, an employer cannot consider it during the selection process.

The inquiry into whether a particular function is essential initially addresses whether the employer actually requires employees in the position to perform the functions that are identified as essential. If the individual who holds the position is actually required to perform a particular function, the inquiry will then focus on whether removing the function will fundamentally alter the position. This determination of whether or not a particular job function is essential will generally include one or more of the following factors described in the EEOC regulations.

Factors the EEOC Will Consider

The first factor is whether the reason the position exists is *to perform a specific function*. The EEOC's (1992) technical assistance manual provides the following example: An employer plans to hire someone for the sole purpose of proofreading documents. The ability to proofread the documents is an essential function of that job, because that is the only reason the position exists.

The second factor in determining whether a function is essential is *the number of other employees available to perform that job function, or among whom the performance of that job function can be distributed*. This may be a factor because either the total number of employees is low or because of the fluctuating demands of business operation.

The third factor is *the degree of expertise or skill required to perform the function*. In certain professions and highly skilled positions employees are hired for their expertise or their ability to perform the particular function. In such situations, the performance of that specialized task would be an essential function.

Evidence the EEOC Will Consider

The *employer's judgment* regarding which functions are essential and *written job descriptions* that were prepared before the position was advertised or applicants were interviewed for the position are key sources of evidence of essential functions identified in the act. However, the legislative history of the ADA indicates that Congress did not intend for these to be the only types of evidence introduced for determining whether a function is essential. Other kinds of evidence that the EEOC will consider include

- The amount of time spent on the job performing the function;
- The consequences of not requiring the incumbent to perform the function;
- The terms of a collective bargaining agreement;
- The work experience of past incumbents in the job; or
- The current work experience of incumbents in similar jobs.

The ADA and the EEOC interpretations give deference to the employer's judgment regarding which functions of a job are essential. Nevertheless, although the inquiry into essential functions is not intended to second guess an employer's business judgment with regard to production standards, whether qualitative or quantitative, nor to require employers to lower such standards, it is incumbent on the employer to demonstrate that its qualifications for a particular position are imposed on all employees in a position and were chosen for legitimate, nondiscriminatory reasons (U.S. Equal Opportunity Commission, 1992). Specifically, although an employer has the right to establish what a job is and what functions are necessary to perform the job activities adequately, the ADA requires that an individual with a disability be considered relative to the job's essential functions.

Identifying Worker Requirements

The preferred starting point for identifying worker requirements is to conduct a job analysis. It is important to note that the ADA does not require employers to develop or maintain job descriptions. However, a written job description that is prepared before recruiting, interviewing, or assessing applicants for a job would be considered as evidence along with other relevant factors. Whether or not the ADA legislative language mandates the development of job descriptions, the American Psychological Association, the Society for Industrial and Organizational Psychologists (SIOP), and many individuals recommend a thorough job analysis as the foundation for a defensible selection system (AERA/APA/NCME, 1999; APA, 1995; Fischer, 1994; Klimoski & Palmer, 1994; SIOP, 1987; Martin, Jones, & McDonald, 1992).

Job analysis often involves a selection specialist who may observe the work performed, conduct interviews with current employees who perform the job in question or their supervisors, examine the environment in which the work is performed, or administer a carefully constructed questionnaire to identify the job duties. A comprehensive job analysis questionnaire may include (a) a description of the duties of the job, (b) an evaluation of the difficulty level of the duties, (c) a consideration of the physical or environmental setting, and (d) ratings of the importance or frequency of each duty. Evaluating whether or not a task is considered an essential function of the job should involve a careful analysis of the most difficult tasks, the most important tasks, and the most time-consuming tasks. The information should then be incorporated into current job descriptions before initiating the selection process. Job descriptions should be reviewed and updated before advertising, recruiting, interviewing, or testing for the position to make sure they accurately reflect the essential functions of a job. When an organization fails to maintain accurate and current job descriptions, their recruiting and selection efforts may be subject to legal risks.

EMPLOYMENT TESTS

For an employment test to be defensible, it must measure knowledge, skills, or abilities that are used on the job or that predict job performance. Employment tests may be used singularly or in combination, depending on the requirements of the job and the preferences of the organization. Four types of employment tests are described in this section: (a) medical exams, (b) physical ability tests, (c) cognitive ability tests, and (d) personality tests.

Medical Exams

The ADA clearly prohibits the use of medical exams before issuing a conditional offer of employment (EEOC, 2000). This restriction does not mean that medical exams cannot be used. What it does mean is that it is necessary to determine first whether the candidate meets all of the other selection criteria. If so, an offer of employment may be extended conditional on the passage of a medical exam. Requiring the passage of a medical exam even at the postoffer stage is only appropriate if the measures taken are related to job success. Wanting a healthy workforce is not a defensible justification for using a medical exam as a selection tool.

Physical Ability Tests

The ADA permits the use of physical ability tests so long as the test does not involve physiological or biological measures. Thus, a candidate may be required to perform actual or simulated job tasks such as lifting or running, but may not have measures of blood pressure or heart rate taken in connection with these activities.

A concern with the use of physical ability tests is that the candidate may be injured by the test itself. Employers may require candidates to provide medical certificates from a physician indicating their ability to perform the physical ability test safely. The medical inquiry must be limited to the ability to perform the task safely and must not elicit other medical information. Employers may also require candidates to agree to assume liability in the event that they are injured while performing a physical ability test. Still another alternative is to administer physiological and physical ability tests postoffer. With this latter alternative, an organization could have its own medical team attest to the safety of administering the physical ability test to the candidate.

Cognitive Ability Tests

Cognitive ability tests are very popular because, when appropriately developed and validated, they are often defensible, cost-effective, and efficient to administer. The constructs measured are those found to be predictive of job success because of their linkage to important or frequently performed tasks and responsibilities.

Unidimensionality has always been a highly valued characteristic of a test because it reduces ambiguity concerning what is being measured. Unidimensionality has become even more important since the passage of the ADA, because the accommodation process becomes more complicated to the extent that multiple constructs are measured. For example, a candidate with dyslexia may have mathematical ability assessed more effectively with a test that does not use word problems.

Another factor to consider with cognitive ability tests is speededness. It is difficult to make interpretable accommodations to a highly speeded test. If, however, speed is an essential part of the job, then there may be limits to the accommodations that may be made for the test and the job. Although many cognitive ability tests are predominantly power tests, time limits are often imposed for administrative purposes. The greater the importance of speed, the more difficult the interpretation of an accommodated test. This should not be construed as an endorsement for the elimination of time limits. There are limits to the amount of time an organization may devote to the administration of cognitive ability tests. When the incidence of requests for accommodation for an organization is low, it makes no sense to eliminate time limits on the chance that an accommodation involving extended time may be requested.

Personality Tests

Typically, personality tests do not have the time constraints associated with cognitive ability tests. Some personality tests, however, are considered medical exams and may only be administered after an offer of employment has been made (EEOC, 2000). Factors to consider in determining whether the test may be considered a medical exam are whether the test is designed to identify physical or mental impairments or results in a medical diagnosis, is typically administered or the results interpreted by a health professional, and whether the procedure is invasive. Based on these factors, tests such as the Minnesota Multiphasic Personality Inventory 2 and the Millon Clinical Multi-Axial Inventory (MCMI) would be viewed as medical exams because they may provide evidence that leads to diagnosis of a mental disorder (for example, those disorders listed in the American Psychiatric Association's most recent *Diagnostic and Statistical Manual of Mental Disorders (DSM-IV)*). By contrast, many personality tests that are designed to be used by employers to measure job-related characteristics such as sociability or conscientiousness are not viewed as medical exams. Even measures of emotional stability are permissible so long as the focus is on differences within the working population at large and not on distinctions between clinical and nonclinical populations. The distinction is that personality tests that are not considered to be medical exams were designed to predict success on the job and were not developed to provide insight into possible physical and mental impairments.

REASONABLE ACCOMMODATIONS

The ADA imposes an affirmative obligation to provide reasonable accommodations to disabled individuals on their jobs and in the selection process. The EEOC guidance is available to employers on reasonable accommodations and undue hardship applicable to the hiring process (EEOC, 1999). The purpose of the accommodation during the selection process is to reduce the distortion in the scores that is caused by the disability. Total elimination of error as a result of the disability is a laudable goal but one that eludes us given the current state of science.

It is useful to distinguish between accommodations that are likely to alter the psychometric interpretation of the test scores and those that do not. An example of an innocuous accommodation is altering the height of a table to accommodate a wheelchair.

Nester (1984, 1993) categorized psychometrically complex accommodations as modifications to the testing medium, time limits, and test content. These modifications are ordered in terms of the severity of the threat to the psychometric interpretation.

Modifying the Testing Medium

The *test medium* refers to the mode of delivery of the test to the candidate. Braille, enlarged print, the use of a reader or an audiocassette are all examples of modifications to the testing medium.

Braille

Translating test material to Braille is analogous to translating a test to a foreign language. Grade 2 Braille is typically used for test materials because it may be read more quickly than Grade 1 Braille.

For security reasons, it is recommended that translations be performed by an organization with an established record of performing such translations. Even so, it is recommended that an independent specialist in services to the blind should review the translation to ensure correspondence with the original material. Graphic and spatial material can be problematic. Tabular information may also be a challenge, with some blind candidates preferring Braille tables and others preferring a linear presentation.

Care should be taken in the transport and storage of Braille material to ensure that the embossed dots are not flattened. Braille material should be cushioned in a package when transported and care should be taken not to place heavy items on top of them. Stacking Braille tests should be avoided.

Enlarged Print

Enlarged print is useful for visually impaired candidates. Enlargement may be accomplished by a professional organization, use of a photocopier with enlargement capabilities, or printing copies of a test with a larger font size. It is helpful to show the candidate a sample of different font sizes from which to choose before enlarging the text, if possible. Enlargement of text may affect the pagination. It is preferable to have more pages than to have awkward or illogical page breaks (e.g., such as breaks in the middle of an extended item).

Enlarged tests may require larger than normal work surfaces and additional time to manipulate the pages. It is also important to remember that the circles that are typically blackened are also enlarged, and the instruction to completely blacken in the circles must be changed. Frequently, candidates place a mark in the circle to indicate their choice of response. If the responses on the enlarged test are transferred to a standard-sized test for scanning, the transference should be done by one staff member and checked by a second member of the staff. The original enlarged version of the test should be retained in the event that there are questions about the responses.

Enlarged print may be problematic when the test is administered on a computer, because the candidate is able to see less of the information on the screen than other candidates. The largest monitor available should be used, and increases in the amount of administration time may be required.

Readers

Reading a test to a candidate is a tedious and time-consuming task that can wear on the patience of both the candidate and the reader. Readers must be able to read well and speak clearly and should be familiar with any technical terms or forms of notation used in the test. Readers should be trained test administrators and not friends or relatives of the candidate. It is useful for the reader to work with the candidate before the beginning of the test to determine what is to be read (e.g., reading passages and instructions but not labels) and ensure that the candidate is comfortable with the pace. In the future, computerized screen readers may replace live readers.

Modifying Time Limits

Extended time is the most frequently requested accommodation and is often used in combination with other accommodations. Providing extra time also affects the psychometric properties and interpretation of test scores.

This accommodation is most appropriate if the test is a power test or a noncognitive test, such as a personality test. If there is a speeded component to the test, then additional time may not be advisable because speed is part of what is measured.

Extended time is most often granted for double time or less. Adopting a policy regarding maximum administration times should be avoided, because it does not take into account the individual needs of the candidate. Some candidates may actually require three times the normal administration time. One solution is to base the accommodation on the recommendation made by an appropriate professional who documented the disability at the candidate's request. Another possibility is to tie the time extension to the essential functions of the job. If the job is one where time is a critical component, then adjustments to time may be governed by these requirements. Organizations wishing to deny extended time on the basis of essential job functions should be prepared with documentation to support their position.

Modifying Test Content

Many accommodations involving changes to the test have a substantial impact on the psychometric interpretation of the test results. Most organizations do not have the resources to develop alternative versions of the test for blind or hearing-impaired candidates. Some organizations waive those test components that cannot be accommodated for the candidate's disability, a practice that poses a few problems. If the test is measuring a construct that is essential for the performance of the job, then waiving the test is inappropriate. As an example, waiving a test dealing with spatial relationships in a graphical format for a job as a draftsperson would be inappropriate because of the inherent nature of the job. In other cases, such as the translation of written material to Braille, the test and the job may both be accommodated to enable the candidate with a disability to perform the essential job functions.

It should be remembered that waiving a test deprives the organization of useful information concerning the candidate's ability. Although waivers may be feasible when a test battery is designed for selecting candidates to a small number of jobs, waivers pose a problem when a test battery is used for a wide range of jobs (e.g., all clerical jobs in an organization). Waiving a component may require that the organization restrict the jobs for which candidates may be considered to prevent them from moving into jobs that require the abilities that were measured by the waived tests.

Another time-consuming alternative used by some organizations is to create a work sample to determine the candidate's ability to perform the essential functions of the job. When such alternatives are used, one must also establish a criterion by which to judge success on the work sample. This alternative is sometimes used for jobs where success is judged by the ability to perform the task.

Some organizations may choose to hire the disabled candidate on an extended probationary period. A disadvantage of this approach is that if the candidate is not satisfactory, the decision is one of termination, not failure to hire. In many ways this last approach is tantamount to waiving the test. This alternative is typically a last resort and one used infrequently by organizations. It is a solution that we do not recommend because it, like waiver decisions, may jeopardize the business necessity defense of the selection procedure.

Combining Types of Accommodations

It is often necessary to adopt combinations of the accommodations described in the previous sections. For example, modifications to the testing medium also often entail extensions of the time limits. Braille takes longer to read than the printed word; enlarged print on a computer monitor reduces the amount of material that can be presented; readers must communicate with the candidate about such matters as which material should be repeated, and portions of an audiotaped test may need to be replayed. Thus, the practitioner must always be alert to the possible necessity of combining various types of accommodations to best meet the needs of the candidate.

CONCLUSION

In passing the landmark Americans With Disabilities Act in 1990, Congress intended to level the playing field for individuals with disabilities by ending discrimination in the workplace and employing qualified individuals to their fullest potential. Little research has been devoted to establishing comparability of examination scores for individuals with disabilities; however, it is important that employers and selection specialists not be intimidated by the law. The use of tests in the preemployment settings offer valuable, objective information to the employer that can be used to compare qualified candidates before the employer must choose among them.

Passage of the ADA has forced organizations to make substantial changes in the way they evaluate and accommodate individuals with disabilities. Applicants with physical and mental disabilities must be evaluated and accommodated with individualized reviews and resolutions. However, with some forethought to the purpose and nature of the test, a well as the setting within which it is given, employers will be able to ensure the integrity of their selection system and will have confidence in their ability to select qualified individuals.

REFERENCES

Americans With Disabilities Act. (1990). 42 U.S.C. § 12101.

American Educational Research Association, American Psychological Association, and National Council on Measurement in Education (AERA/APA/NCME). (1999). *Standards for educational and psychological testing.* Washington, DC: American Educational Research Association.

American Psychological Association. (1995, November). ADA confounds use of psychological testing. *APA Monitor*, 12.

Fischer, R. J. (1994). The Americans With Disabilities Act: Implications for measurement. *Educational Measurement: Issues and Practice, 13*(3), 17–26, 37.

Klimoski, R., & Palmer, S. N. (1994). *The ADA and the hiring process in organizations. Implications of the Americans With Disabilities Act for psychology.* Washington, DC: American Psychological Association and Springer.

Martin, S. L., Jones, J. W., & McDonald, J. A. (1992). *Americans With Disabilities Act: Personnel selection under the ADA.* Rosemont, IL: London House.

Nester, M. A. (1984). Employment testing for handicapped people. *Public Personnel Management, 13,* 417–434.

Nester, M. A. (1993). Psychometric testing and reasonable accommodation for persons with disabilities. *Rehabilitation Psychology, 38*(2), 75–85.

Society for Industrial and Organizational Psychology (SIOP). (1987). *Principles for the validation and use of personnel selection procedures* (3rd ed.). College Park, MD: Author.

U.S. Equal Employment Opportunity Commission (EEOC). (1992). *A technical assistance manual on the employment provisions (Title I) of the Americans With Disabilities Act.* Washington, DC: U.S. Government Printing Office.

U.S. Equal Employment Opportunity Commission (EEOC). (1999). *Enforcement guidance: Reasonable accommodation and undue hardship under the Americans With Disabilities Act.* Washington, DC: Government Printing Office.

U.S. Equal Employment Opportunity Commission. (2000). *EEOC enforcement guidance on disability-related inquiries and medical examinations of employees under the Americans With Disability Act.* Washington, DC: Author.

U.S. Equal Employment Opportunity Commission. (1991, July 26). *Equal employment opportunity for individuals with disabilities; Final Rule.* 29 C.F.R. Pt. 1630.

13

DISABILITY NONDISCRIMINATION IN THE EMPLOYMENT PROCESS: THE ROLE FOR TESTING PROFESSIONALS

SUSANNE M. BRUYÈRE

The focus of this chapter is the role of testing professionals, such as psychologists and other health care providers, in minimizing discrimination and maximizing opportunities for persons with disabilities in the employment process, particularly as it relates to the requirements of the employment provisions (Title I) of the Americans With Disabilities Act of 1990 (ADA). (See chapter 1, this volume, for an overview of the ADA Title II.)[1] An understanding of the basic definitions and key concepts of this disability nondiscrimination legislation is essential for all those interested in the place of testing in the employment process as it relates to persons with disabilities.

This manuscript has been prepared with the assistance of a grant to Cornell University from the U.S. Department of Education, National Institute on Disability and Rehabilitation Research titled, "Improving Employment Practices Covered by Title I of the ADA" (Grant #H133A70005). For further information, contact the author.

[1]A complete copy of a report on this research is available on-line at the Cornell University website: www.ilr.cornell.edu/ped

OVERVIEW OF THE ADA EMPLOYMENT PROVISIONS

In this section we will provide an overview of the ADA requirements, including determining who are covered entities; a definition of disability; the definition of reasonable accommodation under the law, and some examples of workplace accommodations; and an overview of the concepts of direct threat and undue hardship under the ADA.

Covered Entities

ADA Title I applies to private employers with at least 15 employees and to state and local government employers. Title I also specifically includes labor organizations and joint labor–management committees, along with employers, as "covered entities." Labor unions are covered both as employers and as bargaining agents under federal labor laws.

Definition of Disability

The ADA protects qualified individuals with disabilities from discrimination. A "qualified individual with a disability" is a person who meets the necessary prerequisites for a job and can perform the essential job functions with or without reasonable accommodation (EEOC, 1997a). The ADA has a three-part definition of "disability." This definition is not the same as the definition of disability in other laws, such as state workers' compensation laws or other federal or state laws that provide benefits for people with disabilities. Under the ADA, an individual with a disability is a person who

- Has a physical or mental impairment that substantially limits one or more major life activities;
- Has record of such an impairment; or
- Is regarded as having such an impairment. (U.S. EEOC, 1992, p. I-3)

Reasonable Accommodation

A *reasonable accommodation* is any modification or adjustment to a job, an employment practice, or the work environment that makes it possible for a qualified individual with a disability to participate in the job application process, perform the essential functions of a job, or enjoy the benefits and privileges of employment equal to those enjoyed by employees without disabilities.

Accommodations relevant to testing situations are presented in chapter 3. Some examples of common types of accommodations in the workplace suggested by the statute and the Equal Employment Opportunity Commission's (EEOC) guidance include making facilities readily accessible to and usable by an individual with a disability; restructuring a job by reallocating or redistributing marginal job functions; altering when or how an essential job function is performed; providing part-time or modified work schedules; obtaining or modifying equipment or devices; modifying examinations, training materials, or policies; providing qualified readers and interpreters; reassignment to a vacant position; permitting use of accrued paid leave or unpaid leave for necessary treatment; providing reserved parking for a person with a mobility impairment; and allowing an employee to provide equipment or devices that an employer is not required to provide.

In March 1999, the EEOC released comprehensive policy guidance on reasonable accommodations and undue hardship under the Americans With Disabilities Act. The following ADA issues are addressed in the guidance:

- The responsibility of individuals with disabilities to request reasonable accommodation and the way an employer should respond to a request;
- The circumstances under which employers may ask for documentation showing the need for reasonable accommodation;
- Reasonable accommodations for job applicants;
- Reasonable accommodations to provide access to employer-sponsored training programs, services, and social functions;
- New information on many types of reasonable accommodations, including job restructuring, unpaid leave, part-time schedules, modified workplace policies, and reassignment;
- The relationship between the obligation to provide leave as a reasonable accommodation under the ADA and the requirements of the Family Medical Leave Act (FMLA);
- Changes that employers are not required to make to a job, such as lowering production standards or removing a primary job duty; and
- Those instances in which employers may deny a request for a reasonable accommodation because it imposes an undue hardship.

A complete copy of the guidance can be obtained from the EEOC Website at www.eeoc.gov or by writing to the EEOC.

Direct Threat

An employer may require a qualification standard that an individual not pose a "direct threat" to the health or safety of the individual or others. A health or safety risk can only be considered if it is "a significant risk of substantial harm" (U.S. EEOC, 1992, p. IV-9). Employers cannot deny an employment opportunity merely because of a slightly increased risk. An assessment of direct threat must be based strictly on valid medical analyses or other objective evidence and not on speculation (U.S. Equal Opportunity Commission, 1992). Like any qualification standard, this requirement must apply to all applicants and employees, not just to people with disabilities.

If an employee appears to pose a direct threat because of a disability, the employer must first try to eliminate or reduce the risk to an acceptable level with reasonable accommodation. If an effective accommodation cannot be found, the employer may refuse to hire an applicant or discharge an employee who poses a direct threat.

Undue Hardship

An employer is not required to provide an accommodation if it will impose an undue hardship on the operation of its business. Undue hardship is defined by the ADA as an action that is "excessively costly, extensive, substantial, or disruptive, or that would fundamentally alter the nature operation of the business" (EEOC, 1992, p. I-6; EEOC, 1999). In determining undue hardship, factors to be considered include the nature and cost of the accommodation in relation to the size, the financial resources, the nature, and the structure of the employer's operation, as well as the impact of the accommodation on the specific facility providing the accommodation.

THE EMPLOYMENT PROCESS AND THE ADA

The employment provisions of the ADA make it unlawful to discriminate on the basis of disability in a wide range of employment-related actions, including recruitment, job application, hiring, advancement, compensation, benefits, training, and discharge. Title I prohibits both intentional discrimination and also employment practices with discriminatory effect. Specifically, it is unlawful for a covered entity to

- Limit, segregate, or classify an individual in a way that adversely affects employment opportunities on the basis of the individual's disability;
- Participate in a contractual arrangement that has the effect of discriminating against an applicant or employee on account of disability;
- Deny equal jobs or benefits based on an individual's relationship or association with someone with a known disability;

- Fail to make a reasonable accommodation to the known physical or mental limitations of a qualified individual with a disability unless making the accommodation would be an "undue hardship" for the covered entity;
- Deny an employment opportunity because of the need to provide reasonable accommodation;
- Use criteria or tests that tend to exclude individuals with disabilities from employment opportunities, unless the selection criteria and methods are job-related and justified by business necessity; and
- Retaliate against an individual for asserting ADA rights.

In addition, Title I limits the use of both preemployment and postemployment medical examinations and inquiries. An individual with a disability may be subjected to a preemployment medical examination and inquiry only after a conditional offer of employment has been made and only if all entering employees in the job category are subjected to such an examination or inquiry regardless of disability. Postemployment medical examinations and inquiries must be job-related and consistent with business necessity. Employee medical information is to be maintained separately from other personnel information, treated in a confidential manner, and shared only with (a) supervisors and managers who need to know about necessary restrictions on the work duties of the employee and necessary accommodations; (b) first aid and safety personnel, if the disability might require emergency medical treatment; and (c) government officials investigating compliance with the ADA.

EMPLOYERS' REMAINING CHALLENGES IN IMPLEMENTING THE ADA

The employment provisions of the ADA have been in effect for employers of 15 or more employees since July 1994.[2] Thus, most employers have had now more than seven years experience in implementing the ADA. With time and experience, employers, particularly larger employers with more resources, have been able to respond to the law's numerous requirements and change policies and practices accordingly. Challenges remain, however, in certain facets of the employment process, as evidenced by the continued lower unemployment rate for persons with disabilities (U.S. Department of Education, 1998) and the claims of discrimination filed with the EEOC, the governmental body responsible for enforcing the ADA employment provisions. To be as effective as possible as consultants to business and industry in providing testing and other consultative services

---

[2]Employers of 15 or more employees have been covered as of July 26, 1994.

that may relate to applicants or employees with disabilities, psychologists can be assisted by becoming aware of this information about continuing employer challenges in implementing the ADA.

Of the more than 100,000 claims filed with the EEOC in the first six years since the ADA Title I became effective (as of September 30, 1998), more than half (52%) of the claims related to alleged unlawful discharge (see Table 13-1). The next most often cited complaint to the EEOC has been failure to accommodate (29%). With regard to the type of disabilities where claims are filed, the most prevalent disability is back injury (almost one in five or 17%), followed by emotional or psychiatric disability (14%).

During 1998, Cornell University, in collaboration with the Society for Human Resource Management (SHRM), conducted a survey of a random sample stratified by employer size of 1402 of the SHRM membership, on employer practices in response to the ADA employment provisions (SHRM, 1999). The Cornell University survey is a 10-page questionnaire,

TABLE 13-1
Total Number of ADA Charges Received by the EEOC:
July 26, 1992 through September 30, 1998

	Number	% of Total
Disabilities Most Often Cited		
Back impairments	18,242	16.7
Emotional psychiatric impairments	14,945	13.7
Neurological impairments	11,742	10.8
Extremities	10,448	9.6
Heart impairments	4,348	4.0
Diabetes	3,926	3.6
Substance abuse	3,233	3.0
Hearing impairments	3,101	2.8
Blood disorder	2,872	2.6
HIV (subcategory of blood disorder)	1,897	1.7
Vision impairment	2,767	2.5
Cancer	2,609	2.4
Asthma	1,877	1.7
ADA Violations Most Often Alleged		
Discharge	56,775	52.1
Failure to provide reasonable accommodation	31,886	29.3
Harassment	14,025	12.9
Hiring	10,281	9.4
Discipline	8,798	8.1
Layoff	4,683	4.3
Promotion	4,725	3.9
Benefits	4,179	3.8
Wages	3,821	3.5
Rehire	3,524	3.2
Suspension	2,501	2.3

Note: N = 108,939 charges.

which covers questions on employer response to the ADA across recruitment, interviewing, job screening and testing, hiring, promotion and staff development, accommodation practices, and the grievance, termination, and disability management processes. The survey had a response rate of 73 percent of the 1116 eligible respondents. The survey's results are thus based on the responses from the 813 human resource professionals who completed these telephone interviews conducted by the Cornell University Computer-Assisted Survey Team (CAST). Selected results of this survey provide most useful information for psychologists who want to contribute their skills in the preemployment testing or other facets of the employment process, where persons with disabilities are concerned.

For example, one of the items asked the degree of difficulty the human resource professionals experienced in making certain kinds of accommodations across the employment process. It is interesting to note that a smaller proportion of respondents indicated difficulty (9% said "difficult" or "very difficult") in modifying preemployment testing or changing interview questions to comply with the ADA's requirements. By comparison, many more respondents found it difficult or very difficult to know how to make information accessible for the hearing impaired (24%) or for the visually impaired (35%). Also seen as difficult or very difficult in a larger proportion of respondents (30%) was changing coworker or supervisor attitudes about applicants or employees with disabilities.

Other areas where testing professionals should educate themselves is the interplay with other employment and nondiscrimination legislation. Respondents to the Cornell survey indicated a significant degree of uncertainty about how the ADA interacts with the requirements of state workers' compensation legislation, the Family Medical Leave Act (FMLA), and the Occupational Safety and Health Act (OSH Act; Bruyère, 2000; SHRM, 1999).

Finally, of a list of 12 possible alternatives, private sector respondents chose "legal counsel," "safety staff," and "disability staff" as the top three resources to help resolve their ADA issues. This may tell testing professionals where the chief points of intervention may be when trying to make changes in the accommodation process or the culture of acceptance of persons with disabilities within a business organization.

TESTING PROFESSIONALS' CONTRIBUTION TO ADA IMPLEMENTATION

This section provides an overview of the many facets of the employment process where testing professionals can assist employers in clarifying their responsibilities under the ADA and minimize the likelihood of a discrimination complaint. This includes contributions in preemployment recruitment, screening, and testing processes; accommodation processes; promotional opportunities, staff development, and training; and disciplinary process, grievance procedure, and alternative dispute resolution. Excellent references on these topics are the EEOC related *Enforcement Guidances* released in 1999 and 2000 (EEOC, 1999, 2000).

Preemployment Recruitment, Screening, and Testing

Testing professionals can ensure equal access in recruitment for persons with disabilities and the preemployment screening and testing processes in a number of ways. In a shrinking labor pool, employers are increasingly looking to previously untapped labor sources, such as persons with disabilities. For employers who are interested in beginning to recruit persons with disabilities more effectively, testing professionals serving as consultants in this process can assist by learning the community agencies that provide job placement services. Every state has a publicly funded vocational rehabilitation agency dedicated to assisting people with disabilities in obtaining employment. Most communities also have not-for-profit and proprietary agencies that work with people with disabilities. High schools have school-to-work programs for students with disabilities. Employers can contact such agencies and schools to gain access to a pool of potential employees, get assistance in hiring and training workers with disabilities, and learn the facts about effective accommodation approaches. These agencies can also answer questions on legal and compliance issues, adaptive and assistive technology, and how to assess tax credits and other financial incentives for hiring employees from targeted groups. Often these agencies are identified in the white pages of telephone directories under government listings or the yellow pages under headings such as vocational rehabilitation or disability services.

Testing professionals may also contribute to the design of an approach that maximizes accessibility and minimizes disability discrimination in the recruitment, application, preemployment screening, and testing processes. An example is designing a checklist that covers the possible areas of needed accommodation for these processes, such as physical and communication access of recruiting, application, interviewing, and hiring processes. This can include reminders to have employment applications available in alternate formats (large print Braille and audiocassette) or to keep available a listing of agencies providing sign language interpreters. Or it might be a listing reminding those designing application forms or conducting in-person screening interviews of prohibited and acceptable questions that relate to job performance and disability issues. The contribution of the consultant might also be in selecting and administering tests appropriate to the job, not targeted to measuring the disability.

The Accommodation Process

Testing professionals can assist in the accommodation process for applicants and employees with disabilities in a number of ways: verification of whether the person is actually a covered person under the ADA; identification of appropriate accommodations for a particular disability; assistance in modification of a particular job or work space; assistance in modifications that include a change of supervisor's role, coworker interface, or the larger organizational culture; and dispute resolution.

When an accommodation request is made, one of the first questions that an employer, supervisor, or HR person may ask is whether the person is really a covered person under the ADA and therefore entitled to an accommodation. If not obvious, a health care provider's verification may be necessary. The person may be immediately under the care of a practitioner who can provide the needed verification, but this is not always the case. If a neurological or emotional–psychiatric disability, a psychologist or counselor might be an appropriate person to assist with verification. However, if another type of disability is in question, the testing professional may consult with the employer about who may help.

The next most often asked question in the accommodation process, once disability and impairment verification has occurred, is whether the accommodation requested is the most appropriate one. A psychologist may be the best person, depending on the disability and needed accommodation, to make an assessment in this instance, particularly if the disability is cognitive or psychological–emotional. Accommodation also might necessitate job–task redesign, work space redesign, or modification of the work environment. An adaptation to the workplace/work environment is an accommodation that is beyond the work station, such as access to the building bathroom, cafeteria, or other facility. In these instances, testing professionals might consult on a particular request with an industrial or safety engineer or a physical or occupational therapist.

Another role for the testing professional may be in assisting in the modification of the work culture as a whole, the approach of particular supervisors, or the interface with coworkers to make the workplace more receptive to the accommodation process and the needs of individual members who are persons with disabilities. This might include the need for dispute resolution as an added service to employers.

Promotional Opportunities, Staff Development, and Training

The testing professional can assist in the design of a nondiscriminatory process for persons with disabilities in accessing career and promotional opportunities. This might include looking at promotional practices retrospectively over a recent time period across all employees, including identified persons with disabilities. Or it might include proactively ensuring better access by building in periodic career assessments that include attention to persons with disabilities and a scrutinization of career development opportunities such as new responsibilities and training. Equal access to staff development opportunities may include equity in selection for staff development; accessibility of training facilities, accessibility of print and video materials, accessibility for persons with communication disabilities, and accommodations for persons with psychiatric or cognitive impairments.

Disciplinary Process, Grievance Procedures, and Alternative Dispute Resolution

Testing professionals can serve any number of roles in the disciplinary and grievance process with regard to the ADA. Some examples are assisting in the design of a grievance process when accommodation disputes occur; examining the existing grievance process for its viability as a place where these conflicts can be heard; designing an alternative dispute resolution process; and training supervisors, employees, and union leaders in the dispute resolution process.

Nondiscrimination for persons with disabilities also applies to the performance management and disciplinary action components of the employment process. An employer can hold employees with disabilities to the same standards of production–performance as other similarly situated employees without disabilities who are performing the essential functions (with or without reasonable accommodations) of a given job. However, an employer may not discipline or terminate an employee with a disability if the employer has refused to provide a requested accommodation that did not constitute an undue hardship and the reason for unsatisfactory performance was the lack of accommodation.

A consulting testing professional can assist human resource professionals and other employer agents who may be involved in the grievance and disciplinary process both as a preventative measure before claims occur and once a conflict situation has arisen. The human resource professionals or employer agents who may be involved in such a situation might be the employee or labor relations specialist, regional human resource unit managers, employee assistance program professionals, or ombudspersons. The testing professional can assist in the design of a grievance process when accommodation disputes occur as a proactive preventative measure to minimize conflicts. If an existing grievance process is in place, the testing professional can study its viability as a place where these conflicts can be heard. In addition, training can be designed and implemented for supervisors, employees, union leaders, and others who might be involved in the grievance or dispute resolution process within a particular business organization.

NEEDED SKILL AND KNOWLEDGE AREAS FOR TESTING PROFESSIONALS

The focus of this book is on testing and the role that testing professionals can play in providing and adapting testing for persons with disabilities. The purpose of this chapter is to provide background on the employment provisions of the ADA, its impact on employer practices broadly, and the resulting roles that testing professionals can play in helping employers to meet their responsibilities under the ADA. To provide this consultation role effectively, testing professionals must equip themselves with several knowledge and skills areas, such as the requirements of the ADA and subsequent clarification from EEOC guidance; accommodation in the testing process and reliability and validity considerations; accommodation for particular disabilities in the various facets of the employment process; knowledge of community organizations to assist persons with disabilities; knowledge of internal organizations or resource persons that can assist; interplay with other employment legislation; and alternative dispute resolution approaches in the accommodation process.

A brief overview of the ADA employment provisions is provided in this chapter. Further information can be obtained from the EEOC publications listed as references. Those interested in the area of psychiatric disability particularly might be interested in the EEOC publication on the ADA and psychiatric disabilities (1997b). Other authors in this book provide information on accommodation in the testing process and reliability and validity considerations. Other knowledge and skill areas relevant to the ADA and the functioning of psychologists are discussed in Crewe (1994) and Pape and Tarvydas (1994).

Accommodation for Particular Disabilities

Because each person with a disability is unique and each job situation also is unique, each accommodation request must be handled individually. However, with experience in a particular workplace and numerous persons requesting accommodations, accommodation alternatives become more easily identified. As discussed next, community resource organizations and internal company resources might also assist in this process. In addition, another valuable resource is the Job Accommodation Network (JAN),[3] funded by the President's Committee on Employment of People With Disabilities. JAN has a database of employers who have successfully adapted their workplaces to accommodate employees with disabilities. JAN responds to thousands of inquiries per year from employers requesting information on accommodations and similar questions.

---

[3]To reach the Job Accommodation Network, call 800/232-9675, or visit their Website: http://www.jan.wvu.edu/

Knowledge of Community Organizations

To assist employers who are addressing accommodations or other support needs of applicants or employees with disabilities, as well as the individuals themselves, psychologists should become familiar with the. resource organizations within their own communities that can help with particular concerns. As previously mentioned, for recruitment state vocational rehabilitation agencies[4] can help. These agencies, or other community rehabilitation programs, can also help identify appropriate accommodations and other support services. One of the accrediting agencies for these community rehabilitation programs is CARF, the Rehabilitation Accreditation Commission. This accreditation organization now has almost 25,000 programs/services in its roster of accredited programs.[5]

Independent living centers are designed to serve a cross-disability constituency with information and referral services, peer counseling, independent living skills training, and individual and systems advocacy. They may also help identify sources of transportation, accessible or supported housing, home independent living, legal advisement, or other supports.[6]

Knowledge of Internal Organizations or Resource Persons

Often business organizations themselves, particularly in larger companies, have many resources that can be tapped for assistance in the design of an appropriate accommodation. Human resource professionals provide a wide variety of personnel support functions in organizations, and, therefore, are important professionals to consider when assessing accommodation needs. Compensation, benefits, and employee service programs, specifically, are the responsibility of the human resource department. Human resource professionals frequently also handle employment interviews, training, organization development, performance appraisal, disciplinary process, and productivity improvement. All of these areas could affect a person with a disability in the workforce.

Another internal resource for testing professionals working within business are Employee Assistance Programs (EAPs; Farkas, 1989). EAPs are an employee benefit designed to help employees and families of employees whose attendance and job performance are adversely affected by job stress,

---

[4]A particular state vocational rehabilitation agency's listing can be found in the telephone book, or a complete listing through the Council of State Administrators in Vocational Rehabilitation (CSVAR) at Executive Office, P.O. Box 3776, Washington, DC 20007; phone (202) 638-4634; fax (202) 333-5881.

[5]As of August 31, 2000. For further information about CARF, contact 4891 East Grant Road, Tucson, AZ 85712; Voice/TDD (520) 325-1104; fax (520) 318-1129, Website: www.carf.org.

[6]For further information contact: National Council on Independent Living (NCIL) at 2111 Wilson Blvd., Suite 405, Arlington, VA 22201; Phone (703) 525-3406; fax (793) 525-3409; e-mail at ncil@ncil.org, or visit www.ncil.org.

personal problems, or alcohol or substance abuse. EAPs may be housed internal to the business, or the services may be provided by a contract with an external agency. The earlier focus of EAP professionals has been on serving persons who have alcohol and drug addiction problems; these individuals may also be persons who are covered by the Americans With Disabilities Act of 1990. In addition, persons with disabilities of other kinds may also seek support from EAP professionals to help them when a disabling condition or serious illness affects their work and everyday functioning.

Health and safety engineers—industrial hygienists—ergonomic specialists or occupational health professionals may assist in redesigning a work station or assessing an environmental hazard. Ergonomics integrates knowledge derived from the human sciences to match jobs, systems, products, and environments to the physical and mental abilities and limitations of people. Some of the areas that industrial hygienists may get involved in include testing for and possibly removing toxic materials in the work environment; helping to limit disabilities as a result of repetitive and prolonged movement, such as typing at a keyboard, or sitting at a desk all day; and setting limits on exposure levels and providing guidelines for control of chemicals, noise, and radiation in the workplace.

Interplay With Other Employment Legislation

Knowing the regulatory requirements that requirements that surround the workplace and affect employer and employee behavior is necessary to function effectively as a consultant on disability-related issues in the workplace. The focus of much of the discussion of this chapter has been the ADA. However, understanding the FMLA, the OSH Act, state workers' compensation laws, and the National Labor Relations Act (NLRA) might also help the psychologist functioning as a consultant to the workplace. A more thorough treatment of the interplay between this legislation is presented in Bruyère and DeMarinis (1999).

The FMLA establishes a minimum labor standard with regard to leaves of absence for family or medical reasons for employers with 50 employees or more. Some employers raise questions about a perceived conflict between the FMLA provision allowing employers to ask for certification of a serious health condition and the ADA restrictions on disability-related inquiries by employees. The EEOC has responded with development of a fact sheet explaining the differences between the two pieces of legislation.[7]

The OSH Act of 1970 has as its core the recognition that every

---

[7]The EEOC fact sheet, the *Family and Medical Leave Act, the Americans With Disabilities Act, and Title VII of the Civil Rights Act* can be ordered by writing or calling the EEOC's office of Communications and Legislative Affairs at 1801 L St., NW, Washington, DC, 20507, telephone (202) 663-4900, TDD (202) 663-4494.

worker has a right to a workplace that is free from recognized hazards. Therefore, when a potential hazard is identified, the OSH Administration, through the Labor Department, develops a standard against which workplace practices or conditions should be measured. Some of the issues surrounding this legislation that may affect the functioning of consulting psychologists in the workplace is the interplay with prohibitions in employment screening, medical confidentiality of records, and accommodations required under the ADA.

Workers' compensation programs are government-sponsored and employer-financed systems for compensating employees who incur an injury or illness in connection with their employment. They are designed to ensure that employees who are injured on the job receive timely compensation for their losses without proof of fault. Workers' compensation laws allow employees, or their survivors, to file claims for economic losses as a result of work-related injuries or occupational diseases. Benefits provided under workers' compensation laws include medical care, disability payments, rehabilitation services, survivor benefits, and funeral expenses. Some of the areas for concern in this interplay of legislation relate to clarifying for individuals with disabilities and for employers some of the significant aspects of workers' compensation legislation as it relates to the protections provided by the ADA. These include such questions as whether an injured worker is a protected person under the ADA; when an employer can ask about a worker's previous workers' compensation claims; hiring persons with a history of an occupational injury and applying the direct-threat standard; reasonable accommodation for persons with disability-related occupational injuries; light-duty issues; and exclusive-remedy provisions in workers' compensation laws.

The NLRA protects workers from the effects of unfair labor practices by employers and requires employers to recognize and bargain collectively with a union that the workers elect to represent them (Gold, 1998). Among the main principles of the NLRA are the idea of exclusivity of representation, the policy against direct dealing, and the duty to provide information. Seniority rights gained through collective bargaining are also among the most valued benefits of having a unionized workplace. All of these areas may yield conflict for individuals seeking to invoke protection from laws such as the ADA (Bruyère, Gomez, & Handelmann, 1996).

Alternative Dispute Resolution Approaches

Section 513 of the ADA provides, "Where appropriate and to the extent authorized by law, the use of alternative means of dispute resolution, including settlement, negotiations, conciliation, facilitation, mediation, fact-finding, mini-trials, and arbitration, is encouraged to resolve disputes arising under this act" (1990, § 12212). In some ADA cases, mediation or other forms of dispute resolution may provide a swift, satisfying, and low-cost solution where conflicts arise surrounding an accommodation request or alleged disabilities discrimination. Testing professionals consulting in business organizations who are equipped to deal effectively with alternative dispute resolution may find a ready mechanism for their consultation services in resolving conflicts about accommodation issues in the work environment.

CONCLUSION

This chapter provides background about testing of persons with disabilities in the employment context and disability nondiscrimination considerations under the ADA. I have provided an overview of the requirements and key definitions of the ADA, together with a discussion of what appears to be the greatest challenges continuing for employers in implementing the ADA employment provisions. I have detailed the testing professional's potential contributions to preemployment recruitment, screening, and testing, as well as to the accommodation process, promotional opportunities, and the grievance process. I have provided some suggestions for enhanced skill and knowledge development to maximize services as a consultant in the area of disability nondiscrimination in the workplace. Resources for additional information include the EEOC, the Cornell University Program on Employment and Disability, School of Industrial and Labor Relations, and the Disability Business and Technical Assistance Center Website at www.adata.org and their ADA Information Hotline at 800-949-4232. In addition, chapter 16 provides additional resources.

REFERENCES

Americans With Disabilities Act. (1990). 42 U.S.C. § 12111–12213, Pub. L. No. 101–336.

Bruyère, S. (2000). *Disability employment policies and practices in private and federal sector organizations*. Ithaca, NY: Cornell University, School of Industrial and labor Relations, Extension Division, Program on Employment and Disability.

Bruyère, S., & DeMarinis, R. (1999). Legislation and rehabilitation service delivery. In M. Eisenberg, R. Glueckhauf, & H. Zaretsky (Eds.), *Medical aspects of disability: A handbook for the rehabilitation professional* (pp. 679–695). New York: Springer.

Bruyère, S., Gomez, S., & Handelmann, G. (1996). The reasonable accommodation process in unionized environments. *Labor Law Journal, 48*(10), 629–647.

Crewe, N. (1994). Implications of the ADA for the training of psychologists. In S. Bruyère & J. O'Keefe, *Implications of the Americans With Disabilities Act for psychology* (pp. 15–23). Washington, DC: American Psychological Association and Springer.

Farkas, G. M. (1989). The impact of federal rehabilitation laws on the expanding role of employee assistance programs in business and industry. *American Psychologist, 44*(12), 1482–1490.

Gold, M. (1998). *An introduction to labor law* (2nd ed.). Ithaca, NY: Cornell University Press.

National Institute on Disability and Rehabilitation Research. (1998). *Chartbook on work and disability in the United States, 1998.* Washington, DC: Author.

Pape, D., & Tarvydas, V. (1994). Responsible and responsive rehabilitation consultation on the ADA: The importance of training for psychologists. In S. Bruyère & J. O'Keeffe (Eds.), *Implications of the Americans With Disabilities Act for psychology* (pp. 169–186). New York: Springer and American Psychological Association.

Society for Human Resource Management (SHRM). (1999). *The ADA at work: Implementation of the employment provisions of the Americans With Disabilities Act.* Alexandria, VA: Author.

U.S. Equal Employment Opportunity Commission. (1992). *A technical assistance manual on the employment provisions (Title I) of the Americans With Disabilities Act.* Washington, DC: Author.

U.S. Equal Employment Opportunity Commission. (1997a, Feb. 12). *EEOC enforcement guidance on the effect of representations made in applications for benefits on the determination of whether a person is a "qualified individual with a disability" under the Americans with Disabilities Act* (No. 915.002). Washington, DC: Author.

U.S. Equal Employment Opportunity Commission. (1997b, March 25). *EEOC enforcement guidance on the Americans With Disabilities Act and psychiatric disabilities* (No. 915.002). Washington, DC: Author.

U.S. Equal Employment Opportunity Commission. (1999). *Enforcement guidance: Reasonable accommodation and undue hardship under the Americans With Disabilities Act.* Washington, DC: Author.

U.S. Equal Employment Opportunity Commission. (2000, July 27). *EEOC enforcement guidance on disability-related inquiries and medical examinations of employees under the Americans With Disabilities Act (ADA)* (No. 915.002). Washington, DC: Author.

14

THE AMERICANS WITH DISABILITIES ACT AND EMPLOYMENT TESTING

NANCY TIPPINS

Since the Americans With Disabilities Act (ADA) was passed in 1990, employers have struggled to interpret the act as it relates to employment testing, to apply it uniformly, and to ensure fair and consistent treatment of all employment candidates. Despite the language of the act, the Equal Employment Opportunity Commission (EEOC) regulations, and some case law, there are many questions regarding the ADA and its application.

The intent of this chapter is to describe the problems that employers face in interpreting the act in employment testing situations. After a brief introduction, the chapter describes situations that an employer might face and raises questions that must be addressed. The scenarios address the questions of what is a disability, what is a reasonable accommodation, who is a qualified professional, what is the proper interpretation of an accommodated test score, and what is a preemployment inquiry. Unfortunately, there are more questions asked than answered. However, the intent is not to provide clear direction but to stimulate thought about the ADA and testing in employment settings.

The examples provided are hypothetical aggregates of situations from many different employers and do not reflect real incidents at any one organization. The scenarios are not meant to represent typical or common employment practices of private-sector employers; rather, the goal is to inform the reader of the difficulties some employers face in employment testing under the ADA.

DEFINITIONS

Many of the problems employers face in interpreting the ADA stem from their understanding of the definition of what constitutes a disability. Despite the act's specific language, employers are still unclear about who has a disability, what is a major life activity, what is an essential function, and what is a reasonable accommodation. Although many employers are familiar with these definitions, the problem comes at the point of interpretation.

The next two scenarios highlight questions of definition and demonstrate the problems employers have in determining what is a disability, deciding on a reasonable accommodation, and treating job candidates fairly and consistently.

Scenario 1

> All secretarial positions at this company require qualifying on a general ability battery and meeting the current standard of 60 wpm on a typing test. Secretaries at this company are considered interchangeable and frequently fill in for one another.
>
> An internal applicant for a secretarial position had an accident that injured her hand and required surgery. The surgery left one hand partially impaired. At the time of application, it was not clear how long this impairment would last, and the possibility existed that the impairment might be permanent. The candidate took the test battery for a secretarial position and qualified on the general ability battery but failed to meet the standard for the typing test. The candidate then claimed a disability and requested a test waiver on the typing test as a reasonable accommodation. The manager for whom the candidate would work had a past work relationship with the applicant and claimed that his secretarial job did not require typing. He wanted to set the typing speed for his position at 20 wpm.

- Did this candidate have a disability? For many employers, it is not clear if this candidate had a disability. Temporary disabilities are excluded in the ADA. Yet at the time the candidate took the typing test, no one knew how long the limitation might last. Because the candidate did not claim to be disabled until she failed to meet the standard, the employer had legitimate reasons to question the claim of disability. Another problem is the question of whether a major life function was affected. Major life activities have been defined as performing manual tasks, walking, seeing, hearing, speaking, breathing, and learning. Although typing is certainly a manual task, it appeared that only typing performance was impaired.

- What are the essential functions of the secretarial job? Is typing required or not? Essential functions are "fundamental job duties of the employment position the individual with a disability holds or desires" (29 C.F.R. 1630.2 (n)). This company had specifically stated in job announcements and company policies that all secretarial positions included typing duties and required typing speed of 60 words per minute. The manager who wanted to hire this candidate attempted to make his secretarial position different from all the others, although the company's policy required secretaries to be competent and able to fill in for each other. This manager's action raises the difficult question of what is a job? Is it a single position with a unique set of requirements? Or is a job a collection of positions with similar requirements? In this scenario, the company's policy and the manager's preference are at odds.

- Assuming this candidate did have a disability, what would be a reasonable accommodation on a timed typing test? On the job? Is a waiver appropriate? Is 20 wpm an appropriate accommodation given the company's policy of interchangeable secretaries? What if the position was in a bargaining unit? Should the employer lower its standards for this candidate?

  If this company takes the position that the candidate has a disability, then it has to decide how to handle her request for accommodation. Most companies with professionally managed selection programs have ADA policies that require a candidate to identify the need for accommodation before testing, rather than afterward. Thus, in many companies, although the candidate could request an accommodation on the typing test immediately after receiving the feedback that she did not qualify on the first administration of the typing test, she would have to wait the normal retest interval on the typing test before retaking it.

Of course, this kind of policy only delays the hard question: If the candidate proceeds with her request for an accommodation, the company still has to grapple with central concerns, which are the request for accommodation and the determination of what is reasonable. If typing is an essential function of the job and the employer has established 60 wpm as the standard, must the company lower its performance expectations? The terms of the collective bargaining agreement for this position could complicate the situation even more. When a reasonable accommodation creates a conflict with the collective bargaining agreement, the company and the union must negotiate a variance to the collective bargaining agreement unless the accommodation creates an undue hardship (Enforcement Guidance: Reasonable Accommodation and Undue Hardship Under the Americans With Disabilities Act, 1999).

Compared to reasonable accommodation in employment testing for physical disabilities, the situation with mental disabilities is much more complex. In addition to being unobservable, conversations with testing professionals, such as personnel psychologists, and staffing personnel suggest that many mental disabilities are poorly understood and that it is more difficult to determine the associated reasonable accommodation.

Scenario 2

A candidate applied for a customer contact job. After being notified of the preemployment screening process that included qualifying on a paper and pencil battery that measures mental ability, a personality inventory that measures sales aptitude, and a structured interview that measures communication skills, he informed the company that he had a learning disability. He followed the company procedure and had a "qualified professional" attest to his learning disability. The qualified professional noted the candidate was always an underachiever and recommended that the company waive all the tests and interviews and give the individual the job based on his past experience.

- Is "learning disability" a disability under the ADA? Is a major life activity affected? Under most interpretations of the ADA, a learning disability is a bona fide disability that is protected. What is less clear is when underachievement stops being a result of motivation or preparation and becomes a result of a true learning disability. By using the words "underachiever," the qualified professional has muddied the waters. A testing professional might wonder from such a vague statement if this candidate does not possess a true learning disability.
- Is a reasonable accommodation from the employer's perspective to use no test at all? Is the company obligated to accept the qualified professional's recommendation to use past experience over its own validated tests? One of the reasons

many employers use professionally developed and validated selection instruments is to avoid the problem of trying to standardize and validate "past experience." To treat all candidates fairly and consistently, the company should provide a scale for past experience that takes into account many kinds and levels of experiences and produces reliable ratings of that experience that predict future job performance. Few companies attempt to develop rating scales for past experience, and fewer still are successful at this. In the private sector, even the largest businesses rarely have enough incumbents in a job classification to develop these kinds of scales empirically. Moreover, staffing personnel are simply not able to determine what a candidate actually did on the job from a cursory presentation (e.g., resume or application) of past experiences.

The qualified professional's willingness to make a recommendation about an alternative selection procedure is both troubling and understandable. In most cases, the qualified professional has been asked to tell the company what kind of accommodation is needed to accurately assess the individual's skill. Yet many professionals who are qualified to discuss a specific kind of disability are not also qualified in the area of employment testing. This company now finds itself in the awkward position of either accepting an uninformed opinion about how to select its personnel or ignoring the solicited opinion.

REASONABLE ACCOMMODATION IN EMPLOYMENT TESTING

Most large employers have carefully developed procedures for determining reasonable accommodation. These procedures usually involve a process in which the candidate is given an overview of the test, an ADA compliance statement, and the process for requesting an accommodation under the ADA. Often this information is offered multiple times in the application and test-scheduling processes.

The employer often has a list of accommodations that may be made automatically without discussion or documentation. If a candidate asks for a higher desk to accommodate a wheel chair, the candidate will not be asked to document that need. Typically these accommodations do not affect the standardized conditions of the test administration.

The process for requesting an accommodation that affects the standard administration of the test requires the candidate to provide documentation from a "qualified professional" who is knowledgeable of the candidate's disability and who can define what the accommodation required is. The employer then decides if the accommodation is reasonable and notifies the candidate. To ensure that similar accommodations are being granted across different geographic locations, these kinds of accommodations that do affect the standardization of the test are usually reviewed and granted from a central location by professionals who work in this area. Although the process appears straightforward, there are many questions that arise in implementation:

- Who is a qualified professional? How does one go about judging "qualified?" Who decides who is qualified?
- What kind of relationship should the qualified professional have with the candidate? How recent should that relationship be?
- What is reasonable? What is the process for determining reasonableness? Is reasonableness relative to the disability or relative to the costs to the organization?
- Should the industrial and organizational psychologist strive to achieve consistency of treatment of individuals with similar disabilities? Should the policies and procedures be administered consistently across people with differing disabilities?

Here are some examples that illustrate the dilemmas faced.

Scenario 3

A candidate for a craft job reviewed the test preview for a cognitive battery and requested an accommodation for his disability, test anxiety. His qualified professional attested to his disability and recommended two times the standard amount of time given for the test battery.

- Is test anxiety a disability? Does it impede a major life activity? Reasonable accommodation is made only when there is a legitimate disability. If test anxiety is not a disability, then an accommodation need not be made. The Tenth Circuit of the U.S. Court of Appeals found that test anxiety does not impede a major life activity and is not a disability. That decision was later upheld by the Supreme Court (*McGuinness v. Regents of the University of New Mexico*, 1999).
- Is two times the normal time limit reasonable? Does the employer have the right to explore this question?

    The question of what is reasonable arises frequently in discussions of disabilities that are not well-understood and that are rarely claimed. Little if any research exists on test anxiety and possible remedies. Thus, the employer has every reason to question how the qualified professional arrived at two times the normal amount of time and not 1.5 times or some other amount.

At the same time, questioning the qualified professional's opinion puts the company in a precarious situation. On what basis is the company challenging the professional's opinion? Can the company challenge the level of expertise? Should the company? In medical disability cases, companies sometimes hire their own experts and challenge the opinion of the individual's expert. At the same time, there are likely to be many fewer medical disability cases than cases questioning the reasonableness of an accommodation in employment.

Another issue raised in this scenario is whose perspective is relevant in the decision about reasonableness. Although twice the normal amount of time on a cognitive battery may be reasonable from the perspective of someone whose disability is test anxiety, it may not be reasonable from the perspective of the company.

Some companies have avoided judging who is a qualified professional to avoid unseemly professional turf issues. Yet there seem to be some clear cases where reviewing the credentials of the qualified professional or relationship to the individual with a disability are relevant.

Scenario 4

Another candidate for a craft job reviewed the test brochure for the mental ability battery and requested an accommodation for his disability, which is dyslexia. His qualified professional recommended the candidate receive twice as much as the standard time limit on the test battery. In discussions with the candidate and the qualified professional, the employer found out that the qualified professional is the candidate's brother-in-law. He never tested or examined the candidate but read 15-year-old archival information about the candidate's learning disability that was provided to him by the candidate.

- Is this professional qualified? Is it a conflict of interest to act on behalf of a family member? Is it an ethical problem? If the qualified professional was not related to the candidate, would it be acceptable to use documents produced by the candidate to judge the extent of the disability and make a recommendation for accommodation?

The scenario described tells us nothing about the qualified professional's credentials but reveals a great deal about the relationship of the qualified professional and the disabled individual. In many professions, treatment of family members may present an ethical problem. Making a professional judgment without examining the individual directly may also be an ethical dilemma in some professions. The use of out-of-date archival information may present an ethical problem simply because a qualified professional in most fields would be expected to know the period of time certain information is useful.

The ADA requires employers to treat each request on a case-by-case basis. At the same time, employers must treat all candidates fairly. Normally, fairness implies consistency across candidates. Clearly, the ADA exempts employers from strict standardization in some reasonable accommodations. Yet situations remain that seem to indicate inherent unfairness and inconsistency. Consider the consistency in these scenarios.

Scenario 5

Two individuals with visual impairments applied for a clerical position that required qualification on a clerical aptitude battery. Both have the same educational background. Neither has worked before. The first candidate read Braille so the test battery was translated to Braille for him and the test was administered to him with extended time limits. The second candidate did not read Braille. The test battery contained a reading comprehension test so it did not make sense to have the test read to the second candidate. The accommodation requested for this candidate is a complete waiver of the test, and qualification for the job will be determined by performance in training.

- Is it fair to treat differently two candidates with visual disabilities who apply for a job at the same time? The second candidate clearly has an easier selection process. Should the employer provide this option to both? Would the situation be different if they had applied at different times?

   The idea that each applicant with a disability must be treated individually and in accordance with his or her disability and accommodation needs exists throughout the ADA. An accommodation that works for one candidate may not work for another. Yet the second candidate who does not read Braille is getting farther into the selection process than the first because there is simply no other way for the employer to assess his skills. Is this fair? Is there an alternative? One might suggest that the company provide both candidates the opportunity to attend training and have their performance assessed, but then the company loses its ability to do any prescreening before training.

It is impossible to say whether the situation would have been different if the two applications had been separated by several months. However, it is logical to guess that the inconsistency of treatment would have been less noticeable if more time had elapsed between the two applications. The same logic would also apply to geographically dispersed applications. The disparities are more apparent when the two candidates are in the same city as opposed to different ones.

Another example of the consistency problem follows.

Scenario 6

An employer has a detailed process of granting accommodations for employment testing like the one described earlier. For individuals with mental disabilities, the process is scrupulously followed. Candidates whose documents are not in order are not processed. However, candidates with obvious physical disabilities (e.g., someone who uses a wheelchair) are not required to submit detailed documentation, and most accommodations are granted even though many alter the conditions under which the test was originally validated. Thus the employer might require a candidate with a mental disability to visit a qualified professional and have extensive testing and diagnosis performed before the request of extending the time limits is granted. On the other hand, a candidate with a visual disability may request to use a reader and extended time limit and those requests are granted without any documentation.

- Is this fair? The disparate treatment accorded individuals with mental and physical disabilities probably reflects society's biases as well as practical concerns. Many employers have a higher comfort level with accommodating a physical disability that is observable. Mental disabilities are not as observable, and many employers require documentation from a qualified professional. Some candidates are not above malingering to receive longer test limits or other assistance that increases the probability of their qualifying. Similarly, many employers fear that a request for "proof" of the need for accommodation may be offensive when the disability is obvious. Note that the 1993 *Technical Assistance Manual on the Employment Provisions of the ADA* does not require an employer to document physical disabilities; however, the inconsistencies in how individuals with disabilities are treated can lead to real and perceived problems.

Another side to the consistency problem involves variations in the accommodations recommended by qualified professionals. Here is another example.

Scenario 7

One very large employer keeps records on accommodations recommended by qualified professionals in the area. One professional always recommends 150% of the time limits for a battery of cognitive tests for candidates with dyslexia and another always recommends 200% more time on the same battery.

- To what extent should the employer try to treat candidates consistently? What should the role of the employer be? Does he or she have an obligation to challenge the recommendations of the qualified professional? Although it is possible that each of the two professionals described is treating each disabled individual who comes to be assessed, it is odd that each professional always comes up with the same answer. The ADA is silent on what the employer's role is in this case.

INTERPRETATION OF ACCOMMODATED TEST SCORES

A third type of problem relates to the interpretation of accommodated test scores. Many alterations to the test administration process affect the standardized conditions under which the test was validated and the associated normative information. Although extended breaks or use of a fat pencil are less likely to affect standardization, extended time limits clearly do. Often the effect of an accommodation (e.g., use of a reader) is simply not known. The question for the employer is how to interpret the score.

- Should we use the same cut score?
- Do we extend the time limits and expect the same level of performance?
- Is the test still a valid predictor of future success on the job?

In many cases, it appears that the employer has simply gone through the motions of administering the test and the meaning of the result is unknown.

Scenario 8

An employer tests candidates for entry-level manager positions. The test battery consists of a cognitive ability battery that focuses on verbal and numeric reasoning and a situational judgment inventory. The battery has time limits that were carefully set so that 90% of the test takers complete 90% of the items. In response to appropriate accommodation requests, the employer extends the time limit on the battery. In the past five years, 99% of the test takers who requested an accommodation and received 1.5 to 2.0 times as much as the normal time limit have completed 98% of the items.

■ What does the employer do with this information? How does the employer use the test scores? Is an 80% on the standardized test equivalent to 80% on the accommodated test? In this scenario, the accommodation appears to have increased the number of items accommodated individuals attempt. Potentially, the test has changed from a speeded test to a power test. Presumably, increasing the number of items increases the number of items correct for many candidates. Assuming strict psychometric equivalence is naive. In many cases, the accommodation (e.g., extra time) actually changes the construct measured. Asking the question, "Is it fair?" may be the wrong question to ask. The more relevant question may be "Is the test score useable?" Some employers simply ignore the discrepancies between accommodated and unaccommodated test scores and use them as though they were the same. Once the candidate and the employer agree on an accommodation, the resulting test score will be used and compared to the appropriate standard.

This scenario highlights a major problem almost all employers in private industry who use preemployment testing have. Virtually no one has sufficient data to conduct the research that would be required to make a sensible interpretation of a test score given under accommodated conditions. By the time a subject pool is divided into groups that are homogenous in terms of the disability and the accommodation, the sample size is too small for statistical analysis.

OTHER SELECTION CONCERNS

Another aspect of the ADA that has affected and confused those who manage employee selection programs is the preoffer inquiries and the content of the test. The ADA forbids preoffer inquiries regarding the existence, nature, or severity of a disability before an offer of employment. Applicants may be asked about their ability to perform job functions and may be required to take a job-relevant medical exam that is consistent with business necessity only after a conditional offer is made but before the applicant begins work. *The Enforcement Guidance: Disability-Related Inquiries and Medical Examinations of Employees Under the Americans With Disabilities Act (ADA)* (2000) specifically includes psychological tests that are "designed to identify a mental disorder or impairment" (p. 5) as a prohibited inquiry.

Cognitive testing has long been an essential component of preemployment testing. The current emphasis on competition and service differentiation has highlighted the importance of "soft skills." As a consequence, many employers have incorporated personality measures and biodata measures into test batteries in an attempt to measure those traits and skills. Although personality traits do not define a disability, some of the measures of traits (i.e., items) are related to possible disabilities.

Scenario 9

> A company has devised a biodata form with the following questions:
> - My coworkers can count on me to be at work every day. (always–never)
> - Compared to your coworkers, how many days of work have you missed? (more than average–fewer than average)
> - My friends tell me I am a good listener. (strongly agree–strongly disagree)
> - Standing in front of large groups and speaking is no problem for me. (strongly agree–strongly disagree)
> - Is it acceptable to ask questions about attendance and dependability in a personality inventory preoffer? Or do the responses to those questions point to a disability? Measuring dimensions like conscientiousness and dependability through measures such as biodata forms may give the impression that the employer is more interested in determining a disability than assessing work-related dimensions. Many employers are rewriting (and revalidating) items such as these to avoid the unintended appearances.
>
> - Is it acceptable to ask questions that allude to certain physical abilities such as listening, speaking, or standing before the offer?
>   Again, some employers are dodging this question by writing biodata items that avoid the problem altogether. Other employers are arguing that good listening skills are essential functions of jobs like customer contact positions and that it is appropriate to measure that skill.

CONCLUSION

More than 10 years after the ADA was signed into law, employers still struggle with the practical aspects of implementing the act. Case law regarding the selection process per se is sparse enough to leave many unanswered questions. Most employers want to comply with the ADA, to treat all candidates fairly and consistently, and to develop selection procedures that meet their business needs. Yet guidance in many situations is lacking. Until more guidance is provided through testing practice, case law, and other legal interpretations, employers must use what information is available and address these situations carefully.

REFERENCES

McGuinness v. Regents of the University of New Mexico. (1999). 183 F.3d 1172 (10th Cir.), *cert. denied*, 120 S. Ct. 332. *See also* 170 F.3d 974 (10th Cir. 1998).

U.S. Equal Employment Opportunity Commission. (1993). *Technical assistance manual on the employment provisions of the ADA.* Washington, DC: Author.

U.S. Equal Employment Opportunity Commission. (1999). *Enforcement guidance: Reasonable accommodation and undue hardship under the Americans With Disabilities Act.* Washington, DC: Author.

U.S. Equal Employment Opportunity Commission. (2000). *Enforcement guidance: Disability-related inquiries and medical examinations of employees under the Americans With Disabilities Act (ADA).* Washington, DC: Author.

15

ISSUES OF SPECIAL CONCERN IN LICENSING AND CERTIFICATION

MICHAEL ROSENFELD, SHELBY KEISER, AND SHARON GOLDSMITH

Examinees with disabilities take tests in a number of different contexts. Licensing and certification examinations are contexts in which governmental and professional agencies use assessment procedures to evaluate whether or not eligible candidates possess the knowledge and skills required for competent practice. Although some industries and companies also use certification testing, their intent is usually to ensure minimum levels of competence, safety, and productivity. Certification tests in industry are really a form of employment testing. Requirements for these types of examinations are covered in chapter 12.

The focus of this chapter is on credentialing examinations conducted by governmental and professional agencies. Licensing and certification examinations used by governmental and professional agencies are typically designed to be consistent with the *Standards for Educational and Psychological Testing* (AERA/APA/NCME, 1999). The primary purpose of licensure or certification is to protect the public. The *Standards* state,

> Licensing requirements are imposed to ensure that those licensed possess knowledge and skills in sufficient degree to perform important occupational activities safely and effectively. The purpose of certifica-

tion is to provide the public (including employers and government agencies) with a dependable mechanism for identifying practitioners who have met particular standards. (1999, p. 156)

In addition to the use of examinations, many credentialing agencies also set education, training, or experiential requirements as a way to ensure that those holding a particular credential have met their standards. Credentialing agencies hold the dual responsibility of providing assessment measures that are valid and fair to candidates as well as designing procedures that will protect the public from practitioners who cannot function in a safe and effective manner.

THE AMERICANS WITH DISABILITIES ACT

The Americans With Disabilities Act (ADA) provides comprehensive civil rights protection to disabled individuals in the areas of employment, public accommodations, state and local government services, transportation, and telecommunications. Its intent is to increase job opportunities and access for disabled individuals. (Refer to chapter 1 for a more complete description of the ADA.)

The ADA contains five major titles. We are concerned in this chapter with two: Title II describes the responsibilities of state licensing agencies. Title III delineates the responsibilities of private certification agencies. The ADA requires credentialing agencies to provide two general types of accommodations. The first type involves accessibility of facilities to individuals with disabilities; the second type involves modifications to the means by which the examination is delivered (e.g., large-size print, extended time). These accommodations should be designed so that examination results accurately reflect the candidate's knowledge and skills rather than reflecting the individual's impairment, except where the knowledge and skills that would need to be modified are themselves factors the test is designed to measure.

According to the ADA, an individual with a covered disability (see Section 36.104) who is eligible to take a licensing or certification examination has the right to request a "reasonable accommodation." A reasonable accommodation is one that would provide the candidate an equal opportunity to demonstrate that he or she possesses the knowledge and skills necessary to perform the "essential functions of the job." Under the ADA, test accommodations should be tailored to the documented needs of the disabled candidate and to the essential functions of the job. The ADA defines the essential functions of the job as "the fundamental job duties of the employment position the individual with a disability holds or desires." It also states "essential functions of the job do not include marginal functions of the position" [1990, § 1630.2(n)].

The ADA was not intended to guarantee that individuals with a covered disability would be successful in passing credentialing examinations. Rather, it was designed to ensure that they would have a fair opportunity to demonstrate whether or not they possess the knowledge and skills required for safe and effective performance in their occupation. This chapter will describe the kinds of accommodations that are frequently provided by credentialing agencies, the documentation of a disability required by credentialing agencies, the psychometric implications of test accommodations, and the responsibilities that credentialing agencies have in deciding whether or not to provide the requested accommodations.

TEST ACCOMMODATIONS

The language of ADA Section 309 that applies the standard of equal access to education and testing for professional licensure and certification is specific:

> Any person that offers examinations or courses related to applications, licensing, certification, or credentialing for secondary or post-secondary education, professional, or trade purposes shall offer such examinations or courses in a place and manner accessible to persons with disabilities or offer alternative accessible arrangements for such individuals. (1990, § 309)

The means for providing accessibility is through accommodations. Accommodations are defined as alterations or adjustments in an activity or a program that serve to ease the effect of the disability in a particular situation. The purpose of accommodations is to facilitate equal access to a program or activity for the disabled individual. In an academic program, an accommodation may be something as simple as supplying a textbook in advance of a class to allow for its timely copying into an alternative format, such as audiotape. In the workplace, accommodations could range from adjustments in the work schedule to the provision of auxiliary equipment, such as an access ramp or electric lift.

Determining a Disability and Appropriate Accommodations

Decisions about the type of test accommodation are related to the purpose of the test. Certification and licensing examinations are very different from clinical assessments. For the clinician conducting a psychoeducational assessment of an individual with a clearly documented disability, almost any type of accommodation may be used in administering the assessment so long as these adjustments do not affect the psychometric characteristics of the testing instruments. However, if the purpose of the evaluation is to determine the existence of a possible disability, such as a learning disability, it would not be appropriate to provide extended time for the examinee to complete the various tasks because the purpose of the testing is to identify possible deficit areas in cognitive processing. *The Standards for Educational and Psychological Testing* (AERA/APA/NCME, 1999) pointed out that "the disability may, in fact, be directly relevant to the focal construct." Thus, a nonstandard test administration could fail to yield valid information about the very components of information processing that the clinician is attempting to measure.

Psychoeducational evaluation is frequently used to establish an individual's eligibility for accommodations under the ADA (Gordon & Keiser, 1998). In assessing children or adults to determine disability under the ADA, it is important for the clinician to keep in mind the following:

1. *The law's definition of disability differs from a clinical diagnosis.* The ADA defines *disability*, for the purposes of coverage under its provisions, as a physical or mental impairment that *substantially limits* one or more major life activities (ADA, 1990, § 3). Other parts of the definition address stereotypes, stigmas, and misperceptions that cause people to be treated as if they have an actual disability (ABA Commission on Mental and Physical Disability Law, 1997). However, clinicians must be aware that the law itself, accompanying regulations, and case law all affirm that the determination of disability hinges on a substantial limitation to a person's functioning in comparison to others' ability to engage in the same activity (*Federal Register*, 1991). This means that when a clinician intends to provide documentation for an individual to receive accommodations under the ADA, she or he must address issues beyond that of *DSM* (American Psychiatric Association, 1994) diagnosis alone. The substantial limitation language in the law requires that the clinician explain test scores or identified deficits in terms of actual functional limitations.

2. *In documenting a need for accommodation, the ADA requires impartiality, not advocacy.* The following reason for referral, frequently given in psychoeducational reports submitted by individuals requesting accommodations, reflects an inappropriate bias on the part of the evaluator: "Susan was referred by her dean for evaluation of a possible learning disability to obtain test accommodations on the XYZ licensing examination." The evaluator must be prepared *not* to issue a diagnosis of disability if it is not warranted, and in any case should thoroughly document the rule-out process followed before reaching any diagnostic conclusions.

3. *For a person to be covered under the ADA, the identified condition must be substantially limiting to the individual relative to the average person in the general population* (EEOC Directives Transmittal #915.002, 1995; *Federal Register,* 1991). Thus, when measuring reading or mathematics skills or the various areas involved in information processing, the clinician must consider the examinee's scores compared with the overall standardization sample for the particular measure, rather than a narrow normative group. For individuals attempting to pass rigorous professional licensing or certification examinations, the question is not whether their performance falls below the average range for highly trained professionals. Instead, the ADA regulations (EEOC and Department of Justice, 1991) clearly indicate that the comparison group for determining a functional impairment is the general population.

4. *Accommodations must be reasonable and effective.* An appropriate accommodation must "match" the identified functional limitation so that its application mitigates the impact of the disability on a particular task or activity. Accommodations are task-specific. That is, a wheelchair user would require access to a school or office building by means of a ramp, lift, or flat ground-floor entrance. However, lacking functional impairments beyond the inability to walk, the individual would not require additional testing time in an examination task. Accommodations are also unique to the individual. One learning-disabled individual might benefit from additional testing time, and for another an audiotaped version of the test would be a better choice.

Once the clinician has clearly documented the need for accommodations, she or he can play an important role in determining how accessibility to a particular program or activity can best be accomplished for the disabled individual (Gordon & Keiser, 1998). A broad range of assistance can be provided depending on the individual's needs and circumstances.

Adjustments to Time

Providing additional testing time or breaking the test into smaller increments are two common ways to accommodate individuals with disabilities. Extra time may help some individuals with learning disabilities overcome limitations in reading skills. The clinician should determine an appropriate amount of additional time by assessing the extent of the individual's functional impairment relative to the average person. She or he should also consider what accommodations the individual generally uses.

For example, a candidate with dyslexia who ordinarily uses an additional 15 minutes per hour for taking classroom tests should receive a similar time increment for a certification exam.

Off-the-clock breaks of varying amounts that do not involve additional testing time are useful to ease the effect of fatigue associated with a disability or to allow a diabetic to monitor blood glucose levels. Individuals with attention deficit/hyperactivity disorder (ADHD) might also benefit from breaks, allowing them to refocus attention on the testing.

Adjustments to Facilitate Physical Access

There are numerous adjustments to the physical conditions of a testing situation that can assist an individual with a disability. For example, an amanuensis or scribe can handle writing tasks for an individual with limited motor skills. Answers to a written examination can also be dictated to a taperecorder. Ramps, enlarged doorways, adjustable-height tables, orthopedic chairs, and footstools are all means of providing physical access to a testing situation.

Lighting can be improved and glare reduced through use of a table lamp and adjustment of window blinds. Individuals with low vision could also benefit from a reader or from a taperecorded version or voice-synthesis rendition of an examination, if the test does not measure reading ability. Enlarged print, either for printed material or on a computer screen, can easily be provided in many testing situations.

Various other physical and technological aids are used as accommodations. Book stands, lecterns, podiums, and slant boards all provide an alternative for those who cannot sit and write at a desk or table. Computer technology offers a wide range of options for many individuals as well, with large trackballs, breath-activated cursor controls, custom keyboards, and the like. (See chapter 3 for a more complete discussion of test accommodations.)

THE DOCUMENTATION PROCESS

Because licensing and certification organizations administer examinations associated with ensuring professional proficiency, they have an obligation to request documentation to verify a need for accommodations (CLEAR, 1996). Regulations accompanying the ADA state that medical documentation must be provided that describes the nature of the condition and how the condition limits the individual's performance of a major life activity (*EEOC Regulations*, 1995). In other words, although accommodations are task-specific and tailored to a specific activity, the determination of whether or not one is covered under the ADA is made by considering evidence that indicates impairment to a major life activity.

Documentation is needed to verify the presence of a disability and the nature of the functional limitations that impede access to a testing activity. ADA regulations state that medical or other documentation should "describe the extent to which the impairment limits the [individual's] major life activities" (*EEOC Regulations*, 1995).

Agencies may wish to develop guidelines for the documentation of disabilities or to use existing guidelines. Guidelines for the documentation of learning disabilities and ADHD were developed in 1997 by the Association on Higher Education and Disability (AHEAD) and the Consortium on ADHD Documentation, respectively. These guidelines were developed by groups of professionals in response to the need for clear standards of documentation for the two most common disorders for which accommodations are requested. At present, many organizations and agencies administering certification and licensing examinations provide information, in their test registration materials or on their website, about their guidelines (1997) for documentation when an individual requests a test accommodation. Many of these involve a set of general guidelines that apply to documentation of all disabilities and additional guidelines for the documentation of learning disabilities and or ADHD.

The following checklist provides licensing and certification organizations with guidelines for responding to requests for accommodations under the ADA:

1. *Develop policies and procedures.* In consultation with legal and disability experts, licensure and certification agencies should develop specific policies and procedures for handling requests for accommodations. Every agency should include in its policy a written commitment to maintaining confidentiality concerning requests and supporting documentation.

2. *Be consistent in application of policy and procedures.* It is essential that the same standards be applied to all applicants for test accommodations. Failing to do so leaves an agency vulnerable to legal challenges as well as a psychometrically compromised examination. Agencies should establish clear procedures so that examinees can easily understand application and documentation requirements.

3. *Consult with experts when necessary to assist in understanding documentation.* Given the complexities of disability documentation and the many misperceptions about the meaning of disability under the ADA, it is often useful to consult with specialists in physical, psychiatric, and learning disabilities as part of the review process. These experts can verify the di-

agnosis, clarify the functional limitations, affirm the recommended accommodations, and generally assist in interpreting the data. Experts can also help to identify some of the more common problems with documentation, such as the following:

- No history of a developmental problem in the materials documenting a learning disability or ADHD. These two conditions are developmental in nature, so one would expect to see chronic difficulties in learning or focusing and attention dating back to childhood or adolescence.
- Failure to demonstrate a current significant impairment. As noted previously, accommodations are provided under the ADA for individuals who are, at the time the accommodation request is made, substantially impaired in a major life activity.
- Failure to explain lack of previous problems. For developmental disorders originating in childhood or adolescence, why was no accommodation previously required and is needed now? The explanation should relate to the individual's functional limitations rather than the difficulty of the examination.
- Justification for requesting accommodations is that they were provided previously. Because accommodations are task-specific, it may be that the basis for providing accommodations in the past is not applicable to the current situation. Also, documentation justifying previous accommodations may not meet the current standard of the licensure agency.
- Equating educational modifications with test accommodations under the ADA. The basis for providing remedial support under education entitlement laws such as the IDEA is different from the ADA's requirement to provide equal access. Thus, services provided in the past may not be relevant for test accommodations under the ADA.
- Insufficient clinical data to support diagnosis of a disability. Documentation must provide detailed clinical data that are interpretable by commonly recognized professional standards.

PSYCHOMETRIC IMPLICATIONS OF TEST ACCOMMODATIONS

A request for a test accommodation by a candidate eligible to take a licensing or certification examination is in effect a request for a nonstandard test administration. Willingham et al. (1988) indicated that the purpose of a modified test administration is to "provide a test that eliminates, insofar as possible, sources of difficulty that are irrelevant to the skills and knowledge being measured" (Willingham et al., 1988, p. 3). It should be remembered that standardized testing conditions were developed and used to provide candidates an equal opportunity to demonstrate relevant knowledge, skills, and abilities and to provide a common basis for interpreting test scores. The use of standardized testing conditions is particularly important in high-stakes testing contexts, such as licensing or certification. Accommodations for disabled candidates called for in the Rehabilitation Act of 1973 and the ADA reflect the first instances in which testing organizations have been required to modify testing conditions or the format of an examination for a particular subgroup of test takers. This requirement raises a number of questions regarding the meaning and comparability of test scores obtained by nondisabled candidates under standard conditions and by disabled candidates obtained under nonstandard conditions.

COMPARABILITY OF SCORES OBTAINED IN STANDARD AND ACCOMMODATED TEST ADMINISTRATIONS

Research on the comparability of test scores obtained in standard and accommodated test administrations is complicated by the need to tailor the accommodation to the needs of the candidate and to the essential functions of the job. As indicated in chapter 2 of this book, the requirement for test accommodations opens the possibility of a huge number of potential accommodations if one considers the types of disabilities as well as the severity or level of each disability. Little research on the effects of accommodations on test scores has been conducted in the licensing and certification context because of the relatively small numbers of candidates requesting specific types of accommodations in a particular licensing or certification program. Most of what is known about the effects of accommodations on test scores is based on information obtained from college admissions testing where there are very large candidate populations. Even in this context some of the findings are limited by relatively small sample sizes. Many of the relevant findings have already been discussed earlier in this book (see chapters 2, 6, and 11). In a report to the National Research Council, Mehrens (1997) summarized the results of comparability studies as follows:

> The research suggests that scores obtained under standardized and accommodated conditions are reasonably comparable with respect to such aspects as reliability, factor structure, and test content. There is evidence that the correlations between test scores and college grades are lower for tests given under accommodated conditions and there

is some overprediction of college grades for some accommodations. (p. 20)

Another important issue is whether or not the scores obtained from a test administered with special accommodations can be equated with those from a standard test administration. This issue was discussed in "The Score" (APA, 1993). This article considered various equating strategies and the technical difficulties associated with each approach. The authors concluded, "There is no standard technical solution available for precisely equating a modified administration of a cognitive test, which itself has been modified, to the standardized form—at least, in those situations where the modification is one that will have an effect on test scores" (APA, 1993, p. 8).

The information presented in this chapter and in other chapters in this book describe the best data currently available to investigate the comparability of test scores of disabled candidates taking examinations under nonstandard conditions with the scores obtained by nondisabled candidates under standard conditions. It should be emphasized that these studies were based on college admission testing data, conducted with multiple-choice items, and were predominately measures of verbal and quantitative abilities. No results were presented that evaluated the effect of testing accommodations on computer-based tests, performance tests, or constructed-response examinations. These results, therefore, may be of limited utility to credentialing agencies.

We do not currently have definitive answers about the comparability of test scores obtained under standard and accommodated testing conditions. Also, given the huge number of potential accommodations and the relatively small number of candidates requesting each accommodation in a particular licensing or certification context, we are not likely to have definitive answers for a very long time. In fact, as Mehrens indicated, we may never have definitive answers. As a result, credentialing agencies will need to rely on their best professional judgments to decide whether to provide a requested accommodation to a particular candidate. Their decisions will need to consider both the nature and level of the candidate's disability as well as the essential functions of the job.

ADA-RELATED RESPONSIBILITIES OF LICENSING AND CERTIFICATION AGENCIES

Licensing and certification agencies have a number of responsibilities that must be attended to as a result of the ADA. The Council on Licensure, Enforcement, and Regulation describes a number of these responsibilities (CLEAR, 1996).

Document Essential Functions of the Job

Credentialing agencies need to prepare up-to-date job analysis information that can be used to establish the essential functions of the particular job or profession. Credentialing agencies must be able to demonstrate that their examinations assess essential job functions. This requirement is similar to the validity requirements specified in the *Standards* (1999). The *Standards* recognize content validity as the primary strategy for documenting the validity of licensing and certification examinations. Standard 14.8 maintains that job analysis is the primary basis to be used in defining the content domain of an examination. Because most credentialing agencies develop their examinations to be responsive to the requirements of the *Standards*, they are very likely to be able to identify essential functions of the job that are related to public protection.

Describe the Eligibility Requirements for the Examination

Credentialing agencies frequently set educational or experiential requirements or qualifications that must be met by candidates before they are eligible to take a licensing or certification examination. These requirements must be clearly stated, must be consistent with the essential functions of the job, and readily available to candidates. Requirements of this type are consistent with the ADA's concept of a qualified individual with a disability (ADA, 1990, § 1630.2(m)). The act clearly states that a person must be qualified to perform the essential functions of the job in question with or without a reasonable accommodation. If a disabled candidate is not eligible to take a particular examination, the credentialing board does not need to consider the request for an accommodation.

Decide on Which Accommodations to Provide

As indicated earlier, the ADA requires that decisions regarding accommodations be tailored to the individual needs of the candidate and to the essential functions of the job or occupation in question. When deciding on the appropriateness of an accommodation a credentialing agency first needs to be sure that the candidate requesting it is qualified or eligible to take the examination. If he or she is not eligible, the request need not be considered any further. If the candidate is eligible to take the examination, the agency must consider whether or not the candidate will be able to perform the essential functions of the job. For example, it would be unreasonable to expect a candidate who could not see to perform the essential functions of the job of a surgeon or building inspector because both jobs are so dependent on visual ability. If it is judged that the candidate can perform the essential functions of the job, the next issue that must be considered is whether or not the accommodation requested would fundamentally alter the construct being measured. That is, if a written, multiple-choice test was designed to measure knowledge of real estate law, and the accommodation requested was to have the test read aloud to the candidate, that would not alter the construct being assessed. In this instance, the accommodation would be reasonable. However, if this same test had been designed to assess reading comprehension then this request for an accommodation would be unreasonable.

If a credentialing body was using a performance test to assess an examinee's skill in fitting clients with hearing aids, and as an alternative to the performance test the examinee requested a written multiple-choice test assessing knowledge of the anatomy of the ear as an accommodation, this request would be inappropriate. The test requested by the candidate would change the construct being measured from the ability to install a hearing aid properly to knowledge of the anatomy of the ear. Many requests for accommodations are unlikely to alter the construct being measured. For example, requesting a more comfortable chair to sit on when taking an examination or the provision of special paper that will not cause the candidate an allergic reaction are unlikely to alter the construct being assessed and would be reasonable. When deciding on whether or not to offer a requested accommodation, credentialing bodies need to consider the purpose of the test, the constructs it is designed to measure, how the constructs will be measured, and the inferences that will be made from the test score. A reasonable accommodation is one that provides the candidate a fair opportunity to demonstrate the relevant knowledge and skills. Credentialing bodies must balance the issue of fairness toward the candidate with their responsibility for public protection. They have the right to refuse a requested accommodation if the candidate is not qualified to take the examination, if the accommodation requested would fundamentally alter the construct being assessed, or if the accommodation requested places an undue burden on the credentialing agency. An undue burden would be related to the cost or difficulty of developing or administering a particular accommodation.

Decide Whether or Not to Flag Test Scores

Chapter 6 in this book discusses the issue of flagging in great detail. The purpose of flagging a test score is to inform and caution users that the score was obtained under nonstandard conditions and might not have the same meaning as other scores obtained under standard conditions. As indicated earlier in this chapter, it is the responsibility of the credentialing agency or the testing organization to decide whether or not to provide an accommodation requested by a candidate. If the agency provides the accommodation, then the resulting score is deemed to be a reportable score.

Some credentialing agencies flag test scores and note the type of test accommodation provided. We believe this is important for the agency's own record-keeping functions as well as providing the possibility of conducting research on test accommodations at some later date. Other agencies may flag scores and report them to test users. In either case, special care should be taken to ensure that the flagged scores are kept secure from unauthorized personnel and uses.

Keep Appropriate Records

Credentialing agencies need to ensure that they have policies and procedures in place for maintaining the security of requests for accommodations and the associated documentation, for both research and legal purposes. Agencies will need to demonstrate that they have responded to requests for accommodations, have used a rational and defensible process for arriving at decisions regarding those requests, and have transmitted their decisions to candidates in a timely manner. Data on test scores can be aggregated over time and may eventually provide the agency an opportunity to conduct research on the comparability and validity of test scores obtained by disabled candidates under accommodated testing conditions.

CONCLUSION

The testing requirements of the ADA require that credentialing agencies provide facilities that are accessible to disabled candidates and that they provide appropriate modifications to the means by which the examination is delivered. This chapter has described test accommodations that are frequently provided in certification and licensing examinations, the type of documentation that should be provided to credentialing agencies, the psychometric implications of test accommodations, as well as the major test-related responsibilities of credentialing agencies to be responsive to the ADA and to testing guidelines.

REFERENCES

American Bar Association Commission on Mental and Physical Disabilities. (1997). *Mental disabilities and the Americans With Disabilities Act* (2nd ed.). Washington, DC: Author.

American Educational Research Association, American Psychological Association, & National Council on Measurement in Education (AERA/APA/NCME). (1999). *Standards for educational and psychological testing.* Washington, DC: American Psychological Association.

American Psychiatric Association. (1994). *Diagnostic and statistical manual of mental disorders* (4th ed.). Washington, DC: Author.

American Psychological Association, Division of Evaluation, Measurement, and Statistics. (1993, Jan.). Psychometric and assessment issues raised by the Americans With Disabilities Act (ADA). *The Score, 15*(4), 1–15.

Americans With Disabilities Act of 1990. (1990). 42 U.S.C. §§ 12111–12213, Pub. Law No. 101-336.

Association on Higher Education and Disability. (1997, July). *Guidelines for documentation of a learning disability in adolescents and adults.* Columbus, OH: Author.

Council on Licensure, Enforcement and Regulation (CLEAR). (1996, July). *The Americans With Disabilities Act: Information and recommendations for credentialing examinations.* Lexington, KY: Author.

Department of Justice Regulations. (1991, July). *Federal Register, 56*(144).

Equal Employment Opportunity Commission and the U.S. Department of Justice. (1991, Oct.). *Americans With Disabilities Act Handbook.* Washington, DC: Author.

Equal Employment Opportunity Commission. (1995, March 14). Directions transmittal #915–002.

Federal Register. (1991, July 26). Vol. 56(144).

Gordon M., & Keiser S. (Eds.). (1998). *Accommodations in higher education under the Americans With Disabilities Act.* New York: Guilford Press.

Mehrens, W. A. (1997, Sept. 19). *Flagging test scores: Policy, practice, and research.* Background paper for the BOTA Planning Meeting on Test Score Flagging Policies, National Academy of Sciences/National Research Council, Washington, DC.

Rehabilitation Act of 1973, Section 504. (1973). 29 U.S.C. § 701 *et seq.* (1973).

Willingham, W. W., Ragosta, M., Bennett, R. E., Braun, H., Rock, D. A., & Powers, D. E. (1988). *Testing handicapped people.* Boston: Allyn and Bacon.

VI

SOURCES FOR FURTHER
INFORMATION

16

RESOURCES FOR FURTHER INFORMATION ABOUT THE ASSESSMENT OF INDIVIDUALS WITH DISABILITIES

JANET E. WALL

The preceding chapters of this book afford readers the opportunity to expand their knowledge of issues related to the assessment of individuals with disabilities. Printed material, however, cannot keep up with the speed of change in this area. For this reason, information is being provided about organizations, Internet sites, and other resources that can help testing professionals stay updated with the latest initiatives and details on specific topics related to assessing individuals with disabilities. Finding the most current information will help the reader investigate clarifications and refinements of the legislations that have resulted from case law, new legislation, regulations, and national, state, and local policies that attempt to strengthen legislative provisions. The organizations and websites listed in this chapter can shed light on new educational approaches and policies that can be helpful in formulating local policy, influencing program operation, and identifying successful educational practices.

The Internet is an especially rich source of information. Many sites are updated on a regular basis and new sites come on board, thus providing timely information on new legislation and regulations, new standards, and suggestions for improved practices. Often this information is available at no cost. In other cases publications can be ordered directly thorough the organization's website.

There are literally hundreds of sites relevant to assessing individuals with disabilities. The ones listed in this chapter were selected because they are the most likely to contain the latest and most comprehensive information related to the issues discussed in this book. For example, not all clearinghouses and information sources about disabilities could be listed; the ones chosen provide the widest coverage, have links to sources of information about specific disabilities, or have in-depth information relating to assessing individuals with one or more specific disabilities.

At the time of this writing, all URLs (universal resource locators or website addresses) were accurate and active. Occasionally, of course, websites change addresses or become inactive, so it is possible that some of these addresses may no longer function. In those instances, a simple search for the organization through a search engine will likely identify the current web address. The information about the content of sites, the mailing address, and phone numbers were also accurate at the time of this writing; however, as with URLs, changes may occur.

I have tried to group the organizations and websites for more efficient access, but the reader should understand there is some overlap. The first section listed provides information about the Joint Committee on Testing Practices (JCTP) and its member organizations. The JCTP is made up of representatives of professional organizations whose members are often substantially involved in assessment. One goal of the JCTP is to develop products that will improve testing practices. This book grew out of a JCTP working group project. Later sections cover legal information, assessment and testing information, employment information, education information, and clearinghouses and information centers on disability-related topics.

Space limitations make it impossible to provide information about websites for every type of disability. Instead, the site descriptions note when clearinghouses and other sites provide links to information about specific disabilities. Information about a specific disability can be especially helpful for testing professionals who wish to obtain more knowledge about that disability in preparation for working with a test-taker.

THE JOINT COMMITTEE ON TESTING PRACTICES AND ITS MEMBER ORGANIZATIONS

Joint Committee on Testing Practices (JCTP)

www.apa.org/science/jctpweb.html

This site provides information about JCTP activities and products, including the Code of Fair Testing Practices in Education, a videotape titled, "The ABC's of School Testing," a casebook on responsible test use, and a statement on the rights and responsibilities of test takers.

American Counseling Association (ACA)

5999 Stevenson Ave.
Alexandria, VA 22304
(703) 823-9800

www.counseling.org

This site provides information about the ACA and its publications. Section E of the ACA Standards of Practice, listed under resources, includes standards for assessment.

Association for Assessment in Counseling (AAC)

aac.ncat.edu/

The AAC is a division of the ACA that emphasizes the need for appropriate use of assessment instruments by individuals within the counseling community. The website includes, under resources, a list of some key documents in assessment. Many members are willing to answer questions related to assessment concepts and their applicability to assessing individuals with disabilities.

American Educational Research Association (AERA)

1230 17th St., NW
Washington, DC 20036
(202) 223-9485

www.aera.net

This site includes information about the AERA. its publications, and other material of interest to researchers.

American Psychological Association (APA)

750 First St., NE
Washington, DC 20002-4242
(202) 336-6000

www.apa.org

This site includes information about the APA and about psychology, both for professionals and the public. Information on testing and assessment can be found at

www.apa.org/science/testing.html

This site includes information about the *Standards for Educational and Psychological Testing*, a Testing Information Clearinghouse, FAQ/Finding Information About Psychological Tests, and links to other testing-related sites. The disabilities issues homepage can be found at

apa.org/pi/acip/texthomepage.html

This site includes information about the ADA, a publication titled, "Enhancing Your Interactions With People With Disabilities," and information about books and articles dealing with disability issues.

American Speech Language Hearing Association (ASHA)

10801 Rockville Pike
Rockville, MD 20851
(301) 897-5700, TTY (301) 897-0147

www.asha.org and www.professional.asha.org

These sites include information about ASHA and about communication disorders, audiology, and speech-language pathology.

National Association of School Psychologists (NASP)

4340 East West Highway, Suite 402
Bethesda, MD 20814
(301) 657-0275, TTY (301) 657-4155

www.naspweb.org

This site provides information about NASP including, under NASP information, position statements on topics such as school psychologists' involvement in assessment. There are also links to federal government sites with information about topics such as the Individuals With Disabilities Education Act (IDEA) regulations.

National Council on Measurement in Education (NCME)

1230 17th St., NW
Washington, DC 20036
(202) 223-9318

www.ncme.org

This site includes information about the NCME and its publications. It has links to the JCTP, the Code of Fair Testing Practices in Education, the Code of Professional Responsibilities in Educational Measurement, and Competencies in Assessment and Evaluation for School Counselors.

National Association of Test Directors (NATD)

1230 17th St., NW
Washington, DC 20036
(202) 223-9485

www.natd.org

This site provides information on assessment in the K through 12 educational setting. The site offers information on many topics of interest to educators to include current practices, school district policies, assessment standards.

LEGAL INFORMATION

U.S. Department of Justice

950 Pennsylvania Ave., NW
Washington, DC 20530-0001

www.usdoj.gov

The disabilities information section of this site provides information about the ADA. The publications section includes a variety of free material about the ADA; these publications are available in standard print, large print, audiotape, Braille, and computer disk formats.

For general ADA information, answers to technical questions, information about free ADA material, and so forth, telephone: (800) 514-0301 (voice), (800) 514-0383 (TDD).

The departments' ADA homepage is located at

www.usdoj.gov/crt/ada/adahom1.htm

This site includes a full-text version of the ADA, ADA Regulations and Technical Assistance Manuals, and links to other federal ADA resources.

Equal Employment Opportunity Commission

1801 L St., NW
Washington, DC 20507
For technical assistance telephone: (800) 669-4000 (voice) or (800) 800-3302 (TTY).
For publications telephone: (800) 669-EEOC (voice) or (800) 800-3301 (TTY).

www.eeoc.gov

This site provides information about the laws enforced by the EEOC, including the ADA and the Rehabilitation Act of 1973, and the text of "Procedures for Providing Reasonable Accommodations for Individuals With Disabilities."

U.S. Department of Education, Office for Civil Rights

Customer Service Team
Mary E. Switzer Building
330 C St., SW
Washington, DC 20202
(202) 205-5413 or (800) 421-3481

www.ed.gov/offices/OCR/

This site includes an overview of disability discrimination laws and a compendium of federal statutes related to testing.

ASSESSMENT AND TESTING INFORMATION

ACT

ACT National Office
2201 North Dodge St.
P.O. Box 168
Iowa City, IA 52243-0168
(319) 337-1000

www.act.org

This site describes the assessment products offered by ACT, as well as other ACT testing programs. There is information about test registration procedures, testing options for students with disabilities, and ACT policy for documentation to support requests for testing accommodations.

Association of Test Publishers (ATP)

1201 Pennsylvania Ave., Suite 300
Washington, DC 20004
(202) 857-8444

www.testpublishers.org

This site provides answers to frequently asked questions about tests.

CTB McGraw-Hill

20 Ryan Ranch Road
Monterey, CA 93940
(800) 538-9547

www.ctb.com

This site includes a section on assessment accommodations and "Guidelines for Using the Results of Standardized Tests Administered Under Nonstandardized Conditions." There is also a glossary of assessment terms.

Educational Records Bureau (ERC)

222 East 42nd St., Suite 100
New York, NY 10017
(212) 672-9800

www.erbtest.org

This site describes the testing programs offered by ERC, including the Independent School Entrance Examination.

Educational Testing Service (ETS)

Rosedale Road
Princeton, NJ 08541
(609) 734-5410

www.ets.org

This site provides information about several testing programs, including the Scholastic Assessment Test (SAT) and the Test of English as a Foreign Language (TOFEL). The disabilities and testing section of this site provides information about testing accommodations, ETS policy statements about documentation of a learning disability and documentation of attention-deficit/hyperactivity disorder (ADHD), and links to several organizations with disability information.

GED Testing Service

CALEC
One Dupont Circle NW, Suite 250
Washington, DC 20036
(202) 939-9475

www.acenet.edu/calec/ged/home.html

This site provides information about the General Educational Development (GED) testing program, which helps adults obtain a high school diploma. There is information for test takers with disabilities, including GED policies for the documentation of a disability. There are also links to disability resources.

Graduate Management Admissions Council (GMAT)

1750 Tysons Blvd., Suite 1100
McLean, VA 22102
(703) 749-0131

www.gmat.org

This site provides information about MBA programs and the Graduate Management Admissions Test. There is information for test takers with disabilities.

Graduate Record Examination Board (GRE)

GRE-ETS
P.O. Box 6000
Princeton, NJ 08541-6000
(609) 771-7670

www.gre.org

This site provides information about tests for graduate school. There is information about registration procedures for test takers with disabilities and about documentation criteria.

Law School Admission Council

P.O. Box 40
Newtown, PA 18940
(215) 968-1119

www.lsat.org

This site provides information about law schools and the Law School Admission Test (LSAT). There is information about accommodated testing for candidates with documented disabilities and guidelines for documentation.

Medical College Admission Test (MCAT)

MCAT Program Office
P.O. Box 4056
Iowa City, IA 51143
(319) 337-1357

www.aamc.org/students/mcat/start.htm

This site provides information about the Medical College Admission Test (MCAT). A section under frequently asked questions provides information about requesting special testing accommodations.

The Psychological Corporation

555 Academic Ct.
San Antonio, TX 78204
(800) 211-8378

www.hbtpc.com

This site has links to several kinds of testing programs, including psychological assessment; speech and language assessment; occupational and physical therapy assessment; postsecondary admissions tests for programs in pharmacy, veterinary medicine, nursing, and allied health; and the Miller Analogies Test that is used in graduate school admission. There is a link to Harcourt Educational Measurement at www.hemweb.com.

Riverside Publishing

425 Spring Lake Dr.
Itasca, IL 60143-2079
(800) 767-8420

www.riverpub.com

This site provides information about this company's products, which include educational assessments and tests for clinical and special-needs use. There are links to sites with information about testing and disabilities.

EDUCATION INFORMATION

U.S. Department of Education, Office for Special Education and Rehabilitative Services

(202) 205-8241 Voice/TTY

www.ed.gov/offices/OSERS

This site has links to the Office of Special Education Programs (OSEP), the Rehabilitation Services Administration (RSA), and the National Institute on Disability and Rehabilitation Research.

OSEP

www.ed.gov/offices/OSERS/OSEP

This site includes information about the IDEA, including recent reports to Congress about its implementation. There is information about technology for students with disabilities and reports on research about the education of children with disabilities.

The Federal Resource Center for Special Education (FRC)

1825 Connecticut Ave., NW, Suite 900
Washington, DC 20009
(202) 884-8215 (voice) or (202) 884-8200 (TTY)

www.dssc.org/frc

This site has information on the Special Education Technical Assistance and Disabilities Network. There is also information about the IDEA and other legislation related to special education. There are links to several federal agencies.

Council of Chief State School Officers (CCSSO)

One Massachusetts Ave., Suite 700
Washington, DC 20001-1431
(202) 408-5505

www.ccsso.org

This site includes information about CCSSO, its projects and publications, such as "Including Students With Disabilities in School-to-Work Opportunities" and the "Annual Survey of State Student Assessment Programs."

ERIC Clearinghouse on Assessment and Evaluation

1129 Shriver Laboratory
College of Library and Information Sciences
University of Maryland
College Park, MD 20741
(800) 464-3742

www.ericae.net

This site includes the ERIC search system, a test locator, and a list of assessment and evaluation resources on the Internet.

ERIC Clearinghouse on Counseling and Student Services

201 Ferguson Bldg.
University of North Carolina at Greensboro
P.O. Box 26171
Greensborno, NC 27402-6171
(336) 334-4114

www.ericcas.edu

This site provides documents, digests, and other related information relevant to the counseling community. Many documents relating to the assessment of individuals with disabilities are available from this site. This site actively disseminates education information through conferences, book publications, and document archiving.

HEATH Resources Center (National Clearinghouse on Postsecondary Education for Individuals With Disabilities)

American Council on Education
One Dupont Circle NW
Washington, DC 20036
(800) 544-3284 or (202) 939-9320 (both are voice and TTY)

www.heath-resource-center.org

This site serves as an information exchange about educational support services, policies, procedures, adaptation, and opportunities at American postsecondary institutions. HEATH publishes a biannual survey of college freshmen with disabilities.

Association on Higher Education and Disability (AHEAD)

P.O. Box 21192
Columbus, OH 43221-0192
(614) 488-4972

www.ahead.org

This site has many links and resources, covering colleges, legal issues, specific disabilities, and technology.

Consortium for Equity in Standards and Testing (CTEST)

CSTEEP
Campion Hall, Boston College
Chestnut Hill, MA 02467
(617) 552-4521

www.csteep.bc.edu/ctest

This site includes "Spotlights" on Testing Students With Disabilities and on Standards-Based Reform and Students With Disabilities. There are links to related websites.

Education Commission of the States

707 17th St., #2700
Denver, CO 80202-3427
(303) 299-3600

www.ecs.org

This organization works with states' educators and legislators improve educational performance in schools. Statements and policy comments on assessment and accommodations are provided for viewing on this site.

National Association of State Boards of Education

277 South Washington St., S. 100
Alexandria, VA 22314
(703) 684-4000

www.nasbe.org

This site is rich in access to reports, policy statements, and briefs related to several educational issues including assessment of students with disabilities.

National Center on Educational Outcomes

University of Minnesota
350 Elliott Hall
75 East River Road
Minneapolis, MN 55455
(612) 624-8561

www.coled.umn.edu/NCEO

This site includes information about the participation of students with disabilities in national and state assessments and standards-setting efforts. There is information about testing accommodations for students with disabilities, material about high-stakes testing of students with disabilities, alternative assessments, and out-of-level testing. Some research and technical reports can be downloaded. Publications include an assessment series.

National Center for Educational Statistics

1990 K St. NW
Washington, DC 20006
(202) 502-7300

nces.ed.gov

This site provides access to reports about the education of students with disabilities. It also includes information about the National Assessment of Education Progress (NAEP) and the inclusion of individuals with disabilities.

National Center for Research on Evaluation, Standards, and Student Testing (CRESST)

301 GSE&IS, Mailbox 951522
300 Charles E. Young Drive North
Los Angeles, CA 90095-1522
(310) 206-1532

cresst96.cse.ucla.edu/index.htm

This site provides reports and materials relating to assessing students with disabilities, testing accommodations, and related assessment issues.

National School Boards Association

1680 Duke St.
Alexandria, VA 22314
(703) 838-6722

www.nsba.org

This site provides policy guidelines and updated information on Congressional activities related to educational issues, including special education.

EMPLOYMENT INFORMATION

Office of Disability Employment Policy, U.S. Department of Labor

1331 F. St., NE, Suite 300
Washington, DC 20004
(202) 376-6200 (voice) or (202) 376-6205 (TTY)

www.dol.gov/dol/odep

This office was new at the beginning of 2001. It includes programs and staff that were formerly a part of the President's Committee on Employment of People With Disabilities. The site describes the office, its programs, and publications.

Disability Employment and Initiatives Unit, U.S. Department of Labor

Room N-4641, Employment and Training Administration
200 Constitution Ave., NW
Washington, DC 20210
(202) 693-3821

www.wdsc.org/disability/htmldocs

This site, called ETA disAbility Online, provides information about programs and services under the Workforce Investment Act of 1998 that affect individuals with disabilities.

Program on Employment and Disability (PED)

School of Industrial and Labor Relations
106 ILR Extension
Cornell University
Ithaca, NY 14853-3901
(607) 255-7727 (voice) or (607) 255-2891 (TTY)

www.ilr.cornell.edu/ped

This site describes the PED mission and services. There is information on the ADA, employment and disability policy, transition from school to adult life, and vocational rehabilitation.

Council on Licensure, Enforcement and Regulation (CLEAR)

403 Marquis Ave., Suite 100
Lexington, KY 40502
(859) 269-1289

www.clearhq.org

This site provides information about CLEAR and its publications, including "The Americans With Disabilities Act: Information and Recommendations for Credentialing Examinations."

CLEARINGHOUSES AND INFORMATION CENTERS ON DISABILITY-RELATED TOPICS

Council for Exceptional Children (CEC) and ERIC Clearinghouse on Disabilities and Gifted Education

1920 Association Drive
Reston, VA 20191-1589
1-888-CEC-SPED, (703) 620-3669 (local), (703) 264-9446 (TTY)

For the Council for Exceptional Children

www.cec.sped.org

This site includes information about CEC and its publications and about IDEA.

For the ERIC Clearinghouse on Disabilities

www.ericec.org

This site includes a list of ERIC fact sheets, minibibliographies, and digests on disability topics. There are answers to frequently asked questions about specific disabilities. There are also links to information about the ADA, IDEA, and the Rehabilitation Act of 1973.

National Information Center for Children and Youth with Disabilities (NICHCY)

P.O. Box 1492
Washington, DC 20013
(800) 695-0285

www.nichcy.org

This site provides information on the IDEA, information about specific disabilities, and links to many disability organizations.

National Council on Disability (NCD)

1331 F St, NW, Suite 1050
Washington, DC 20004-1107
(202) 272-2004 (voice) or (202) 272-2074 (TTY)

www.ncd.gov

This site describes NCD's mandate. There is a list of NCD publications, including reports on national disability policy. There is a youth/family information page to help individuals with disabilities understand their rights under the ADA, IDEA, and other legislation.

DB-LINK (National Information Clearinghouse on Children Who Are Deaf–Blind)

Teaching Research
345 N. Monmouth Ave.
Monmouth, OR 97361
(800) 438-9376 (voice) or (800) 845-7013 (TTY)

www.tr.wou.edu/dblink

This site provides information related to deaf–blind children and youth. There are fact sheets, including one on the psychological evaluation of children who are deaf–blind, and bibliographies, including one on assessment.

National Deaf Education Network and Clearinghouse

Gallaudet University
800 Florida Ave., NE
Washington, DC 20002-3695
(202) 651-5051 (voice) or (202) 651-5052 (TTY)

clerccenter.gallaudet.edu

This site provides information the clearinghouse, its services, and its publications.

National Center for Learning Disabilities (NCLD)

381 Park Ave. South, Suite 1401
New York, NY 10016
(212) 545-7510 or (888) 575-7373

www.ncld.org

This site provides numerous resources on learning disabilities, including information on school testing issues. There is a list of national organizations on learning disabilities.

AUTHOR INDEX

Numbers in italics refer to listings in the reference sections.

Farris, E., 173, *189*
Finn, S. E., 105, 114, *116*
Fischer, R. J., 197, *204*
Foote, W. E., 108, *116*
Fow, N. R., 107, *116*
Fowler, L., 147, *170*
Fox, R. W., 126, *132*
Frank, R., 110, 111, *116*
Frisbie, D. A., 144, *146*
Frost, M., 107, *116*
Fullerton, D., 110, *116*

Gaskill, F. W., 109, *116*
Gatchel, R. J., 110, *117*
Geisinger, K. F., 36, 39, *41, 42,* 98, 99, 106, *117*
Ginter, E. J., 123, *132*
Glock, M. D., 49, *57*
Gold, M., 218, *220*
Goldman, H. H., *118*
Goldstein, A. A., 50, *57,* 72, 82, 127, *132*
Gomez, S., 218, *219*
Gordon, M., 238, 239, *248*
Gordon, W. A., 109, *118*
Gramling, S., 109, *116*
Greene, R. L., 114, *117*
Grimes, J. P., 73, 75, 77, *82*
Grisso, T., 108, *117*
Gronlund, N. E., 47, *57*
Gustafson, M. S., 107, *116*
Gwin, R., 114, *117*

Hagen, E. P., 148, 158, *171*
Haith, M. M., 148, *171*
Hall, S. A., 107, *117*
Hallahan, D. P., 73, *81*
Hallmark, R., 147, *171*
Hammill, D. D., 147, *170*
Handelmann, G., 218, *219*
Handler, L., 105, *118, 119*
Hannah, J. M., 73, *81,* 151, *170*
Hardy, G., 106, *119*
Haring, N. G., 73, *81*
Haring, T., 73, *81*
Harkness, A. R., 105, *117*
Harris, G. T., 106, *119*
Harry, B., 107, *117*
Hart, D. S., 106, *120*

Harvey, R., 110, *117*
Harvill, L., 105, *119*
Hauser, R. M., 13, 25, 29, 98, 99, 127, 128, *132,* 142, *146*
Havey, J. M., 147, *171*
Haynes, S. N., 105, *117*
Heaney, K. J., 14, 20, 28, 29, 30, 176, 183, 184, *189*
Hegstrom, K. J., 148, *171*
Henderson, C., 4, 8, 183, *189*
Herrmann, D., 110, *118*
Heubert, J. P., 13, 25, 29, 98, 99, 127, 128, *132,* 142, *146*
Heumann, J. E., 125, 129, *131*
Heward, W. L., 73, *82*
Hewlett, S., 110, *117*
Hieronymus, A. N., 144, *146*
Hilsenroth, M., 105, *119*
Hood, A. B., 121, *132*
Hoover, H. D., 144, *146*
Horn, J. L., 74, *82*
Howell, T., 110, *117*
Hu, S., 148, *171*
Huang, D. D., 107, *117*
Hutton, J. B., 147, *170*

Imhof, E. A., 147, *170*
Impara, J. C., 123, *132, 171*

Janda, L. H., 148, *170*
Jirele, T., 38, 40, *41, 42*
Johnson, R. W., 121, *132*
Jones, J., 197, *204*
Jordan, S., 107, *117*

Kamil, B., 21, *30*
Kaplan, B. A., 38, 39, 40, *41, 42,* 183, *189, 190*
Kaufman, A. S., 78, 79, *82,* 148, 155, 156, 168, *170*
Kaufman, J. M., 73, *81*
Kaufman, N. L., 78, 79, *82,* 148, 155, 156, 168, *170, 171*
Keiser, S., 238, 239, *248*
Keller, J. W., 147, *171*
Kennedy, C., *118*
Khadavi, A., 106, *120*
Kim, S. W., 107, *117*

Kinney, R. K., 110, *117*
Kirwan, J., 110, *117*
Klein, M., 110, *117*
Klimoski, R. J., 40, *41, 42,* 197, *204*
Klonoff, P. S., 109, 110, *117, 118*
Kok, C. J., 106, *118*
Kolpan, K., 109, *119*
Krause, J. S., 111, *116*

Laing, J., 93, *99*
Lamb, D. G., 110, *117*
Laurent, J., 147, *170*
Lee, H., 148, *170*
Lehman, I. J., 49, *57*
Leisen, M. B., 105, *117*
Lewis, L., 173, *189*
Lewis, R. B., 149, *171*
Lilienfeld, S. O., 105, *117*
Livingston, S. A., 98, *99*
Livneh, H., 110, *117*
Locke, K. D., 105, 114, *118*
Lombana, J. H., 123, *132*
Lutkus, A. D., 182, *189*

McCallum, R. S., 79, *81*
McCormick, L., 73, *81*
McDaniel, F., 38, *41*
McDonald, J. A., 197, *204*
McDonnell, L. M., 14, 19, 25, *30,* 98, 99, 128, 139, *146*
McGrew, K. S., 127, *132*
McLaughlin, M., 14, 19, *30,* 98, 99, 128, 139, *146*
McLoughlin, J. A., 149, *171*
McNeil, J. M., 3, 4, *8*
Madaus, G., 137, *146*
Mahaffey, C., 60, *70*
Mahrle, C. L., 124, *131*
Malec, J., 110, *117*
Malony, H. N., 108, *119*
Mandinach, E. B., 182, 185, *189*
Markwardt, F., 78, *82*
Martin, S. L., 197, *204*
Maruish, M., 147, *170*
Masling, J. M., 105, 114, *117*
Matano, R. A., 105, 114, *117*
May, D. C., 95, *99,* 184, *189*
Mazzeo, J., 182, *189*
Mebane, D. L., 108, *119*

Mehrens, W. A., 25, 26, *30,* 49, *57,* 95, 97, 99, 181, 185, *189,* 243, *248*
Melton, G. B., 108, *118*
Merritt, R. D., 106, *118*
Messick, S., 25, *30*
Meyer, G. J., 105, *118*
Milani, A. A., 21, *30*
Miller, S. A., 148, *171*
Milliren, J. W., 109, *118*
Monahan, J., 106, *118*
Morey, L. C., 105, 106, *118*
Morison, P., 14, 19, *30,* 98, 99, 128, 139, *146*
Morrison, T. L., 105, *118*
Muir, S., 147, *170*

Naglieri, J. A., 148, 163, *171*
Neimeyer, R., 110, *117*
Nelson, L. D., 105, *118*
Nestor, M. A., 19, 25, *30,* 106, *118,* 200, *204*
Nieberding, R., 124, *132,* 147, *171*
Noble, J., 182
Novatkoski, I., 39, *41*
Nyquist, R., 111, *118*

Oakland, T., 148, *171*
Oehler-Stinnett, J., 147, *171*
Olds, S. W., 148, *171*
O'Leary, J., 109, *115*
Olsen, K., 144, *146*
Olson, J. E., 140, *146*
Olson, J. F., 18, 50, 56, *57, 77, 82,* 127, *132*
Omar, M. H., 128, *132*
Oppenheim, S., 106, *120*
Orleans, J. H., 97, *99*

Palmer, S. N., 40, *42,* 197, *204*
Papalia, D. E., 148, *171*
Pape, D., 215, *220*
Parente, R., 110, *118*
Pate, J. L., 106, *115*
Petrila, J., 108, *118*
Phillips, S. E., 25, 26, *30,* 46, *57,* 139, *146*
Pieterse, M. J., 107, *116*
Pincus, H. A., 114, *118*

Piotrowski, C., 147, *170, 171*
Plake, B. S., 123, *132, 171*
Polatin, P. B., 110, *117*
Pomplun, M., 128, *132*
Powers, D. E., 19, *31, 42, 100, 190, 248*
Poythress, N. G., 108, *118*
Presse, N., 123, *132*
Prigatano, G. P., 109, *118*
Pruitt, P., 126, *132*
Pryor, E. S., 94, 112, *119*
Pullin, D. C., 14, 20, 28, *29, 30,* 125, 176, 183, 184, *189*

Quinsey, V. L., 106, *119*

Ragosta, M., 19, 26, *30, 31,* 38, 40, *41, 42,* 91, *99, 100,* 183, *189, 190, 248*
Reagan, T., 107, *119*
Rees, A., 106, *119*
Reilly, R. R., 36, *42*
Reschly, D. J., 73, 75, 77, *82,* 148, *171*
Reynolds, S., 106, *119*
Rice, M. E., 106, *119*
Robinson, N. M., *30,* 28, 91, 94, *100,* 185, *190*
Rock, D. A., 19, *31,* 38, 39, 40, *41, 42, 100, 190, 248*
Rodevich, M. A., 106, *119*
Roeber, E., 143, *146*
Rogers, R., 108, *119*
Rosenfeld, M., 89, *99,* 109, *119*
Rothchild, B., 182, *189*

Salvia, J., 149, 150, *171*
Sattler, J. M., 148, 149, 158, *171*
Scalise, J. J., 123, *132*
Schwartz, K., 105, 114, *118*
Schwartz, N. S., 108, *119*
Shapiro, N. S., 106, *119*
Sharfstein, S. S., *118*
Sherman, S. W., 28, *30,* 91, 94, *100,* 185, *190*
Shriner, J. G., 127, *132*
Silverstein, B., 19, *31*
Silverstein, R., 21, *30*
Simmens, S. J., *118*
Siskind, T. G., 128, *132*

Sloan, P., 105, *119*
Slobodzian, J., 17, *30*
Slobogin, C., 108, *118*
Smith, D. K., 148, *171*
Smith-Knapp, K., 110, *119*
Spataro, R., 107, *116*
Spiegel, A. N., 127, *132*
Staal, M., 114, *117*
Startup, M., 106, *119*
Steege, M. W., 73, *81*
Steinberg, A., 107, *119*
Stinnett, T. A., 147, *171*
Stricker, L. J., 40, *41*
Swerdlik, M., 147, *170*

Tanenbaum, R. J., 89, *99*
Tarvydas, V., 215, *220*
Tenopyr, M. L., 36, *42*
Thomas, A., 73, *82*
Thorndike, R. L., 148, 158, *171*
Thurlow, M. L., 19, *31,* 56, *57,* 72, *82,* 127, *132*
Tillman, M. H., 107, *119*
Tindahl, G., 50, *57, 82*
Tonsager, M. E., 105, 114, *116*
Trexler, L. E., 109, *119*
Tucker, B., 21, *31*
Tun, C. G., 110, 111, *120*
Tun, P. A., 110, *120*

Uzzell, B., 109, *116*

Vander Kolk, C. J., 107, *120*
VanValin, P., 110, *116*
Vasta, R., 148, *171*
Viney, L., 110, *120*
Voelkl, K. E., 182, *189*

Wacker, D. P., 73, *81*
Wandry, D., 126, *132*
Wanlass, R. L., 106, *119*
Watkins, C. E., 147, *171*
Watkins, C. E., Jr., 124, *132*
Webb, P. M., 109, *119*
Webster, C. D., 106, *120*
Wechsler, D., 148, 149, 150, 151, 153, 166, *171*

SUBJECT INDEX

Attention deficit disorder (ADD), 38, 182
  documentation and, 61–63
  overprediction of performance, 38, 93
Attention deficit hyperactivity disorder (ADHD), 61, 258, 242
  guidelines for documenting, 62, 73, 241
Audiotape, or oral presentations, used in testing, 19, 37, 178, 212
  extra time requirement, 52, 53
Auditory disabilities. *See* hearing impairments

Barlett v. New York State Board of Law Examiners (1998), 18
Best Practices in School Psychology III, 73
Board of Educ. of Northport-East Northport Union Free School Dist. v. Ambach (1983), 24
Board of Trustees of the University of Alabama v. Garrett (2001), 17
Board on Testing and Assessment (BOTA), 96–97
Braille, 19, 37, 72, 130, 148, 179, 188
  in employment testing, 200, 203, 212, 228
    extra time requirement, 53
    problem employment scenario, 228–229
    testing difficulties with, 39, 51, 52, 92
Brookhart v. Illinois State Board of Education (1983), 24

Calculator use, in tests, 54
CARF. *See* Rehabilitation Accreditation Commission
CAS. *See* DAS-Naglieri Cognitive System
Census Bureau, U.S.
  definition of disability, 3
  definition of disability for children, 3–4
Civil rights. *See* Federal disability rights statutes; Office for Civil Rights
Clinical assessment, of disability
  determining treatment needs, 105
  versus disability law, 238
  emotional reactions, 109–110
  forensic, 108

neuropsychological, 109
rehabilitation, 109
use of psychological testing, 105
Code of Fair Testing Practices in Education, 90
Cognitive ability tests, 147–170, 198–199. *See also names of individual tests*
  problem employment scenarios, 230–232
College Board, 23, 65, 97
  and flagging, 181
Communications, 145
Community rehabilitation programs, 216
Computer-based testing (CBT), 54–55
  as accommodation, 53
  postsecondary, 175, 187–188
Consortium for Equity in Standards and Testing (CTEST), 262
Cornell University, 205n
  ADA study, 210–211
  Computer-Assisted Survey Team (CAST), 211
  Program on Employment and Disability (PED), 219, 265
Counselors, school. *See* Counseling assessment
Council for Exceptional Children (CEC), 266
Council for the Accreditation of Counseling and Related Educational Programs (CACREP)
  standards for counselors, 122
Council of Chief State School Officers (CCSSO), 56, 143, 261
Council on Licensure, Enforcement and Regulation (CLEAR), 266
Counseling assessment, 121–131
  ADA regulations and, 126
  documentation requirements, 130
  guidelines for, 125–126
  legislation affecting, 125–127
  providing assess to services, 127–128
  psychometric issues, 128
  role of counselor, 123
  score reporting, 130–131
  Section 504 regulations and, 126
  testing accommodations, 129–130
  types of, 124–125
Criterion-referenced tests (CRTs), 47
  in large-scale assessments, 136
CTB McGraw-Hill, 257

Educational testing. *See* Elementary and secondary schools; Postsecondary admissions testing

Education Commission of the States, 262

Education Department. *See* Department of Education, U.S.

Education of All Handicapped Children's Act, 71

Education Testing Service (ETS), 258
 test-score flagging settlement, 21–22, 97, 181

Elementary and Secondary Education Act (1965), 22

Elementary and secondary schools. *See also* Counseling assessment; Individual educational program; Large-scale educational assessments
 federal disability rights statutes, 22–25
 determining testing accommodations, 64

Emotional reactions, related to injuries, 109–110

Employee assistance programs (EAPs), 216–217

Employers, and ADA. *See also* Testing professionals
 challenges in implementing, 209–211
 "direct threats," 207–208
 "reasonable accommodation," 206–207
 "undue hardship," 208

Employment scenarios, 222–231

Employment testing, 17–18, 80–81, 193–203. *See also* Employers, and ADA; Testing professionals
 cognitive ability tests, 198–199
 and disability nondiscrimination, 205–219
 "essential functions" requirement, 195–197
 federal disability rights statutes, 17–18
 job-relatedness requirement, 18
 medical exams, 197–198
 personality tests, 199
 physical ability tests, 198
 problem scenarios, 222–232
 qualification standards, 194–195
 "reasonable accommodations," 199–203

Enforcement Guidance: Disability-Related Inquires and Medical Examinations of Employees Under the ADA, 67, 232

Enforcement Guidance: Reasonable Accommodations and Undue Hardship Under the ADA, 68, 224

Equal Employment Opportunity Commission (EEOC), 194, 219, 221, 256
 ADA guidelines, 60, 195–196, 207, 215
 determination of "essential functions," 195
 evidence to determine discrimination, 196
 factors to consider, 195–196
 number of ADA complaints, 1992–1998 (table), 210

Equity, and individuals with disabilities, 4–5
 defined, 4
 nonbiased in determining, 5

ERIC Clearinghouse on Assessment and Evaluation, 261

ERIC Clearinghouse on Counseling and Student Services, 262

ERIC Clearinghouse on Disabilities and Gifted Education, 266

"Essential functions"
 in employment testing, 194–195, 236
 problem employment scenarios, 222–225

ETS. *See* Education Testing Service

Exam Accommodations Reference Manual, 65

Facility accommodations
 and postsecondary admissions testing, 177

Fairness, of testing, 34–35
 investigation of test components, 35
 studies of, 39
 validity for all test groups, 35

Family Medical Leave Act (FMLA), 207, 217

Federal disability rights statutes, 12–16, 23–25. *See also individual statutes*
 accommodations determinations, 19–20
 discrimination protection, 12
 for elementary and secondary schools, 22–25
 in employment testing, 17–18

KAIT. *See* Kaufman Assessment and
Adult Intelligence Test
Kaufman Assessment and Adult Intelligence Test (KAIT)
accommodations of, 168–169
description of, 166–168
recommended use of subtests (table),
169
use with visual impairments, 168
Kaufman Assessment Battery for Children (K-ABC), 79, 149
accommodations of, 155–158
description of, 155
recommended use of subtests (table),
157
use with hearing impairments, 155–
156
use with motor impairments, 156–157
use with visual impairments, 156

Labor Department. *See* Department of
Labor, U.S.
Large-print formats, 17, 19, 35, 37, 51,
52, 72, 148, 179
in employment testing, 200–201, 203,
212
for multiple-choice tests, 52
Large-scale educational assessments, 20,
135–145
accommodations decisions, 138–141
accountability of, 142–143
communications between officials, 145
criterion-referenced tests (CRTs), 136
features of, 130–131
infrequency of, 136
norm-referenced tests (NRTs), 136
review of instructional practices, 140
stakes of, 137–138
state content standards of, 140
validity of, 141–142
Law School Admission Council, 259
Law School Admission Test (LSAT) program, 20, 259
overprediction of performance, 93
studies of special administrations, 93
Learning disability, 16, 24, 92, 95, 185,
224
documentation and, 61, 62, 73
increase in requests for, 182–183
in licensing and certification exams,
241–242

overprediction of performance, 38, 92,
183
problem employment scenario, 224–
225
Legal policy requirements, 12–18
Licensing and certification, 235–247
ADA-related responsibilities, 244–245
disability determination, 237–240
documentation process, 240–242
eligibility requirements, 245
flagging, 246–247
job analysis, 245
psychoeducational evaluation, 238–239
psychometric implications, 242–243
record-keeping, 247
test accommodations, 237–240
test-scoring, 243–244
Low-stakes assessments, 137–141

*McGuinness v. Regents of the University of
New Mexico* (1999), 222
Magnifying devices, 179
Medical College Admission Test
(MCAT), 259
Medical exams, 197–198, 231
allowable under ADA, 209
Millon Clinical Multi-Axial Inventory
(MCMI), 199
Minnesota Multiphasic Personality Inventory 2, 199
Mobile County Bd. of Educ. (1997), 25
Moderate-stakes assessments, 137
Motor impairments, 53, 106
problem employment scenario, 229–
230
verification needed, 213, 241
Murphy v. United Parcel Service (1999),
17

National Academy of Sciences, 28
National Assessment of Educational Progress (NAEP), 56, 127
National Association of School Psychologists (NASP), 254
National Association of State Boards of
Education (NASBE), 262
National Association of Test Directors
(NATD), 255
National Center for Learning Disabilities
(NCLD), 268

ABOUT THE EDITORS

Ruth B. Ekstrom recently retired as principal research scientist in the Center for Higher Education at Educational Testing Service in Princeton, NJ. She received her BA in psychology from Brown University, her MA from Boston University, and her PhD from Rutgers University. She is a fellow of the American Psychological Association (APA) and has served on the APA Committee on Psychological Tests and Assessment. She has been cochair of the Joint Committee on Testing Practices.

Douglas K. Smith received his BA in psychology from Emory University (1969) and his MEd (1970), EdS (1972), and PhD (1977) in school psychology from Georgia State University. He was designated a Nationally Certified School Psychologist by the National School Psychology Certification Board in 1988, and he had served as Wisconsin delegate to the National Association of School Psychologists and president of the Wisconsin School Psychologists Association (WSPA). He served as membership chair of WSPA and was cochair of the Joint Committee on Testing Practices/Working Group on Assessment of Individuals With Disabilities and a member of the Test-Taker Rights and Responsibilities Working Group.